MAKING REAL MONEY IN RENTAL PROPERTIES

A Street Smart Guide to Finding Money-Making Opportunities in Any Market

Susan J. Underhill

with
Ken Upshaw

PROBUS PUBLISHING COMPANY
Chicago, Illinois
Cambridge, England

ISBN 1-55738-253-0

Printed in the United States of America

IPC

1 2 3 4 5 6 7 8 9 0

To Bernie and June
and Ethel, my Gram

without whose stubborn genes all of this
would not have been possible.

Table of Contents

■ ■ ■ ■ ■

Preface

■ ■ ■ ■ ■

Much of what you will read in this book refers to my experiences in Chicago. Although the experiences are localized, the concepts are universal. These are the concepts that I learned on the streets and in the neighborhoods of Chicago. I call my ideas "street smart" because they present real world ideas that work. Most importantly, this book is designed to teach a "street smart" attitude. Where most other books outline traditional investment strategies, this book attempts to teach intuition. Where most other real estate advisors appeal to your fantasies and your dreams, my strategies involve attitudes about people. Real estate is, after all, about people, not parcels of land or structures. Real estate is about the places people live, the places they work, the places they shop, the land on which they raise their food, the places they go for recreation. Real estate is about people because, without people, real estate has no value. To understand fully the value of real estate, then, one must understand people and the myriad ways in which they give value to real estate.

A Strategy for All Economic Seasons

When I bought my first rental property—a five-flat in a blue-collar neighborhood of Chicago—I was a single mother with two young daughters. At the time I knew of only one reason to buy rental property: cash flow. I wanted to make some extra money each month.

To find the right property, I relied on the instincts I had gained from growing up in the city and living in apartment buildings. At the time, I had no knowledge that these instincts were special. Only later, when I observed other people attempting to invest in real estate and falling short of my successes, did I realize the value of my intuition.

The rules that I present in this book are the same rules I have followed for more than 25 years of real estate investing. Viewed by many as quaint, conservative, even foolish during the halcyon years of the 1970s and 1980s, these rules now seem prudent, even shrewd, to many whose portfolios are sagging under the weight of extreme leverage and negative cash flow.

Because of my success, I have never deviated from my original game plan—to invest only in rental properties that generate cash flow. That is what this book is all about: an investment strategy that works in all economic seasons; a strategy born of the neighborhoods in which I grew and formed my attitudes; a strategy that will miss some of the gold during real estate booms, but will continue earning solid profits during the inevitable busts.

In this book, you will learn the strategy that has served me so well. And along the way you will learn:

- How to scout the neighborhoods and which neighborhoods to scout.

- Where to look for the right building.

- How to look for the right building.

- What kind of building to look for.

- How to recognize and deal with real estate brokers who try to steer you the wrong way.

- How to size up a building by driving past it.

- How to figure true cash flow.

- How to figure whether a building is a good investment.

- How to do a thorough walk-through inspection of a building.

- How to negotiate a good deal.

- How to finance the deal you negotiate.

- Why no-money-down deals are usually unrealistic.

- Why you have to be patient.

- How to do all this in a business-like manner.

Along the way, you will encounter a few myths that will be dismantled and you will learn how well suited you are for this undertaking. Nothing you read will be terribly sophisticated—or even new, for that matter. Some will seem so obvious as to be unnecessary. Yet if you read all the way through you will obtain a new attitude toward real estate investing that will serve you well no matter what specific strategy you ultimately embrace. Because the strategy is not the most important element in real estate investing—the attitude is.

Susan J. Underhill

Introduction

■ ■ ■ ■ ■

How to Use This Book

Many books are started, few are finished. The reason: people typically do not read through a book from start to finish. Most books require several sittings to complete; but the motivation that often accompanies the first sitting tends to dissipate after a few days, with the result that often only the first 25 or so pages get read. How many books have you picked up in the past year, started to read, then left open to page 25 or so, only to be placed back on the bookshelf during a spate of cleaning and straightening?

For the reader who is not likely to finish this particular book, it has been organized so that the entire concept can be grasped in one sitting. The introduction to each chapter expresses, as succinctly as possible, the specific concept included in that chapter. The remainder of the chapter expands on the concept, providing specific tips and illustrations. Finally, each chapter concludes by summarizing the information just read.

Read for Concept First

This book is about a new attitude. It is important for the reader to attain that attitude first, before reading each chapter in detail. After completing this short introduction, go directly to the concept section of Chapter 1 ("In This Chapter . . ."). Then read the concept section of Chapter 2, and continue through the book in that manner. It is best to read each chapter introduction in order, as each builds on the previous chapters. When all 27 concept sections have been completed, a task that should require approximately 30 to 45 minutes to accomplish, the reader will have grasped the entire concept behind this unique approach to real estate investing. After this initial scan, the reader will know what this book intends to teach. Only then should the text of each chapter be read. Go now to Chapter 1, "In This Chapter . . ."

Section I

■ ■ ■ ■ ■

Are You Prepared to Invest in Rental Properties?

One

■ ■ ■ ■ ■

Rental Properties and the American Dream

In This Chapter

The American dream is based on ownership of property. Real estate investment includes dozens of different strategies, but for the individual investor a strategy of investing in older apartment buildings holds the most promise. Buying rental properties is the most viable strategy for three reasons:

1. Rental properties potentially produce positive cash flow—money in your pocket every month.

2. Rental properties require less capital than other types of real estate as they generate their own operating capital.

3. Most potential investors in rental properties have experience as consumers of real estate—as an apartment dweller, a homeowner, etc. This experience forms a strong foundation of skills from which to draw.

Dreams

This is a book about dreams and practicalities.

Most of us aspire to realizing the American dream: the opportunity to make a fortune regardless of the circumstances of our birth. At the heart of the American dream is the ownership of land.

Why Rental Property?

Dreams are all well and good, but one must also be practical. Ownership of property, by itself, holds no guarantee of wealth. Whatever riches are to be obtained from investing in real estate must be squeezed from hard work and careful planning. The wealth is there, but remains elusive to all but the most capable.

Real estate investment offers dozens of strategies that can be followed successfully in the pursuit of profits: investing in single family homes, subdividing land, new construction, rehabbing older properties, flipping contracts, lease-options, exchanges, buying distressed properties—the list goes on. With each strategy, one can find hundreds of investors who have turned that plan to their advantage. Of all the strategies, however, investing in older apartment buildings is the most viable for the individual investor. Why?

- **Cash flow:** Apartment buildings combine all the typical advantages of a real estate investment—tax benefits, leverage, equity building, inflation hedging, investment security—with the most important advantage of all: cash flow (profits at the end of each month).

- **Operating capital:** Most real estate investment strategies require significant operating capital as well as initial investment capital. With rental properties, the investor can work with less money because the property itself generates the money to maintain the investment plus it returns cash flow to the owner.

- **Experience:** Most real estate investment strategies require specific skills and knowledge. The apartment building owner, however, typically can draw on his or her own experience as a foundation for the skills necessary for success. All that is needed is some specific information and a little gentle coaching.

In Summary

Of all the real estate investment strategies, purchasing rental properties is the most viable for the individual investor. Rental properties produce cash flow, require little or no operating capital, and involve skills that many potential investors have already acquired through their own experiences.

Two

■ ■ ■ ■ ■

I Don't Know Whether Patience Is a Virtue, But With Real Estate Investing, It Is Essential

"Patience is virtuous on the wine rack—and in the real estate business."

Sanford R. Goodkin

In This Chapter

This book is about a new attitude. In the field of real estate investing there is not a lot new under the sun in regard to strategy: any number of books teach a viable game plan. Success, however, depends not so much on strategy as on the attitude with which one approaches the game. One of the essential ingredients in this new attitude is patience. The investor who is not patient has two alternatives: one is to develop patience; the other is to abandon any illusions about doing well in real estate investing.

Overnight Success Is a Dream

Overnight success is rare in any field—but particularly in real estate invest-ing. Patience is essential. The late night TV gurus and the direct mail wizards, of course, would have one believe the opposite. Most of these real estate wonders would have us believe that a simple investment formula can produce immediate results:

> "I bought six properties in six weeks and put $80,000 in cash into my pocket. I was skeptical when I first read your ad, but I'm sure a believer now," reads the personal endorsement on one seminar ad.

The gurus sell dreams, not reality. They sell strategies that might work once in a thousand transactions. But then the *Wunderkinder* might not attract as many customers if they were to run a more honest advertisement:

> "Follow the long steady road to financial security! Buy your first property within 12 months; look forward to adding additional proper-ties slowly. Minimum investment capital required: $10,000."

The fast-talking medicine-show marvels are not alone in misleading the unwary. Even the best books on real estate investment spend very little time explaining to the novice investor the attitudes that lead to success. Most focus almost entirely on such sterile topics as strategies, types of properties, methods of financing, and formulas for assessing the viability of a particular deal. Few mention the difficulty involved with locating the right property. Even fewer discuss the disappointments one will encounter along the way—or the temptations. None mentions the essential characteristic of patience.

Shoppers versus Buyers

Most Americans love to buy things: appliances, clothes, automobiles. Ac-quiring nice things is an essential part of the American dream. For many Americans, unfortunately, the important part of acquiring something all too often is the initial pleasure of buying it. Such people can be classified as buyers. Buyers tend to be impatient: loath to postpone the thrill of the purchase, buyers often buy the first item they encounter rather than shop-ping for a better price or a better value. Buyers often purchase items for which they have little use—objects that end up cluttering the closet or the basement until a garage sale pulls them out of hiding. Impulsive by nature, buyers refuse to compare prices and may pay thousands of dollars more than they should for an automobile or some other major purchase.

Shoppers, on the other hand, are a hardy breed who often won't buy even an undershirt without shopping at least five stores for the best value. Compulsive rather than impulsive, the veteran shopper will often shop all day only to return home having made no purchase at all. A true shopper may haggle for weeks over $50.00 on the price of an automobile. To be satisfied with any purchase, a good shopper must be convinced that they have paid the lowest possible price for the highest quality available. Patient to a fault, the shopper nevertheless has much to teach the would-be real estate entrepreneur.

Characteristics of a Shopper

1. **Strategy.** A shopper usually does not leave the house without a strategy in mind—which stores to shop, where the best values are likely to be found. Rarely does a shopper purchase the first item without comparing price and quality in several other stores. Only then is the shopper satisfied that the first item is indeed a good value.

2. **Value.** A shopper always has a goal in mind—to get the best value. A shopper is not satisfied with a purchase unless he or she spent the least amount of money possible to obtain the best quality available.

3. **Criteria.** Consciously or unconsciously, a shopper routinely judges a potential purchase against five specific criteria: Quality, Price, Aesthetics, Function, and Personal Satisfaction. These criteria act in accord with one another, each at times exerting the greatest influence on the decision, but none ever being ignored.

Five Criteria by Which a Shopper Judges a Purchase

1. **Quality.** Quality has importance only in relation to price. The item may not necessarily be of the highest quality, but the relationship between quality and price must be in balance, which yields a measure of value.

2. **Price.** For a shopper, the price of an object must always be in line with the price of similar or identical objects from other sources. This can only be determined by spending time in comparison shopping.

3.   **Aesthetics.** A shopper knows intuitively when an item is attractive and whether it will blend with its proposed surroundings.

4.   **Function.** A shopper strikes a balance between beauty and function. The function of a porcelain statue, for instance, is to be beautiful and to harmonize with its surroundings, while an electric drill may be quite ugly but will get the job done.

5.   **Personal satisfaction.** A shopper tends to be extremely independent in the assessment of value, beauty, and function. Although a shopper will often ask for another opinion, decisions are rarely based on what pleases someone else. They are based, rather, on an independent set of criteria. For a shopper, the most satisfying aspect of a purchase, of course, is the almost smug knowledge that the best deal was struck.

Characteristics of a Buyer

1.   **Impulsive.** A buyer often buys on impulse, caring little about price and everything about the item itself. A buyer attaches great pleasure to the act of acquiring, while a shopper derives great pleasure from the process of shopping for value.

2.   **Impatient.** A buyer lacks the patience to shop for quality and price. Not often concerned with value, a buyer simply falls in love with something—a car perhaps—and pays the asking price on the spot.

3.   **Impressionable.** A buyer is commonly taken with appearances rather than quality, and often applies only one criterion: Do I like it? This criterion, of course, may vary from day to day, depending on the mood of the buyer.

Are You a Buyer or a Shopper?

In the field of real estate investing, there are plenty of buyers. Buyers in real estate exhibit the same characteristics as buyers among the general population: impatience, impulsiveness, and impressionability. For the investor who is more a buyer than a shopper it's time to change attitudes.

How Patient Must You Be?

The majority of properties on the market are not good investments. The rare property that meets all the criteria of a good investment is elusive and must be teased out from among the masses of unsuitable candidates. The search can often take as long as 12 months or more. It is possible, albeit unlikely, for the first property one encounters to be the perfect acquisition. More likely, the search will last far longer than one at first can imagine.

Author's Note: My first rental property, a five-flat, took nearly a full year to locate—a year of searching the paper every Sunday, calling about the ads, doing the numbers, driving by, submitting offers, and all the other tasks associated with the search for the right building.

My most recent acquisition, a 40-unit building, required less than a month. An agent who had handled the purchase of another property for me called when this building went on the market. I looked at it, ran the numbers, and submitted an accepted offer.

A friend who profited from my advice and assistance looked for nearly a year before finding the right property. He kept the building one year, did some minor repairs, and sold it for twice what he paid.

What are the Criteria for a Good Property?

To be considered a good rental property, a building must meet four specific criteria:

1.   The property must produce a positive cash flow.

2.   The building must be in good condition, with little deferred mainte-nance.

3.   The location must be suitable for attracting good tenants.

4.   The building must be able to be purchased with a reasonable down payment.

Why Does It Take So Long?

Notwithstanding the claims of many self-styled real estate investment con-sultants, truly good deals in real estate are difficult to find. No matter which strategy one chooses to pursue, the inevitable result is a long, tedious slog through the morass of real estate agents, newspapers, and multiple listing services or, if one prefers, lists of repossessions or tax sales. The search is destined to be long because the criteria are so strictly drawn: positive cash flow, good condition, suitable location, reasonable down payment.

Buyer Beware

As the search for the right building grinds on at an impossibly slow pace, the temptation will arise several times to settle for a property that comes close to the established criteria. The agent handling the sale, of course, will attempt to minimize every flaw and encourage the buyer to go ahead with the purchase. Often such encouragement is difficult to withstand.

Apart from the agent, however, a feeling of impatience on the part of the buyer is inevitable as building after building is checked out and found wanting. Here and there a particular building will stand out: this one is strikingly beautiful, another has just been rehabbed and promises relatively low maintenance, a third is available for no money down, and a fourth is in a wonderful location.

Each time an appealing building comes along the temptation to buy becomes very strong. When the criteria are applied in an unimpassioned manner, however, the building proves to be a poor investment, or at best a marginal risk. Most often the problem is that the building will not generate cash flow. In such a circumstance, walking away from a building is often quite difficult, particularly when an agent is whispering in one's ear that the building is a perfect arm-chair investment, that it makes money every month, that it won't last long at this price. The best action at that moment is to move on to the next property. The worst temptation, though, is to justify buying a building by minimizing the problems: the leaky roof can be fixed, rents can be raised, the vacancy rate can be improved, expenses can be lowered, the sagging floor can be straightened, the present tenants can be replaced with better tenants, the trains that pass by so closely will not bother the tenants if the building is made to look better, and so on.

What Happens When a Buyer Succumbs to Impatience?

There are any number of charming folksy sayings that apply when a buyer loses patience and goes ahead with a flawed deal: "The chickens come home to roost"; "It's time to pay the piper"; "You asked for it, now you've got it"; and "How am I going to pay the mortgage this month?"

Does Patience Really Pay Off?

Author's Note: Sometime around 1975, I began thinking about buying a new house. The home I lived in at the time was very nice, but I longed for something larger, with more character, more personality. I began looking. With a concept clearly in mind of the type of house I wanted, I searched the neighborhoods where I wanted to live. Most of my Sunday afternoons were given to attending open houses. Early in the search I was motivated by anticipation; as I entered the front door of each succeeding house I could, with little effort, imagine my furniture arranged tastefully in the various rooms. I envisioned family dinners in the dining rooms and festive parties in the living rooms.

In a relatively short time I found a house that suited me. But I had a limited amount of money to work with, and the offer I made was rejected, as was the second and the third. I was devastated; I had already figured where my furniture would go. In my mind, I already owned that house.

Disappointed but undaunted, I continued looking and putting in offers. But my resources were simply too limited to afford the houses I wanted. Disappointment followed disappointment, until finally I decided that the best approach was not to imagine living in the house, but rather to deal with every offer in a purely business-like manner. Somewhere, I knew, there would be the perfect house. I just had to keep looking.

Early in my search I noticed a particular house for sale that was striking in its beauty. I had attended an open house, noticing its unique character as well as some problems with deferred maintenance. From the outside it looked like a small castle; on the inside it was a dream house.

I knew that this particular house was beyond my resources. The price was over $200,000, a price I could not afford.

But I liked the house so much that I drove by it often. Week after week the "For Sale" sign remained, and I continued to dream with no hope of ever owning the house. I continued making offers and being rejected at other houses. Then one week, three months or so later, there was another open house at the little castle, with a different listing broker.

I went inside, eager just to walk through the house again, and it was just as wonderful the second time. The price had come down a bit, to $175,000—still not even close to a price I could afford. Two months later, there was another open house, another Realtor. I walked through again. This time the price was $160,000.

Because I was the only person in the house at the time I struck up a conversation with the agent. I told him how much I loved the house and how much I wanted it. He suggested I make an offer. I said the offer I could make would never be accepted. He asked how much I could offer. I told him $115,000. He said, "Let's write it up and see what they say."

As long as he was willing to write it up, I was willing to sign, never expecting even a counter offer. A day and a half later, he called and said he had a counter offer—$117,500. I immediately signed the contract, nearly a year after beginning my search.

At this writing I have lived in my little castle over 14 years. Comparable homes in the area are now priced from $600,000 to over $1 million.

"Patience is bitter, but its fruit is sweet."

Jean Jacques Rousseau

In Summary

Even the best books on real estate investment spend very little time teaching the attitudes that lead to success. None mentions the essential characteristic of patience. Patience is characteristic of a shopper, from whom the would-be investor has much to learn. When making a purchase, a shopper always has a strategy in mind, as well as a goal—to find the best value. In order to identify value, the shopper uses five criteria: quality, price, aesthetics, function, and personal satisfaction. A buyer, on the other hand, tends to be impulsive, impatient, and impressionable. To be successful, a real estate investor must emulate a shopper, not a buyer.

The majority of properties on the market are not good investments: the rare property that meets all the criteria of a good investment is elusive and difficult to find. No matter which strategy one uses, the search for the right property is long and tedious; inevitably, one will feel impatient and willing to settle for a property that comes close to the criteria. The worst temptation, however, is to justify buying a building by minimizing its problems. Patience is essential.

Three

■ ■ ■ ■ ■

The Virtues of Real Estate as an Investment Commodity

In This Chapter

Real estate as an income-producing business has traditionally received secondary notice from most writers; primary attention has been paid to the other, more exciting advantages of real estate. In this chapter you will learn why real estate investment has been so popular through the years but also why the traditional strategies are not as viable in tough economic times. Each of the characteristics that has made real estate the most sought-after of all investments is presented here in detail: investment security, appreciation, inflation hedge, leverage, tax benefits, equity growth, and cash flow. Although each is discussed separately, all are interrelated. Keep in mind that these advantages continue to be important considerations in any real estate investment strategy. When the economy turns down, however, cash flow assumes primary importance and the other advantages represent the icing on the cake, assume secondary importance. It is just those times when the street-smart strategy of investing in rental properties proves its long-lasting worth.

The Advantages of Investing in Real Estate

Real estate has always been a favored investment because it offers a selection of advantages that few other investments can match: security, appreciation, leverage, tax shelter. Each of these benefits plays an important role in any real estate investment strategy, even a strategy that focuses entirely on cash flow. When the economy turns sour, however, most of the benefits of real estate investing reveal serious flaws, while a strategy that focuses on developing cash flow will sail through most economic conditions. When good economic times create increased property values, nevertheless, the true value of investing in rental properties becomes even more evident.

Advantage #1: Appreciation

Over the long term, well located properties normally grow in value regardless of short term economic conditions. This growth in value results both from the forces of supply and demand acting on a piece of property and from the perception that real estate has an intrinsic value that is lacking in paper investments and in the dollar itself. Appreciation depends upon continued high demand, however, while tough economic times often witness an overall decline in demand for real estate and, in some locales, an actual decrease in real estate values over the short term.

Advantage #2: Investment Security

Investors typically look for investments that will not lose value regardless of economic or social conditions. Gold is the most obvious example of a commodity that holds its value through the years—primarily because of its scarcity, secondly because of its beauty, and in modern times because of its industrial usefulness. In spite of its popularity, nevertheless, gold experiences short term price volatility because of its relationship with other investment products. There are times when the price of gold is quite high and other times when gold can be bought relatively cheap. Next to gold, land has been the most consistently desirable commodity through the ages. In modern times, this has given real estate an aura of security that may be misleading.

Investors looking for security have long felt that, because the supply of land is fixed, continued demand will always force the price higher. To many investors, this perceived market pressure mistakenly appears to make real estate more secure than other investments. Just like gold, however, the value of real estate in recent years has experienced tremendous volatility, belying conventional wisdom and causing many investors to question the sagacity of their assumptions about real estate. The fact is, nevertheless, that as a long-term investment real estate is more secure than most other investments and the risk of loss from declining value is less than with most other commodities. In the short term, however, localized market forces can wreak havoc with real estate prices.

Booms and Busts. In difficult economic times, demand for even the most desirable real estate can dry up. In Houston, Texas during the mid 1980s, for example, rising oil prices first created a boom-town environment that attracted thousands of people from all over the United States. Houses were built at a feverish pace; office buildings sprang up at break-neck speed. Then, when the price of oil on the international market suddenly plummeted, the boom ended, suspending the demand for housing and office space. Real estate values crashed and thousands of homeowners and investors suffered huge losses. What happened in Houston is typical of real estate booms everywhere, a phenomenon that must be understood to be avoided. The aftermath of a boom, of course, is a period of stagnating or falling prices, such as occurred in Houston.

Economic Cycles. For most of this century, the U.S. economy has experienced alternating cycles of prosperity and recession. Caused by the same supply and demand forces that create real estate booms and busts, these economic cycles have a profound effect on real estate values.

Speculation. As with any investment-quality commodity, real estate is subject to speculative investing. This means that there are investors willing to spend money for property that has a low present value but has the potential of significantly increasing in value. An example might be a blighted inner-city neighborhood that stands in the path of possible gentrification. Any investment in that area is speculative because the area might remain in poor circumstances indefinitely. Less obvious is the speculation that occurs during a real estate boom such as the one that occurred during the 1980s.

Through the last half of the 1980s, real estate became more and more a speculative investment in specific areas around the country. In Orange County, California, and Washington, D.C., for instance, the growth in real estate prices far outstripped the rate of inflation for several years. This surge spilled over to other areas like southern Florida and Las Vegas. There, when the market heated up, many homeowners and other potential buyers no longer appraised a home for its livability or its amenities; rather, many prospective buyers were drawn to the housing market solely on the basis of profiteering. In Las Vegas, as a consequence, demand for new houses for awhile so exceeded available supply that prospective buyers could be found standing in line waiting for the precise moment when a new house would be offered for sale. Some would arrive one or two nights early and camp at the spot, waiting. Out-of-town buyers, frustrated by the expense and time involved in traveling to the city every week just to try to place an offer, would pay local inhabitants to wait in line for them.

The growth in prices that resulted from this feverish speculation tended to exceed the rate of inflation by a significant amount. But the spiraling prices were based on nothing concrete—just the faith that prices would continue to rise. At some point in every price spiral speculative fever burns itself out and prices actually decline, as occurred in Los Angeles and Las Vegas. As with all speculative markets, prices ultimately rose to heights that could not be supported by new buyers. Without entry level buyers to feed the market from the bottom, the pyramid collapsed under its own weight and prices fell dramatically, leaving the last feverish buyers holding deeds for properties that in many cases were worth less than the mortgage they had taken against it. Whenever speculation takes over the real estate market, which occurred in spades during the 1980s, the short-term security of an investment in real estate declines significantly.

Advantage #3: Inflation Hedge

Real estate has traditionally been viewed as an excellent hedge against inflation. As inflation reduces the value of the dollar, the price of real estate tends to increase at a comparable rate. This assumes, of course, a steady appreciation of the value of the real estate, which we have said is a fairly safe assumption for the long term but can be problematic in the short term. Because of capital gains taxes and other expenses associated with the sale of a property, the only way real estate can be a reliable inflation hedge is when the price of real estate appreciates more quickly than the overall rate of inflation, an assumption that is, by nature, highly speculative.

The major fallacy of real estate as a hedge against inflation, however, lies elsewhere. Rather than increasing in price as the *result* of inflation, real estate much more likely has *contributed* to the rate of inflation by appreciating in value in response to the market forces of supply and demand.

Advantage #4: Leverage

Real estate investing offers one advantage that most other investments lack: leverage. Few Americans pay the entire cost of a real estate acquisition. Most purchasers actually pay only a fraction of the price from their own capital; they borrow the rest from a bank, a savings and loan, or from some other source. This is known as leverage. Leverage is the ability to borrow a large percentage of the purchase price of a commodity. Thus, the real estate investor can control properties worth large amounts of money with an investment of relatively little cash, often as low as 10% of the purchase price. Such leverage is made possible because of the intrinsic value of the real estate, a value that is lacking in most other forms of investment. A lender can feel relatively safe lending against the value of the real estate, knowing that in the event a foreclosure becomes necessary, the property can be sold for sufficient cash to pay off the loan. In a period of price stagnation or decline, of course, that is not a safe assumption.

There are two excellent reasons why lenders are willing to make highly leveraged loans for the acquisition of real estate: high yield and low risk. The combination of these two benefits makes real estate lending highly popular among financial institutions. Through the years, the interest rates charged for mortgages have typically run 2% to 4% higher than the rate of inflation. This yield, while small in itself, generates huge profits for lending institutions when one considers the volume of business conducted. Second, although an unhealthy economy increases the number of foreclosures dramatically, the rate of foreclosures continues to run quite low when compared with the overall volume of real estate loans. This is true because of the extreme caution exercised by lending institutions.

In a real estate boom such as occurred the late 1980s and into 1990, however, such caution can be circumvented by lenders eager to cash in on a rising market. During that heady period many lenders, encouraged by the opportunity to reap huge profits, invested in projects that turned out to be high risk ventures, with the unfortunate result that billions of dollars were lost and hundreds of financial institutions went out of business. As many discovered, the price of throwing caution to the wind can often be the proverbial whirlwind. In the aftermath of this frenzy, lending requirements have become more restrictive than ever.

Advantage #5: Tax Shelter Benefits

Even though a well maintained building will actually appreciate in value over time, the tax code assumes that its value will decline, allowing the owner to list this depreciation as a business expense. The resulting deduction lowers taxable income even though no cash has been spent. Prior to passage of the Tax Reform Act of 1986, this tax shelter benefit fueled much of the boom in commercial property construction because of the wide-spread growth of limited partnerships. As a limited partner in a real estate syndicate, an individual could benefit from the tax savings derived from a huge development project. In many cases, this feature alone created profits for the individual investor; consequently many projects were started that offered very little economic benefit other than tax savings. The Tax Reform Act of 1986, however, changed all of that. It allows losses from passive investments, like a real estate limited partnership, to offset only income derived from other similar types of passive investments, thereby effectively eliminating the tax benefits of limited partnerships. When the owner is actively involved in a real estate venture, however—as you will be—the tax shelter benefit remains a significant factor in the profitability of the property.

Advantage #6: Equity Growth

Equity is the difference between a property's market value and the amount of the mortgage on the property. As the mortgage is repaid, the owner builds an increasing amount of equity in the property, independent of the equity that develops as a result of appreciation. Later, the equity that has been accumulated can be used to refinance the property or as security against other acquisitions. The truth is, however, that during the first ten years of ownership equity build-up as a result of repayment of the mortgage is not a very large sum as most of the monthly mortgage payment goes to pay interest.

Advantage #7: Cash Flow

Rental properties also may provide cash flow—money in your pocket after paying all the expenses and the debt service each month. Unfortunately, locating properties that actually produce cash flow has become more and more difficult in recent years. First, the price of real estate has climbed faster than the growth of rents. Likewise, the cost of taxes, utilities, and maintenance has increased at a higher rate than rents. As a consequence, monthly rent collections often do not cover expenses and debt service. Nevertheless, such properties can still be found by the patient, business-like real estate investor.

Advantage #8: Enhanced Value

The value of a particular property can be enhanced any number of ways—by fixing it up, by raising the rents, by subdividing, by expanding the building, by re-zoning the property. Part of the art of investing in real estate is the ability to envision a property's full potential. A perfect example is Las Vegas, Nevada. In the early 1950s this arid semi-desert in southern Nevada was good for little more than sheep-herding and mining. While the rest of the country passed laws prohibiting gambling, however, Nevada's laws continued to allow games of chance. A few visionaries (gangsters, perhaps, but gangsters with a vision) recognized a tremendous opportunity for profit and established an oasis of casinos in an otherwise nearly worthless valley. Forty years later, Las Vegas is a thriving metropolitan city in the desert, supported in large part by the huge casinos but also having attracted a variety of other businesses.

In Summary

Real estate has been viewed as an excellent investment-grade commodity through the years for the following reasons:

1. Its value has tended to appreciate and to keep pace with inflation.

2. Its purchase can be leveraged.

3. There is a finite supply coupled with increasingly greater demand.

4. Its value can be enhanced through a change of usage.

5. Present tax codes allow paper depreciation of the structures to provide a tax shelter.

6. It is possible to derive rental income from the property.

But times have changed; real estate is not necessarily the investment it once was. As a hedge against inflation, as a high demand commodity, as a highly leveraged yet secure investment holding, real estate has had little equal for decades. But the risks are far greater today than they were only a few years ago. A property that produces positive cash flow, however, remains a good investment choice, particularly during difficult economic times.

Four

■ ■ ■ ■ ■

A Business Is a Business Is a Business, and Investing in Rental Properties Is a Business

In This Chapter

Rental property owners often refer to themselves as landlords. The term itself has become so ubiquitous that few of us question its origins, which hark back to medieval times when the owner of the land was the lord of the manor and the tenants—who could never hope to own land or housing themselves—remained in a subservient state. Because there was nowhere else to go, tenants were subject to the landlord's wishes and whims. The lord, on the other hand, need not be concerned with sound business practice; if he needed more money he could simply raise the rents.

Today's successful landlord, by contrast, is first and foremost a businessperson. Real estate investing involves negotiations, lawyers, brokers, deeds, loans, taxes, regulations, courts, paperwork, and a great deal of insight and oversight. A typical business involves three fundamental elements: a product, a customer to buy that product, and capital with which to operate the business. Rental properties are no different. The product is housing, the customer for the housing is the tenant, the investment capital is the down payment, and the operating capital is the rent. Along with correctly identifying both customer and product, the landlord must be adept at anticipating and managing expenses, raising capital, appraising property values, and negotiating deals.

The Elements of a Business

There are three fundamental elements of any business venture: the product, the customer, and the capital.

The Product: Housing

A business must have a product to sell. With rental properties, the product is housing—a place to live. Housing, of course, is one of the basic needs of mankind; everyone needs a place to live. Who could ask for a better product to sell than one that always has been and always will be in demand? In good times or in bad, there will always be a market for housing.

On the other hand, there is not necessarily a good market for the particular housing each property owner provides. Overbuilding can create a glut of new apartments and consequently a high vacancy rate. In some neighborhoods, the sheer number of older apartment buildings can create a highly competitive atmosphere that results in high vacancies and depressed rents. Through it all, however, certain types of buildings continue to attract large numbers of quality tenants. This is the product we want to sell. This is the kind of rental property that will form the foundation of our business plan. In the chapters to come, you will learn how to identify such properties and how to run buildings in a manner that will make them highly desirable to the clientele for which they are intended.

The Customer: The Tenant

When Marshall Field moved west and settled in Chicago, he had a vision of owning his own drygoods store. He brought his vision to reality and great wealth to himself and his family through a unique combination of personal thrift and hard work. From the beginning, his business was founded on a very simple philosophy—*the customer is always right*. Through the years, Field's philosophy has become so commonplace that the phrase itself now sounds trite. When applied to the business of operating rental property, however, it holds a special significance. Treating the tenant as a *customer* means *paying particular attention to the kind of customer to whom the product will be sold and gearing the product to the customers one hopes to attract.*

A successful business is built on developing a clientele, servicing that clientele and maintaining that clientele. To thrive, a business must know its customer thoroughly and be certain that it offers a product that the customer will buy. In the rental property business the customer is the prospective tenant who will live in the building.

Capital: Rental Income

Businesses operate on capital. The business of rental properties is no different. There are two kinds of capital: investment capital and operating capital. Investment capital is the money used to acquire the property and to make improvements. Operating capital is the money used to pay the bills.

There are plenty of so-called real estate advisors who would have us believe that a real estate empire can be built with very little capital. Their catch phrases are "No money down" and "Other people's money." Don't be fooled. These catchy ideas sell a lot of books and entice a lot of paying customers to their seminars, but those ideas have little to do with the real world of real estate investment. This is not to say that no-money-down deals don't occur and that creative financing can't play a significant role in reducing out-of-pocket expenses. However, a primary cause of failure in real estate investing, as in any business venture, is under-capitalization. Most real estate deals require capital.

A Word About Profit

Other than having fun, there is only one reason for a business to exist—to make a profit. Real estate is no different and the catch phrase is "cash flow." In its simplest terms, cash flow means money in the investor's pocket every month. Identifying a product and a customer is only the first step in building a successful business. Rental properties also involve expenses: the cost of acquisition, utilities, repairs and maintenance, cleaning, advertising, insurance, and on and on. If the venture is to show a profit, the rental income must exceed expenses plus debt service (the mortgage payment).

For some time, however, the price of property has grown at a faster rate than the price of rent. As a consequence, positive cash flow has become more and more difficult to obtain. Consequently, when the search for suitable properties begins it soon becomes obvious that many real estate agents have their own way of defining profits. They throw around phrases like *"cap rate"* (the rate of capitalization), *pretax earnings* and *after tax earnings, appreciation dollars, equity accumulation, depreciation dollars, tax savings, temporary negative cash flow*, etc., all of which is designed to convince a buyer that a particular piece of property is a good investment, when in fact it probably isn't. Our strategy, however, is to *make money regardless of economic conditions or the current tax code*—and that means Cash Flow. The rental business must show profit on its own, not sometime in the future after tax losses or when the building is resold.

The Business of Real Estate Investing

Investment in rental property is a business first and foremost. Although the investment characteristics of the property itself—appreciation, leverage, tax benefits—are potentially lucrative, they play a minor role in our long term business plan. Real estate that is purchased solely as an *investment* is subject to favorable economic conditions to produce a reasonable profit, while real estate that is purchased as a *business* can be operated through good times or bad. In other words, in an uncertain economy one cannot rely on the appreciated value of the property to make money. Therefore, one must rely solely on the business itself—rental income—for profits.

As with any business, there will be successes and there will be occasional failures. Property values are subject to situations that are often beyond the control of the individual investor, no matter how diligent. If the largest employer in the area closes down, for example, property values will fall no matter how carefully the owners maintained their buildings. During an economic recession fewer people are looking for apartments and the competition for tenants can become fierce. Or, a property next door may be poorly managed and attract objectionable tenants, making it more difficult to attract good tenants to our building.

Real estate investing is not a risk-free venture. But with a good business plan and the right attitude, one can minimize the risks and maximize the potential. Just keep in mind that to be successful one must offer the right product to the right customer for the right price, while at the same time keeping expenses under control. Those who approach their venture with the greatest amount of foresight and dedication are the most likely to succeed.

In Summary

Investment in rental property is a business first and foremost. The business of investing in rental properties involves a product: housing;

a customer: the tenant; and investment and operating capital. A successful investor in rental properties must rely solely on the business itself—rental income—for profits. Real estate investing is not a risk-free venture. As with any business, there will be successes and there will be occasional failures. But a good business plan can minimize the risks and maximize the potential.

Five

■ ■ ■ ■ ■

You've Got to Have a Plan

In This Chapter

Successful businesses have a plan. A plan may only be in the mind of the entrepreneur, but it is a plan nevertheless. A real estate investor also needs a plan, and the purpose of this book is to develop one. This plan will include six key components: The first is self assessment—how prepared are you to invest in rental properties? The second is investment capital—how much do you have; how much can you raise? The third element of the business plan is a statement of goals and objectives. The fourth element is strategy—how to identify and locate the appropriate property. The fifth element is to identify the product that will be sold. And the sixth element is to identify the potential customer.

The Six Components of a Business Plan

No matter how small, a business is much more likely to succeed if all the available assets have been identified and a clear plan has been formulated. That plan must include a strategy, but also should identify the investor's motivations and sensitivity to risk. It is helpful to use a form so that the plan is committed to in writing and can be reviewed periodically. Figure 5.1 can be used for that purpose. On that form there are six sections, each devoted to one of the six essential components of a business plan.

Section 1: Self Assessment

"Know thyself," the ancient philosophers advised us. An eager investor, unfortunately, will be tempted to pass over this part and go straight to the strategy. That would be a mistake. You must take stock of yourself first. What kind of investor are you? What motivates you? How sensitive are you to loss? What kinds of risks are you willing to take? How involved do you want to be? How much experience do you have?

Some of the strategies that will be presented later in the book depend on specific personal characteristics for success; if an investor lacks one or two key elements it could prove disastrous. By analyzing yourself carefully, you obtain a profile upon which your investment strategy will be built.

Section 2: Investment Capital

Author's Note: My grandpa once told me, "If a man is selling $50 bills on the street corner for 50¢, and you can raise only 49¢, it ain't no bargain."

You may have grand plans for your real estate venture. You may have heard that properties can be had at bargain prices with no down payment and are eager to begin. But the truth is that without capital most plans will fail. How much can you afford to invest? What is your present net worth? How liquid is your capital?

Section 3: Goals and Objectives

An investor who does not know where he or she is going surely won't know how to get there. Establish some goals for yourself—both long term and short term. Where would you like to be in five years? Where must you be in one year if you are to accomplish your five-year goal? What do you want from this venture? What kind of yield are you looking for?

Traditionally, real estate investment contributes to one of four goals: income, tax shelter, capital turnover, and capital appreciation. Unfortunately, swollen real estate values have significantly reduced the opportunity for appreciation and turnover of capital. The Tax Reform Act of 1986 significantly reduced the tax shelter advantages of real estate. What's left? Income, which should be the goal of your real estate investment strategy. This is not to say that each of the other three real estate investment characteristics—tax

Figure 5.1   Personal Business Plan

The objective of this business plan is to summarize, as succinctly as possible, one's readiness, both fiscally and psychologically, to invest in rental properties, and to draft an outline of one's plan to proceed with the business of rental properties. This is not meant to take the place of a formal business plan but rather is meant to highlight the important points that are raised in the book.

SECTION I: SELF ASSESSMENT

MOTIVATION (From Chapter 6):

Why do you want to invest in rental properties?_____

_____

_____

ABILITY TO TOLERATE RISK (From Chapter 7):

Risk is an inherent part of investing in rental properties. Discuss how well you can and do handle financial risk.

_____

Analyze your investment portfolio (Chapter 7, Figure 7-1). How much risk have you been willing to assume?

_____

Assess your level of self-confidence (Chapter 7). Are you able to analyze an investment and make an independent decision?

_____

Assess your emotional state (Chapter 7). Do you maintain a positive state of mind that allows you to handle adversity?

_____

LEVEL OF PERSONAL INVOLVEMENT (Chapter 8):

Investing in rental properties involves a great deal of time and energy. The most successful investors are those who are most involved. Assess how much time you realistically can make available for your venture (Chapter 8, Figure 8-1).

_____

How involved do you wish to be in each stage of the venture, searching for the property, acquiring the property, managing the property, and selling the property?

_____

_____

LEVEL OF SKILL AND EXPERIENCE (Chapter 8):

What specific skills do you have that will help you in your new business? (Example: negotiating, business operations, sales, management, plumbing, carpentry, roofing, electrical, painting and plastering, general repair, accounting, "people" skills.)

_____

_____

SECTION II: INVESTMENT CAPITAL

AMOUNT OF INVESTMENT CAPITAL AVAILABLE (Chapter 9):

How much investment capital do you have on hand or can you raise by selling or borrowing against other assets?

        $_____ Cash on hand

        $_____ Cash I can raise by borrowing against my assets

        $_____ Cash I can raise by selling some of my assets

  $_____ Total cash available for investing (money I can afford to lose without jeopardizing my life-style)

Figure 5.1 Personal Business Plan *(continued)*

SECTION III: GOALS AND OBJECTIVES

ONE YEAR GOALS:

By _____, 199__, I will raise my net worth to $_____.

By _____, 199__, I will raise my annual income to $_____.

By _____, 199__, I will own _____ rental properties.

By _____, 199__, I will own _____ rental units (total # of apartments).

TWO YEAR GOALS:

By _____, 199__, I will raise my net worth to $_____.

By _____, 199__, I will raise my annual income to $_____.

By _____, 199__, I will own _____ rental properties.

By _____, 199__, I will own _____ rental units (total # of apartments).

FIVE YEAR GOALS:

By _____, 199__, I will raise my net worth to $_____.

By _____, 199__, I will raise my annual income to $_____.

By _____, 199__, I will own _____ rental properties.

By _____, 199__, I will own _____ rental units (total # of apartments).

RETURN ON INVESTMENT:

I wish to receive _____% cash return on my investment each year.

ADDITIONAL GOALS:

_____

_____

_____

_____

_____

SECTION IV: STRATEGY

My strategy is to search for and purchase _____ rental properties that generate sufficient positive cash flow to produce my targeted rate of return. Here is how I plan to proceed (Chapters 10 through 24):

_____

_____

_____

_____

_____

_____

_____

_____

_____

Figure 5.1   Personal Business Plan *(continued)*

SECTION V: THE PRODUCT:

The product I will offer for sale is clean, safe, quiet apartments, specifically (include size, type of neighborhood, type of building, age, condition, etc.):

_____

_____

_____

_____

SECTION VI: THE CUSTOMER:

My targeted customer can be described as (include socio-economic level, marital status, number of children, age, neighborhood, type of occupation, etc.):

_____

_____

_____

_____

shelter, capital turnover, and capital appreciation—will not play a part in the long-term success of your venture. But your primary goal should be monthly profits.

Section 4: Strategy

Real estate is a confusing mass of overlapping specialties. There is residential property, commercial property, retail property, industrial property, mixed use property, new property, rehabbed property, land development, commercial leasing, apartment complexes, single family homes, small apartment buildings, distressed properties—and the list goes on. What kind of property do you want to work with and in what neighborhood? Without a clear focus, you will quickly find yourself off the fairway and in the rough, wandering from one project to another, without the expertise to pull the full potential from any of them.

Section 5: The Product

Rental properties are traditionally viewed from the perspective of tenant/landlord rather than the more business-like customer/product perspective. Avoid being drawn into thinking of yourself as a landlord. That old-world concept can create fuzzy thinking. You are a retail business that offers a specific high-demand product: housing. Your business will succeed to the extent that you are able to sell your product to the right customer. As you develop your strategy, you will find that few rental properties will produce a steady income. This fact alone will limit the type of property you work with. What is important, however, is to identify clearly the product that this real estate business is to offer. Then confine yourself to that product; become an expert, learn everything there is to know about your product.

Section 6: The Customer

To be successful, it is not enough for a business to offer a product for sale; the critical step occurs when the customer buys the product. Once you have decided on the type of neighborhood to work in and the kind of real estate projects you plan to pursue, it is essential to identify who your customers are and what they want to buy. Then you provide the product.

Use the Form

Figure 5.1 is a simplified form for a business plan. As you proceed chapter by chapter through this book, it may be helpful to fill in the sections of your business plan. When you have finished with the final chapter, your plan will be in place and you will be on your way to becoming a successful real estate investor.

In Summary

Without a plan, a business is much less likely to succeed. A workable plan assesses the assets and the goals before planning a strategy, which includes identifying both the product that is to be offered and the customer for whom the product is intended. The best kind of plan is committed to writing and reviewed periodically.

Six

■ ■ ■ ■ ■

What Kind of Investor Are You: Urban Pioneer, Yuppie Rehabber, True Believer?

In This Chapter

This is the chapter that works like a mirror. Not the kind of mirror one finds in a lady's dressing room, surrounded by gentle lights designed to enhance one's image by softening and obscuring imperfections. No, this chapter is meant to work like the mirror one encounters, often by surprise, in the clothing section of a department store: wrapping around you on three sides, with the light from dozens of fluorescent ceiling fixtures penetrating every line in your face, it reveals details about yourself that are both unexpected and unflattering. From the stains on your teeth to the bulges around your waist, the department store mirror is unremitting in its reflection of reality.

Like the department store mirror, this chapter will reflect reality. If successful, it will not only reflect obvious realities but will also probe more deeply, searching out the fantasies that have led you to consider real estate as an investment venture.

The purpose of this chapter is to challenge you to look carefully at yourself—what motivates you to consider real estate as an investment, the illusions you bring to this venture, your misperceptions, your fantasies. The investment strategies that will be presented in the pages that follow require a level of commitment that you may not be prepared to make. If so, it's good to determine so early on to avoid approaching real estate investing with unrealistic expectations. It's better that you uncover these now, and determine whether you are really suited for a successful career in rental properties.

In the world of real estate investment there are a number of types of individuals who, if emulated, can lead one to failure. There is the Urban Pioneer, who, regardless of the risk, lays claim to a lovely old building in the heart of the urban ghetto. The Yuppie Rehabber sees every building as a candidate for a total rehab, using the most expensive Euro kitchens and track-lighting. The Social Worker views every sub-standard building as a potential haven for low-income tenants, often ignoring the economic realities of the building. The Slumlord bleeds a building of its resources, putting nothing back into it, until it ultimately fails to shelter life any longer. The True Believer, totally unaware of the concept of balanced books, has a vision that any slice of real estate is a potential diamond mine. The Deal Maker operates for the joy of putting deals together but often ignores the most basic of economic principles when it comes to the operation of the building. The Janitor turns an affinity for buildings into a growing empire, while Mr. Fix-it concentrates on taking care of all the plugged pipes and broken switches while a potential fortune slips away. The Passive Investor, meanwhile, is caught up by the concept of the "armchair investment" and looks the other way while his or her investment capital is squandered.

Each of these tendencies can ruin a potentially lucrative rental business. To counteract such tendencies, one must keep one's eye on the true goal of rental properties—profits.

Character Traits That Hinder A Real Estate Venture

Author's Note: In Chicago there is a neighborhood known as Uptown. Four miles or so north of the Loop, it crowds against Lake Michigan on the east, held back by a narrow strip of park-land and a two-block-wide corridor of upscale apartment buildings and stately older homes. Contained by a strip of cemeteries on the west, this colorful neighborhood has been the subject of numerous sociological studies and has also been home to several generations of migrating Appalachians.

After World War II, many of the graceful six-flats in the area were cut up into rooming houses, often providing a room and a shared bath for as many as 25 or more tenants. Residential hotels that date from the Twenties—long corridor buildings of four or five stories with 80 to 100 studio apartments—dominate the skyline on many of the trash-strewn blocks. Eighty-year-old maple and oak trees shade sidewalks that long ago ceased being safe thoroughfares.

Through the years, Uptown has become home to a widening array of nationalities and races. Shortly after the Vietnam war drew to an ignoble end, scores of refugees carved out a few blocks of Uptown as their own. Here, restaurants and shops have recaptured the images of Saigon that we have seen so often in films and documentaries of the Vietnam Nam era. In this few-square-block area, a long oppressed people can be seen pulling themselves out of the oppression of a long-neglected and abused neighborhood. Only a block away, however, is the intersection of Broadway and Wilson, the most well-known skid row of many in the city. Stand on this corner and see White Appalachians, Native Americans, Hispanics, African-Americans, Asians, Jamaicans, Haitians, a handful of Urban Pioneers, homeless people, prostitutes, drug dealers, emotionally disabled individuals from numerous half-way houses in the area, as well as students from near-by Truman College and a few steadfast natives left over from the 1920s, all going about their business.

I have looked at numerous buildings in the Uptown area. Once I nearly bought one, but the elderly owner was not to be found and the offer to buy could never be delivered. The real estate agent was as frustrated as I was.

I have been caught in a flooded basement in Uptown when the elevator that brought us down refused to take us back up. We clambered from box to chair to crate just like kids scrambling across a mountain brook, picking their way from rock to rock. I have been shown apartments in which the two inhabitants were lying on a filthy mattress in the corner of an unswept room littered with trash and clothing but no furniture, barely covered by a blanket that might have seen service in World War II and hadn't been laundered since. I have inspected apartments while the occupant lay on the sofa in an obvious drug-induced near coma, the fires on the gas burners turned nearly to blow-torch candescence. As I dutifully checked water pressure in the bathroom the stultifying air smothered me in a damp tropical swelter.

Into the mix of seething humanity known as Uptown came one day a husband and wife determined to make their fortune in real estate. The Uptown couple overlooked the hopelessness of most of the inhabitants and saw only two things: here were beautiful buildings just waiting to be restored to an earlier splendor, and these buildings could be bought at fire-sale prices. They bought one of the most beautiful of the vintage Roaring Twenties corridor buildings—one richly adorned with delicately formed concrete scroll-work and fine, filigree-like ornamentation on its ostentatious facade. Like a once-glorious fur coat from a resale shop, however, the building had noticeable blemishes, the result of decades of abuse and neglect—the quintessential Tarnished Lady. But these blemishes could be fixed.

Inside, this once-stately building housed some of the most desolate beings in a neighborhood of disconsolate derelicts and struggling outcasts. Prostitutes carried on a booming business in many of the shabby rooms. In others addicts, alcoholics, dealers, and mental incompetents lived out their sorry existence, away from the view of society and the light of day. But these tenants could be removed.

There was no problem, it seemed to these rosy-eyed novices, that could not be solved with a good mix of sweat and money. Then, with a scrubbed building and a new mix of poor-but-honest tenants, they reasoned, their real estate empire would have been launched.

But dreams, sweat, and money are not always the stuff of happy endings. The hapless tenants, they found, did not want to move, and resisted every effort to extricate them. Oh, the optimistic couple utilized all the available resources: court, sheriff, heavy locks, private guards. But these resources cost a lot of money, and this project was on a tight budget. When the guards were gone, the tenants came back. Expensive locks were only a minor impediment. All efforts to clean out the building failed.

What work was done to the building was soon vandalized; tools or materials left on the sight were stolen or destroyed. The costs were mounting and no end was in sight. It was impossible to attract decent tenants while this motley band of parasites continued to inhabit many of the rooms. No one would feel safe inside their apartments. And of course the squatters no longer paid rent.

With no rents coming in and the seemingly unsolvable problems creating a whirlpool that was sucking their limited resources and their heady optimism into oblivion, the hapless couple faced mortgage payments that could not be met, utility bills that went unpaid, tax levies that were beyond their dwindling reserves.

Finally, all hope gone, they simply abandoned the building, giving it back to the mortgage company and the squatters. Far from improving their own financial situation, they nearly bankrupted themselves. Far from improving the lot of the neighborhood, they left it more damaged than they found it, with a building that would now sink into utter squalor and finally become just one more of the boarded up abandoned hulks that pockmark such desolate neighborhoods.

In the world of real estate investment, one may encounter a broad spectrum of fellow investors. Some allow personal eccentricities to deprive them of the full potential of their ventures. In each case, their behavior as an investor is shaped by personal attitudes that form an impediment to the clear pursuit of their avowed goals.

Certain characteristics are particularly detrimental. In the examples to follow, each type is drawn with broad brush strokes in order to make the point clear. Each of us likely harbors some small bit of each of these characteristics. But by recognizing each of them we can refuse to allow them to influence important investment decisions. If you find yourself identifying too closely with any of these types, however, you might want to reconsider your decision to invest in rental properties.

The Urban Pioneer

In nearly every large city there are lovely old neighborhoods full of turn-of-the-century Victorian houses, stately graystone homes, enchanting brick mansions, captivating rowhouses, charming bungalows and grand old two-flats, three-flats, and larger apartment buildings. Some of these neighborhoods have remained in the hands of the wealthy and have survived the persistent threat of urban decay while others have succumbed to the inexorable flight of the middle class and have suffered from decades of neglect and abuse. To anyone with an appreciation for old-world craftsmanship and gracious living, a drive through these now poverty-stricken neighborhoods brings a sense of sadness and regret. To some, it also excites a latent sense of adventure. Unable to afford the prices of such properties in the established, affluent neighborhoods, these urban pioneers choose to leave the comfort and safety of their present homes to buy one of these elegant old homes or apartment buildings.

Living among squalor and crime, they rehabilitate the building and the grounds, install elaborate security systems, and settle into a life of luxury amid the otherwise bleak urban decay. In pursuit of their dreams, they persevere amongst muggings and break-ins. Some, however, like the attorney who rehabbed a particularly beautiful home on a block of restored Victorian graystones in Chicago, don't survive. Pursued by a purse snatcher and choosing to fight, she lost her life.

If your primary motivation is that of the urban pioneer—to find, restore, and live in charming old buildings in marginal neighborhoods—you will find it very difficult to make a profit with rental properties. For one thing, it will be nearly impossible to attract high caliber tenants to live in your grandly restored building. For another, the costs of restoring the building will likely exceed by far the potential rental income. But most important, the desire to recreate gracious living in the midst of blight will deter you from a fair assessment of the customer/product paradigm upon which your venture depends.

The Yuppie Rehabber

Most cities in the United States have experienced some degree of "gentrifica-tion" in particular areas. Generally, younger middle class professionals move into a neighborhood, purchase an older house or small apartment building and rehabilitate it. It can be very satisfying to locate an older city home or a former warehouse and, after removing nearly everything from the interior, replace the old walls and fixtures with extravagant tiles, expen-sive hardwood, Euro kitchens and elegant baths, lofts and skylights, chan-deliers and track-lighting. It can also be very expensive.

It is often difficult for a rehabber to envision any other use for an old building than upgrading it to such professional standards. The fact is, however, that in most areas of the city where profitable rental properties exist, rehabbing would not only be inappropriate, but far too costly to make economic sense. When the rehab project is for your own residence it makes sense, but as a business, rehabbing such properties can be risky and requires access to huge amounts of capital. In difficult economic periods, rehabbing for profit often follows the same path as new construction—financing dries up, demand is significantly reduced, and profits evaporate.

If you are driven by the need to rehab rather than to make simply livable, to upgrade rather than to repair and paint, to create a living situation that is comfortable for you rather than your prospective tenants/customers, investing in rental properties will likely not be your cup of tea.

The Social Worker

There is no escaping the fact that quality affordable housing for the poor in urban areas is a critical problem. You may be motivated by a desire to acquire some of the substandard buildings in the inner-city and turn them into decent abodes for low-income tenants. This motivation, while noble, is often misdirected and can lead to disaster. While none of us wants to operate like a slumlord—bleeding a building of it's income while refusing to maintain even the basic services—it is quite difficult to operate a good building in a difficult neighborhood. Difficult, but not impossible. Unfortunately, most social worker types tend to ignore the bottom line, and consequently are not only unable to turn a profit, but often operate at a loss and ultimately must abandon their dreams.

Fortunately, if you have a strong inclination toward philanthropy and altruism, investment in rental properties can very well fulfill that disposi-tion. What could be better than providing safe, clean housing for individuals who might otherwise have difficulty finding it? The only way to do it successfully, however, is to do it in a business-like manner.

The Slumlord

The antithesis of the social worker, the slumlord acquires building after building in poor areas of the city for very little money. The modus operandi of the slumlord is then to collect as much cash as possible from each building, often by cutting up apartments into smaller units, creating illegal basement apartments or attic apartments, all the while refusing to make any more than the absolutely necessary repairs. As the building steadily deteriorates, the slumlord often neglects to pay property taxes, water bills or utility bills, pocketing as much cash as possible until the building is rendered uninhabitable. Finally, the slumlord boards up the building and walks away. After bleeding the building of its money, the slumlord leaves the tenants to fend for themselves, having destroyed their homes—as unattractive as they might have been.

Your search for profitable rental properties will likely take you into neighborhoods that attract slumlords. Some of these neighborhoods offer the best income potential and the most consistent supply of good quality tenants. In such areas, the temptation is to ignore some of the upkeep that one might do as a matter of course in other neighborhoods. Certainly, operating like a slumlord can be profitable. But operating an ethical business in such areas can also be profitable, and one sleeps better at night.

The True Believer

True believers are sold on the wisdom of acquiring property—any property—as a means to gain wealth. A true believer has no concept of cash flow. He or she finds a building for sale, likes it, and buys it. A year later, when the building requires huge quantities of additional capital to keep it afloat, the true believer cannot understand what has happened. Never having analyzed the income versus expense aspect of the property, they are unable to determine what went wrong.

Author's Note: Unwary true believers can be drawn into impossible deals by unethical owners. I recall one such person who operated in this manner. He would offer a building for sale to an unwary East European immigrant who, eager to make his fortune in the United States, was not able to evaluate the deal objectively. The terms were these: $20,000 down, a land contract for the balance, and a five-year *balloon. This meant that the buyer would have to find new financing at the end of the five years or forfeit the building.*

The buyer I knew agreed to purchase the property for $365,000 under just those terms. The seller had recently acquired the same property for only $250,000. He accepted the $20,000 down payment and wrote up the contract. During the subsequent five years the buyer faithfully made the mortgage payments, even though he had to put in some of his own money routinely because the property would not pay its own way. At the same time, he religiously upgraded the building, painting and repairing it until it became one of the nicest in the neighborhood. At the end of the five years, the balloon became due, and the buyer searched for new financing. Because he had paid an inflated price for the property, he was unable to obtain adequate financing. The seller, of course, demanded the property be returned, ready to sell again to the next unwary True Believer. The buyer was left with nothing, having forfeited his down payment, plus all the time and money he had put into the building for the past five years.

The Deal Maker

The deal maker derives great pleasure from putting a deal together, start to finish. Finding the right property, he or she makes the offer, negotiates a price, settles on terms, creates a financing package, and closes the sale, paying particular attention to each detail, using every advantage and squeezing every penny that can be wrung from the deal along the way. One gets the impression that money is not the motivating factor with the deal maker; gaining an advantage is. The deal maker is most happy when he or she has pulled the last possible dollar from the seller, often continuing to angle for a better price right up to the closing date by pointing out some flaw in the property that has occurred since the contract was signed. The seller, not wanting to lose the sale, will often agree to a reduction in price just to close the sale. The deal maker is often ruthless in his negotiating tactics, leaving the seller exhausted and angry, resentful and vengeful.

Because the deal maker focuses so carefully on the deal itself, he or she has little time or energy to devote to the property, to the management details, to the cash flow, to the little things that keep a building profitable. A deal maker can all too easily slip into the character of the slumlord, however inadvertently.

Although good negotiating skills will help obtain the best deal in acquiring properties, the deal itself is secondary to all the other parts of a business plan. Focusing attention on the deal can, in fact, be a hindrance to a long term plan. It is tempting, for example, to over-leverage acquisitions to the point that the income will not cover the expenses and the debt service. This is the legacy left by the expansion of the 1980s—property that could not pay its own way, overbuilding, billions of dollars of debt that could not be recaptured.

The Janitor

Thousands of immigrants through the years have found their first jobs as janitors in apartment buildings. Often combining a rent-free apartment with a small salary, these hard-working new-comers to the American dream recognized the value of property ownership and faithfully saved their money for a first down payment, followed by a second and a third, all the while continuing to work as the janitor for their own and for others' buildings. For most, the plan worked. Turning a little capital and a lot of "sweat equity" into ownership gave them independence and a sense of pride they were unable to obtain in their homelands.

Author's Note: By chance, I encountered one such entrepreneur who told me his plan: "Each time one of my children was born, I bought a building. This was their college money," he said. "I have five children and five buildings."

I looked at his shoes, worn at the ball of the foot, broken down at the heel. His patched and dirty navy blue pants and shirt testified to long hours of work and few hours of leisure. His Chaplinesque bearing—slouched, ragged, shuffling—decried his fierce ambition and his self-sacrifice for the future of his children. When I first met him, it was to inquire after the owner—I wished to purchase this property if it was available. When he introduced himself as the owner I was momentarily taken aback. Then I recognized the situation that I had seen repeated all over the city since my early childhood: the janitor with a vision for his children—turning real estate into college tuition, a shot at law school or medical school.

The Janitor suggests a strategy that, if followed carefully, can produce a substantial portfolio of properties with minimal beginning equity. Perhaps this is the way to get started. The Janitor also reveals some potentially problematic characteristics, however. Because of limited focus and a certain naivete, the Janitor can easily function as a True Believer and be victimized by an unscrupulous Deal Maker. Or, as happens more commonly, the Janitor's vision is limited to those buildings that can be managed as both janitor and managing agent. With this limitation, most Janitors will never enjoy the true potential that rental properties offer to the business-like investor.

Mr. Fix-it

Related to the Janitor, Mr. Fix-it is a capable handy-man who views every flaw in a building as repairable and is never afraid to tackle a property in disrepair. Looking through rose-colored glasses, he envisions the property after he has worked his magic on the crumbling plaster, the worn-out plumbing, and the frayed electrical wiring. Recognizing correctly the advantage of buying sub-standard buildings and investing "sweat equity," Mr. Fix-it often underestimates the cost in both time and money to accomplish his goals. Chained to a building that overwhelms him with repairs and tenant complaints, he is consequently unable to develop his real estate business because he spends too much time with a pipe wrench or a paint brush in his hand.

The Passive Investor

The Passive Investor dreams of a real estate empire, even looks for suitable investments. Often he or she invests a little in a limited partnership or a syndicate. Leaving everything to the managing partners, the Passive Investor waits for the profit checks to arrive. Often he or she waits in vain, watching rather as the management fees and other expenses eat up any potential profits. Without any tax advantage (passive losses can offset only passive gains) and showing no profit, the investment looks worse every day. When the building is finally sold, the soft real estate market causes the partners to accept a disappointing price which, after paying the sales commission (to the managing partner?), the legal fees, and the closing costs, is barely able to pay off the mortgage and return the original investment to the limited partners.

Disappointed and looking for something on his own, the Passive Investor contacts a real estate broker and asks him or her to find a good building. Within days, the broker presents a "great deal." The Passive Investor, after briefly driving by the building, decides to make an offer, which is accepted. Sixty days later, the property is bought, complete with a property management contract with the broker.

After a week or so, he drives out to the building to see how things are going, walks through the halls, looks at the huge boiler and goes home. At the end of the month, his first management report arrives from the broker. Pulling it from its envelope, he quickly scans to the end to find out how much money he has made this month. But instead of a check to the owner, the statement indicates a negative balance, with a request from the managing agent to forward a check to cover the short-fall.

What happened? Scanning the rent roll, he discovers that the building has a vacancy rate over 20%. Looking further, another three or four tenants are hopelessly behind in their rent. And what's this? $3,500 to repair the boiler! Real estate, to the chagrin of the Passive Investor, does not lend itself well to passive ownership.

What Motivates You?

Each of the investor types identified above—the Urban Pioneer, the Yuppie Rehabber, the Social Worker, the Slumlord, the True Believer, the Deal-Maker, the Janitor, Mr. Fix-it, the Passive Investor—is driven by a particular motive—a motive that inhibits their ability to be successful. In each case, the motive has been exaggerated for the purposes of identifying it for the reader. Very few investors are as single-minded as these. Your own personality is very likely a complicated jumble of competing influences and impulses. But don't be misled.

There is only one legitimate reason to pursue the business of real estate investment—profit. There may be any number of secondary inducements, but profit is the only justifiable motivation for investing in rental properties. Don't forget to have fun, of course, but every decision you make, beginning now, must first be made on the basis of profit.

This statement is not necessarily as mercenary as it sounds. Good business is good sense. When you pay attention to the bottom line, your customers receive the best product and you assure yourself and them that you will stay in business for the long run. Adam Smith recognized this phenomenon when he told us in 1776, "Every individual endeavors to employ his capital so that its produce may be of greatest value . . . By pursuing his own interest he frequently promotes that of society more effectually than when he really intends to promote it."

The Legacy of the Uptown Couple

Author's Note: What did the Uptown couple do wrong? Their motives seemed so honorable. Their willingness for hard work was obvious. Unfortunately, they were misled by some of the very character traits that made them so attractive as people.

They believed that real estate was their ticket to wealth (the True Believer). Then, they were drawn to the Uptown building in particular because of its faded beauty and its restoration potential rather than its true economic function (the Yuppie Rehabber?). Mistakenly, they assumed that the neighborhood would welcome their efforts to clean up a problem building and create safe, clean housing for the inhabitants (the Social Worker?). Naively, they ignored the dangers of working and owning property in this tough area (the Urban Pioneer?). Like Mr. Fix-it and the Janitor, they tried doing everything themselves but succeeded in doing very little. Worst of all, this earnest young couple failed to analyze the building from a business perspective. They failed to identify who the customer was in this neighborhood. Therefore, they were drawn to a building that met their criteria but not their customers' needs. They also failed to address the true risks of this project—both fiscal and personal. Consequently, they were grossly unprepared for the problems they encountered. Their intentions were noble, but the outcome was disastrous, both for them and for the neighborhood.

In Summary

A number of character tendencies can get in the way of an otherwise promising rental business. Most of these character traits are seemingly harmless or, in several cases, even noble. The truth is, however, that profit alone should be the deciding factor in the acquisition of any property. This does not mean that one cannot operate a clean, safe, quiet building in the best interests of the tenants. On the contrary, to do so is only good business. If a building will not generate profits, however, one will not own it long, unless one has very deep pockets.

Seven

■ ■ ■ ■ ■

How Much Risk Can You Tolerate?

In This Chapter

The ability to tolerate risk involves more than one's financial capacity to lose money. It is not difficult to determine how much money can be lost before infringing upon one's current life-style. More difficult to measure is one's *psychological* capacity for risk. Psychological considerations, of course, are elusive and difficult to measure. Only you can determine how much risk you can reasonably withstand; it is essential, therefore, to be entirely honest. Once the commitment to purchase a rental property has been made, the ability to handle risk will determine your capability for making sound decisions and, by implication, your ability to protect your investment. If your personal assessment reveals at least a moderately high capacity for taking risk, you should be well suited for the strategies outlined in later chapters. If, however, your assessment reveals a low capacity for risk taking, perhaps you should confine your activities to less speculative ventures.

Psychological Capacity for Risk

Chapter 6 exploded some of the myths of real estate investing. By describing graphically the possible results of inexperience and misguided motives, that chapter revealed some of the risks that one embraces when choosing to invest in rental property. The risks, of course, can be mitigated by following certain essential procedures and by being smart, which is the purpose of this book—to teach the reader how to profit from rental properties with the least amount of risk. In spite of our best efforts, however, risk is still a major factor when dealing with rental properties.

Some individuals are just not cut out for taking risk. The potential rental property investor must analyze his or her financial and psychological capacity for risk taking. Because rental properties involve financial risk, the money to be invested must be considered risk capital: money one can afford to lose without significantly changing one's present standard of living. Chapter 9 introduces a simple procedure for determining one's personal cash flow and net worth, and thus one's financial capacity to tolerate risk. An investor's capacity to endure financial risk is therefore relatively easy to calculate. One's psychological capacity for risk, however, is more difficult to assess.

How Prepared for Risk Are You?

Are You an Overly Cautious Investor?

Most successful investors tend to be cautious about their ventures; they realize that rushing into that "chance of a lifetime" without a diligent examination of all aspects of the project can be deadly. Most also realize that there are no guarantees in the world of investment; each project is a unique mix of informed speculation and concrete investment, with some luck mixed in. The overly cautious investor, however, may be uncomfortable with even the mildest level of risk. Are you overly cautious?

Ask yourself these questions:

1. *Do you dutifully evaluate every new investment, analyzing possible outcomes before putting money in?* If so, you are a diligent investor, one who is rightfully cautious about where you put your hard-earned cash.

2. After your evaluation, however, *do you agonize over a new investment, checking every conceivable outcome before deciding to invest?* If the answer is yes, you are probably too cautious with your money to consider an investment in rental properties. Each real estate acquisition is unique, with its own set of problems and risks. Outcomes can be assessed within broad parameters, but unforeseen obstacles can change the outcomes dramatically.

3.   *What kinds of investments are now in your portfolio?* Your present portfolio of investments reveals a great deal about your affinity for taking risks. Is your money primarily in insured cash savings programs, like passbook savings accounts, certificates of deposit (CDs) and insured money market accounts? Have you ventured into mutual funds, which offer a greater return with less liquidity, greater risk of loss and no insurance? Have you ever tried investing in stocks on your own? If so, do you pick the stocks yourself or do you let the broker pick them for you? What other kinds of investments do you have? Where do they fit on the risk continuum?

4.   *Do you now own real estate?* If so, do you own any properties other than your home, and would you consider them high risk or low risk properties? If you now own or have owned real estate, much of the mystery has already been revealed. With some experience under your belt, the perception of risk is likely much less than for the pure novice.

Are You an Anxious Investor?

1.   *Are you the kind of investor who must carefully peruse every statement to determine how well your investments are doing?*

2.   *Do you worry a lot about how to protect your family, your life-style, your position in the community?*

A yes answer to either of these questions indicates a high need for security and a low tolerance for risk. This may be true regardless of your true financial condition. Everyone worries about their finances. We all become frightened at times when we read about savings and loan associations failing or another crash in the stock market. The difference lies in the intensity and the frequency of the feelings. It is one thing to be concerned in a healthy way about one's condition. It is another to be constantly in a state of agitation about one's investments.

Are You Overly Sensitive to the Loss of Money?

1.   *Are you uncomfortable investing your money in an uninsured program?*

2.   *Are you uncomfortable if any of your investments lose money, even for a short time?*

Figure 7.1   Portfolio Evaluation

PORTFOLIO EVALUATION

How much risk have you been willing to tolerate in your investments?

First, enter the value of your portfolio. Second, on the lines provided, enter the dollar value of each type of investment in your portfolio. Third, calculate the percentage of the total portfolio that is represented by that particular type of investment. Fourth, total the percentage for each category to determine how much risk you have assumed in your investment portfolio.

TOTAL PORTFOLIO VALUE: $_____ (100%)

Low risk investments:

____%	$_____	Savings Accounts
____%	$_____	Certificates of Deposit
____%	$_____	Money Market Accounts
____%	$_____	Other
TOTAL ____%		Percentage of portfolio in low risk investments

Moderately risky investments:

____%	$_____	Tax Deferred Accounts
____%	$_____	Mutual Funds
____%	$_____	Retirement Accounts
____%	$_____	Other
TOTAL ____%		Percentage of portfolio in moderately risky investments

Moderate to high risk investments:

____%	$_____	Stocks
____%	$_____	Bonds
____%	$_____	Precious Metals
____%	$_____	Collectibles
____%	$_____	Long-Term Real Estate
____%	$_____	Other
TOTAL ____%		Percentage of portfolio in moderate to high risk investments

High risk investments:

____%	$_____	Speculative Real Estate
____%	$_____	Futures
____%	$_____	Other
TOTAL ____%		Percentage of portfolio in high risk investments

SUMMARY:

LOW RISK:	____%
MODERATE RISK:	____%
MODERATE TO HIGH RISK:	____%
HIGH RISK:	____%
	100 %

For some, the loss of $10 is terribly unsettling. For others, gambling tens of thousands of dollars is part of the thrill of life. I read a story once about a well known businessman who had survived several reversals in his fortunes through the years. At the bottom of one of his periods of loss he was interviewed by a reporter eager to capitalize on the humbled status of a prominent millionaire.

"How does it feel to be broke?" the insensitive reporter asked.

"I'm not broke," came the immediate reply, "only temporarily out of money."

This man's capacity for risk was extraordinary. Most of us are not so immune to the prospect of losing our shirts. If you have never tried a higher risk investment, you must be very cautious in your approach to rental properties. Your investment is not insured; the return on your dollar is not guaranteed. Even though you may feel that you can handle nearly anything, unless you have actually experienced the grinding feeling that comes with losing some of your hard-earned money you cannot adequately anticipate your response.

Are You an Eternal Optimist?

Are you constantly in a positive emotional state about most things?

If so, you will probably be able to tolerate a high degree of risk without any obvious personality consequences. The problem is that your optimism at times may be unrealistic. If you always see the glass as being half full, you might overlook some important details that can lead to problems later. A good dose of healthy skepticism is often called for.

Are You an Eternal Pessimist?

Are you constantly in a negative emotional state about most things?

If the glass always looks half empty, you may miss some important opportunities because of an overly negative perspective. Once into an investment, a period of poor performance can easily throw you into a state of depression that renders you incapable of taking positive action. When dealing with rental properties, there will inevitably be problems. A boiler breaks down in the dead of winter at a cost of thousands of dollars. The rental market changes and suddenly you are faced with high vacancies. If you are a pessimist, these inevitable but temporary setbacks will likely serve to reinforce your negative expectations and consequently lead to emotional gridlock just at the time you need to take clear-headed action.

Do You Lack Confidence?

1. *Are you constantly looking for other people's opinions before investing?*

2. *Do you read every investment book you can obtain in an attempt to find the best possible strategy?*

3. *Do you attend seminars and send for pamphlets and tapes, constantly looking for the sure thing?*

4. *Do you find it difficult to establish a new investment, even after checking it out meticulously?*

If you are considering an investment in rental properties but know very little about the business, a search for information and advice can be helpful. Once you have the information, however, the next step is to take action. If you lack the confidence to act, you can easily find yourself on a merry-go-round of investment seminars, newsletters, books, and courses, always searching for the perfect strategy but never able to throw off the shackles of insecurity. If you have these tendencies, be careful: if you decide to buy a property, that same insecurity can lead to an inability to make decisions, and decisions are a daily part of working with rental properties.

Are You Full of Confidence?

Do you feel confident that you can meet and conquer any adversity?

You are ready to face almost any amount of risk; there is nothing you can't handle. If there is a problem, you feel, there is also a solution. This attitude, if taken to excess, can also be problematic. Some problems are beyond solving, and therefore some situations demand that they be left alone. Like the Uptown couple, excessive optimism and self-confidence, if not regulated by good sense, can lead an investor into dangerous waters.

How Much Risk Should You Be Able to Tolerate?

Rental properties involve risk, particularly during difficult economic times. Tenants lose their jobs and their incomes and are unable to pay the rent. Evictions are costly. Vacancy rates go up. Unexpected expenses arise. All of this is part of the business of owning rental properties. The best emotional profile for a successful real estate investor will therefore reflect a healthy balance of caution and confidence. To be successful in this business, you must be extremely cautious. When the right property presents itself, however, you must have the confidence to act. Later chapters will teach the skills that lead to that kind of confidence.

Risk versus Reward

In business as well as in life, it is axiomatic that greater rewards require greater risk taking. In real estate investing, there is an entire spectrum of risk/reward strategies to choose from. This book will spend little time with the low reward strategies and much more with those that offer higher rewards. At the same time, we will only look at investments in which the outcomes are primarily under the investor's control. In other words, we won't look at investments that are predominantly speculative in nature. Rather, we will look at the business of rental properties, where the potential income can be clearly calculated, expenses can be closely determined, the customer can be identified and the product defined.

In Summary

The ability to tolerate risk involves more than one's financial capacity to lose money. An overly cautious investor might find that rental properties are just too risky. Before investing, it is best to check your emotional profile: are you an anxious investor, overly sensitive to the loss of money, or an eternal optimist? Do you suffer from a lack of confidence? Rental properties involve risk, particularly during difficult economic times. Greater risk, however, usually entails greater rewards, and a healthy mix of caution and confidence should prepare one for a successful career in real estate investing.

Eight

■ ■ ■ ■ ■

How Involved Do You Wish to Be?

In This Chapter

Investing in rental properties is like starting a business: through your actions you can maintain and create value. With other investments—stocks, bonds, CDs, mutual funds—one's investment is entirely under the control of someone else; in fact, in most cases the amount of profit one makes is largely independent of the activities of any single person. Real estate is one of the few investments in which the investor can exercise a strong measure of control.

How actively do you want to participate in the management of your real estate business? The extent of your participation will depend on three factors:

■ How much time you *can* devote to the venture;

■ How much time you *want* to give to the venture;

■ Your level of skill and experience.

How Much Time Do You Have Available?

Take time now to assess how many hours per week you realistically can give to your real estate venture without seriously affecting your career or your family. If you are employed in a demanding job, you might not have the time to complete all the tasks and activities necessary for success. If you have a family, the demands of family life might preclude your giving enough hours to the venture.

Using the Time Assessment worksheet (Figure 8.1), place an x in each box that is routinely committed to an activity each week. Each box you check represents an hour that you cannot give to your business venture because of a prior commitment. For each hour time slot total the open boxes (column 1), then total column 1 to obtain the total time per week that is available to pursue your real estate investment strategy.

How did you do? If you found that you have less than ten hours per week, you probably will not have time enough to do everything necessary for a successful venture. Ten to fifteen hours is difficult. Fifteen to twenty hours is adequate. More than 20 hours is excellent.

Now go back to the worksheet. What kinds of sacrifices can you make to free up more time? Is it possible to cut back on the time you give to your job, to carve out a few extra hours for your new business. Look again at your other commitments. Is there anything else that can be cut? Be honest. Some of those weekly activities that now seem so important may be less significant than a successful future as a real estate entrepreneur. With a different color ink fill in each crossed-out box or portion of a box that could be made available with a little effort. Now total the hours again (column 2). Did you find some more time to devote to your new business? If you did, be assured that each hour you found will pay off handsomely in the future. Next to a lack of capital, the greatest potential contributor to poor performance in rental properties, as with any business, is lack of involvement. No one else will oversee your money and interests as faithfully as you.

How Much Involvement Do You Desire?

Maybe you *have* the time to give to a new business, but you choose not to be actively involved; there are other things you would rather be doing with your time. If that is the case, you might want to look at some alternatives. Not every investor in rental properties actively participates in the process of acquiring and managing rental properties. One way is to invest with one

Figure 8.1 Time Assessment Worksheet

	M	T	W	Th	F	Sa	Su	Total 1	Total 2
6:00 AM									
7:00 AM									
8:00 AM									
9:00 AM									
10:00 AM									
11:00 AM									
12:00 PM									
1:00 PM									
2:00 PM									
3:00 PM									
4:00 PM									
5:00 PM									
6:00 PM									
7:00 PM									
8:00 PM									
9:00 PM									
10:00 PM									
11:00 PM									
			WEEKLY TOTAL						

or more partners. You might be the inactive partner who invests most of the capital while the others do most of the work.

Even with such passive investments, however, you should become interested to the point that you carefully choose the experts with whom you will entrust your money. As you would expect, the less you are involved, the lower the anticipated return on your investment. Conversely, the more active you are, the greater the potential return. If you decide to work with one or more partners, be certain they have the skills that you will have learned from reading this book. Check their resumes carefully; experience is essential if the venture is to prosper. Check their track records: how successful have they been in the past? As you have already seen, the world of rental properties is fraught with pitfalls that only the best professionals are prepared to avoid. If you choose the wrong person or people, the outcome is likely to prove disappointing.

Should you decide that you want to let others do much of the work, you will find that the strategies contained in this book will still serve you well. By knowing and understanding the strategies you will be able to evaluate the effectiveness of those in whose hands you have placed your money and your hopes.

What Skills Do You Have?

Perhaps you have lived in an apartment at one time in your life. Maybe you still do. If so, you already have vast experience as a consumer of rental real estate. If you have never rented, you still have a good understanding of the tenants' needs and desires—tenants need comfort, security, and a clean, working home, just like you do. As a person who has lived somewhere, you already have a basic understanding of the rental business. Very likely, you already have a good understanding of the principles of business as well. Therefore, a perceived lack of skills should not be a hindrance to your getting involved in the business of rental properties.

Perhaps you know nothing about roofs, catch basins, tuckpointing, and the like. Or you feel ignorant about real estate values, financing techniques, property management and such. These are specific skills that can be learned and will be covered later. By applying the knowledge you already have to the skills you will learn elsewhere in this book you can become an expert in rental properties.

How Many Hours Does It Take?

Author's Note: During the first 15 years or so of my real estate career, I worked as a teacher and invested in real estate part-time. I found that the process of acquiring a suitable property required a great deal of time and attention. I would spend most of my weekends searching through newspapers and Multiple Listing books, and the rest of the weekend driving out to see properties. Week-day evenings were often spent talking with real estate brokers, doing the numbers on properties in which I had an interest, and driving by other properties. The acquisition phase of the process required a huge investment of time.

After my third property, as a part-time investor, I found it necessary to hire a management firm to handle the day-to-day details of running the business for me.

I had tried managing my own properties at first and found the time demands too great. Early on, I monitored the management firm very carefully, and found them to be competent and thorough, though not as thorough as I would have been. By using their services, however, I had time to devote to acquiring additional properties.

There were times, however, when I allowed several years to pass before looking for more buildings, content to enjoy the substantial cash flow from the buildings I had. During this period of time, the demands on my time were quite low, by choice.

Then I decided to "retire" from my teaching job and devote full time to real estate. I now spend perhaps 30 to 35 hours per week watching over my properties, although when I enter an acquisition phase, the time commitment is far greater. I continue to use a management firm, but watch their activities closely and remain actively involved with all decisions regarding the management of the property.

How much time will you need to give? As much time as it takes. At first, the time commitment will be great. Later, you will be able to relax and enjoy the fruits of your labor. For now, however, be prepared to give most of your free time to this venture. If you are like me, though, you will find it as enjoyable as a leisure-time activity, or even more so because, in contrast to leisure activities, rental properties are also profitable.

In Summary

Investing in rental properties offers the opportunity to take control of your own investments. The extent of your involvement, however, will depend on how much time you *can* devote to the venture, how much time you *want* to devote to the venture, and your level of skill and experience.

Nine

■ ■ ■ ■ ■

How Much Money Can You Invest?

In This Chapter

Because real estate is not the safe harbor some would have us believe, it is essential to view the money that is set aside for real estate investment as risk capital. The distinction is important. Risk capital is money one can afford to lose without significantly changing one's present standard of living. Not as risky, under most conditions, as stock speculation or futures trading, real estate investing nevertheless is not the same as a certificate of deposit backed by the FDIC. Nor is it as safe as municipal bonds.

The investment strategies that are recommended in later chapters rarely involve no-money-down deals; an investor must plan to put some of his or her own money into each acquisition. Most young businesses fail because they are inadequately capitalized. Starting on a shoe string might be a romantic idea—fun to read about in *Readers' Digest*—but, in reality, when an unexpected calamity leads to a default on the mortgage payment and repossession of the property the pain outweighs any elation one may have experienced early on.

You may already have a good idea of how much money you intend to invest: perhaps you have been saving for a while, planning to use the money for this kind of investment, or you have made some money in other pursuits and now have decided to invest the proceeds in real estate as a form of diversification. On the other hand, you may be the kind of potential investor who has a vague dream of acquiring investment riches but has not yet determined quite how nor where the investment capital is to be raised. Chapter 23 shows the alternatives for financing real estate acquisitions. The purpose of this chapter is to determine how much of your own money you realistically can put into the venture, by analyzing your cash flow and your net worth.

Your Personal Financial Analysis

The best way to determine how much money one can afford to invest is to complete a personal financial analysis, which includes a cash flow statement to determine how much can be saved for a real estate venture and a net worth statement to determine how much money is available right now for the venture. Perhaps you have already done this; most potential investors have not. It is, nevertheless, an excellent analytical tool that will be valuable as your strategy is worked out later. The amount of money you have to work with, after all, is key to the development of a workable investment strategy.

Cash Flow Statement

Figure 9.1 is a sample cash flow statement. Look it over, copy it and fill in the blanks. The purpose of this form is to allocate all expected sources of income for the present year and for each of the next five years or more into fixed and variable categories. Fixed expenses are then matched with fixed income. One's personal mortgage, for example, should be matched with the most reliable source of income, while variable and discretionary expenses such as entertainment can be matched with less secure sources of income. A good idea, however, is to determine a preferred standard of living and then consider all expenses that directly support that standard of living as fixed expenses, even if they have a discretionary component. Variable income, then, is matched with expenses that are considered luxuries—those that could be easily omitted without undue hardship.

Net Worth Statement

The next step is to create a net worth statement. This will establish the amount and the source of any money available for your investment strategy. Make a copy of Figure 9.2, look it over and fill in the blanks. When you are finished, you will know the true value of your assets, such as your home,

Figure 9.1   Cash Flow Statement

CASH FLOW STATEMENT

INCOME: Fixed   Variable

Earned:
  1 Salary $_____ $_____
  2 Commissions   _____   _____
  3 _____   _____   _____
  4 _____   _____   _____

Investment (i.e., stocks, property, etc.):
  1 Interest   _____   _____
  2 Dividends   _____   _____
  3 Capital gains (when sold)   _____   _____

Other:
  1 Child support   _____   _____
  2 _____   _____   _____
  3 _____   _____   _____

Total Income: $_____ + $_____ = $_____
             (Fixed)   (Variable)   (Total)

EXPENSES:

Household:
  1 Mortgage loans or rent $_____ $_____
  2 Property taxes   _____   _____
  3 Property insurance   _____   _____
  4 Utilities   _____   _____
  5 Maintenance (e.g., painting)   _____   _____
  6 Repairs (e.g., electrical repair) _____   _____
  7 _____   _____   _____
  8 _____   _____   _____
  9 _____   _____   _____

Personal:
  1 Food   _____   _____
  2 Clothing   _____   _____
  3 Medical and dental   _____   _____
  4 Non-property insurance   _____   _____
  5 Entertainment   _____   _____
  6 Child care   _____   _____
  7 Child support   _____   _____
  8 _____   _____   _____

Figure 9.1 Cash Flow Statement *(continued)*

Education:
 1 Children   _____   _____
 2 Self   _____   _____

Transportation: _____   _____

Other taxes:
 1 Local   _____   _____
 2 State   _____   _____
 3 Federal   _____   _____

Investment expenses (e.g., mutual funds, stock account, antique autos, etc.):
 1 Management fees   _____   _____
 2 Advisors' fees   _____   _____
 3 Insurance   _____   _____
 4 Debt service   _____   _____
 5 Storage   _____   _____
 6 _____   _____   _____
 7 _____   _____   _____

Other expenses:
 1 _____   _____   _____
 2 _____   _____   _____
 3 _____   _____   _____
 4 _____   _____   _____

Total Expenses: $_____ + $_____ = $_____
                   (Fixed)   (Variable)   (Total)

Calculate how much of your fixed income (as a percentage) goes to pay fixed expenses by dividing expenses by income:

Fixed expenses $_____ ÷ Fixed income $_____ = _____%.
This is the portion of your fixed income that must cover fixed expenses.

Similarly, calculate how much of your total income goes to pay expenses by dividing expenses by income:

Total expenses $_____ ÷ Total income $_____ = _____%.
This is the portion of your total income that is consumed by expenses.

To calculate cash flow, subtract total expenses from total income:

Total income $_____ - Total expenses $_____ = $_____.

Figure 9.2   Net Worth Statement

NET WORTH STATEMENT

A. ASSETS:

CASH:
   1 Savings accounts $_____
   2 Checking accounts   _____
   3 On hand   _____

SECURITIES (Market Value):
   1 Governments   _____
   2 Publicly traded corporate stock   _____
   3 Mutual fund shares   _____
   4 Privately held stock or bonds   _____
   5 Stock options (less exercise cost)   _____
   6 _____   _____

LIFE INSURANCE (Face Value):
   1 Individual   _____
   2 Group   _____

REAL ESTATE (Market Value):
   1 Primary residence   _____
   2 Vacation home   _____
   3 Investment   _____
   4 _____   _____

RETIREMENT INTERESTS:
   1 Profit sharing   _____
   2 Vested pension contributions   _____
   3 Pension and profit-sharing death benefits   _____

DEFERRED COMPENSATION   _____

PERSONAL PROPERTY   _____

AUTOMOBILE:
   1 _____   _____
   2 _____   _____
   3 _____   _____

OTHER ASSETS:
   1 _____   _____
   2 _____   _____
   3 _____   _____

                 (A) Total Assets: $_____

Figure 9.2   Net Worth Statement *(continued)*

B. LIABILITIES:

MORTGAGE DEBT $_____

NOTES:
  1 Notes to banks   _____
  2 Notes to others   _____
  3 Automobile loan   _____

DEBTS:
  1 Debt owed to brokers   _____
  2 Debt owed to insurance companies   _____
  3 Taxes owed   _____

CHARGE ACCOUNTS AND CREDIT CARDS:
  1 _____   _____
  2 _____   _____
  3 _____   _____

CONTINGENT LIABILITIES (e.g., co-signer for loan):
  1 _____   _____
  2 _____   _____
  3 _____   _____

OTHER LIABILITIES:
  1 Personal loans   _____
  2 _____   _____
  3 _____   _____

            (B) Total Liabilities: $_____

    NET WORTH Assets (A) less Liabilities (B): $_____

your car, personal property, stocks, bonds, investments, business interests, insurance, and anything else you own. On the other side of the ledger is the total amount of your liabilities—your mortgage, the loan on your car, and any other financial obligations. Subtracting your liabilities from your assets reveals your net worth in dollars. How does it look? If the figure is negative, you may not be a good candidate for an investment strategy. If the figure is under $10,000, there might not be sufficient cushion to allow you to pursue other than a very conservative strategy. If the figure is over $25,000, you might have some flexibility in planning a strategy.

If your net worth does not support a venture into real estate investing in its present condition, is there anything you can do to alter it? Can you sell your car, for instance, or settle for a smaller home for a time? As with any successful business, the early years of your venture might require sacrifices in life-style that will pay off later. The choice, of course, is yours.

How Solid Is Your Net Worth?

By the time the 1980s drew to a close, thousands of real estate investors across the country were able to flaunt a very high net worth, based on sky-high real estate values. Their net worth was not inflated, but the value of the properties that represented the bulk of their net worth was inflated. When the real estate bubble burst, their financial condition quickly skidded to nearly nothing. Such is the nature of paper worth; if the value of the underlying collateral decreases, so does one's net worth. It is important not to fool yourself into believing you have a large net worth when in fact your net worth is based on speculative values. The loser, if something should go wrong later—and it usually does—will be you.

How Liquid Is Your Net Worth?

Can your net worth be converted to cash easily? If you have a high net worth, but most of it is represented by illiquid assets—expensive paintings, for example—it might be difficult to raise cash for investment purposes. The only source of cash in such a scenario is to sell some of the paintings or to try to borrow against the value of the art collection. If, on the other hand, your net worth is primarily represented by certificates of deposit at the local bank, you have adequate access to the cash to put it to use at your convenience.

Be certain you have sufficient real net worth and liquidity to cover financial emergencies—personal as well as business. Keep in mind also that real estate itself is considered highly illiquid. Even the best of properties require several months to sell. Don't expect that in an emergency you can unload one property to pay the debts of another. Always maintain adequate cash reserves to cover predictable reversals.

How Much Investment Capital Do You Have?

From your *cash flow* statement, how much can you save each month toward an investment fund? Does your cash flow realistically allow you to save money toward a real estate investment strategy? Alternatively, what size monthly payment could you make on a loan against your less liquid assets without endangering your fixed obligations?

From your *net worth* statement, how much liquid cash do you have for investing? How much cash could you borrow against the equity in your home, the value of your life insurance, the value of other investments, without endangering your financial condition?

How much money do you have to work with right now? In six months? In one year? If you have been honest in filling out the forms, you now know the limits of your investment capital. But remember—*invest only the money you can reasonably afford to lose.*

In Summary

Real estate investing involves risk. It is wise, therefore, to assess one's cash flow and net worth to determine how much risk capital is available to pursue the business of investing in rental properties. The simplest way to do this is to complete a cash flow statement and a net worth statement. The temptation will be strong to overstate your net worth, but honesty is important at this stage.

To be useful in an investment strategy, your net worth should be based on a realistic valuation of assets and should be liquid. If your calculations reveal an adequate amount of investment capital, it is safe to pursue an investment in rental properties. If, on the other hand, your net worth is quite small, you should consider deferring your plans until you have been able to raise an adequate amount of capital.

Section II

■ ■ ■ ■ ■

How to Find the Right Property

Ten

■ ■ ■ ■ ■

Finding the Right Apartment Building Can Be Tough

In This Chapter

Investing in rental properties offers great opportunity to the individual real estate investor, but remember, the majority of apartment buildings on the market do not make economic sense. Unfortunately, several factors have combined to drive the price of most apartment buildings beyond a level that can be supported by their rental income. Most of the problems can be traced to the 1970s, a time of rapid inflation and fundamental changes in the real estate market.

Those changes were led by condominium conversions, which forced prices to dizzying heights nearly overnight. The runaway inflation of the 1970s was both a cause and a result of spiraling real estate prices, which were fed as well by a sympathetic tax code that encouraged investment in projects that made no economic sense but created profits for investors through significant tax savings.

In spite of such pressure, buildings can still be found that produce cash flow. Because prices have hit unrealistic levels, however, the search for such buildings will be long and difficult and will lead the prospective investor into areas and neighborhoods where he or she might not otherwise choose to go. More recently, though, a fall in real estate prices has shown signs of returning the cost of rental properties to more realistic levels.

The Bull Market in Real Estate

Most properties on the market will not generate positive cash flow. The reason: unrealistic prices have driven the cost of debt service—the mortgage payment—much too high. For the investor with significant capital, the answer is to take on less debt and thereby reduce monthly costs. The result, of course, is reduced leverage and lower return on the investment dollar. Most investors, however, do not have sufficient capital to cover more than a reasonable down payment. For those investors, the cost of debt service eliminates most properties from consideration.

What has led to this state of affairs? A number of forces have influenced the real estate market over the past two decades, leading to a situation where the value of most property no longer reflects simple income/expense relationships, but is subject rather to the market forces of supply and demand. The causes: condominium conversions, an overly favorable tax code, inflation, and, finally, speculation.

Condominium Conversions

The first wide-spread development to affect rental properties was the condominium craze of the 1970s. Prior to condo-mania, an average 20-unit building in most neighborhoods would very likely support itself from its own rents, even delivering a reasonable profit to the owner in the form of cash flow after expenses and debt service were paid. As an extra incentive, the building would also offer moderate appreciation in value. A tidal wave of condo conversions changed all that.

As condominiums grew from being a novelty on the real estate market to a mainstream alternative to home ownership, the inherent value of thousands of apartment buildings changed virtually overnight. Because of the increased demand for condominiums, a 20-unit building that may have sold for $60,000 as a rental property could suddenly bring as much as $15,000 per apartment if it were divided into condos. This raised the value of the building to a dizzying $300,000. Granted, a fair amount of capital was required to convert the building, and some income was lost during the period of conversion—though not much: tenants were often given first option to buy their apartment at a reduced price. The demand for this new form of home ownership was so great that building after building was converted, often with the unfortunate result that long-term tenants, unable to buy, were forced from their homes. Many were compelled to move several times as each new building was converted. In a short time, apartment buildings had taken on an entirely new system of valuation. This drove the price of most buildings past the level at which a new owner could expect to see cash flow from rentals alone.

Tax Code and Inflation: A Combination Punch

Along with condominium conversion, two other factors conspired to drive the price of properties higher during the 1970s: inflation and favorable tax laws. Because of runaway inflation, an investor could buy a property regardless of the economics of the building, secure that he or she would see sizable profits from appreciation after holding the building for only a year or so. The relationship between inflation and demand for real estate, of course, is circular. As inflation drives prices higher, contributing to greater demand for real estate, the increased demand itself pushes prices even higher, contributing in large measure to an accelerated rate of inflation.

The second factor contributing to escalation of prices was a favorable tax code. Tax laws that favored real estate led to the development of syndicates that purchased apartment buildings primarily for the purpose of passing along tax losses to the limited partners. These syndicates could purchase a building that showed a net loss in operating income, combine that with accelerated depreciation, and present a substantial paper loss to each of the limited partners, who could then shelter a like amount of other income from taxes. Within a few years, the buildings could be sold for a profit (the result of inflation and high demand) and the profits passed to the limited partners, who then paid capital gains taxes at a preferred rate.

Speculation

All of these forces—condo conversions, favorable tax laws, and inflation—combined to force the price of apartment buildings ever higher. Then came the real estate boom of the 1980s. Speculative fever continued to create an unrealistic market for rental properties, one that had little relationship to the gross income that could be expected from collection of rents.

Slowing the Price Growth

More recently, however, the normal cyclical nature of the real estate market has begun to bring the prices of rental properties more in line with realistic economics. Several factors have combined to slow the rise in prices. The Tax Reform Act of 1986 removed the favored status of capital gains, took away accelerated depreciation and required that passive losses be used only to offset passive gains. This triple whammy nearly buried the limited partnership syndication business, removing such buyers from the market and thereby significantly reducing demand. In the meantime, prior over-building by syndications created a surplus of apartments and commercial properties, forcing prices—if not to fall—at least to cease their dizzying escalation. The recession that hit in 1990 dried up many of the sources of easy development money that fueled the expansion of the 1980s, and banks and savings and loan associations became very prudent in the wake of the multi-billion dollar S&L scandal that unfolded in 1989 and 1990. All of this means that rental properties are once again on the verge of becoming an attractive investment for the long-term individual investor.

Author's Note: For those of us who never abandoned the fundamental idea of cash flow as the measure of a good investment, however, all of this ebb and flow in the real estate market has been essentially irrelevant. Finding the right building has never been easy, and the fact that uncontrolled economic forces conspired to make the search more difficult simply raised the sense of victory when I was successful. Never having relied on appreciation, I have been relatively untouched by the recent decline in the real estate market.

Positive Cash Flow Is Still Possible

The basic formula of business is this: *income minus expenses minus debt service equals profit*. In an apartment building, if the income is too low to cover the expenses and the debt service, the building will deliver what is euphemistically referred to as *negative cash flow*. This means that the building is losing money each month. The goal, then, is to find a building that generates enough income to pay the expenses, cover the mortgage payment, and deliver money into your pocket each month. But where to find such a building?

Because inflation, condominium conversions, and syndications have conspired to force the price of apartment buildings to unrealistic levels, profit has become more and more elusive in rental properties. The primary culprit is the high cost of debt service. Even though expenses have risen through the years, rents have risen at a similar pace. But the cost of acquisition has driven mortgage payments to levels that distort the formula. To find a building that generates profit, an investor must locate properties whose price has not been driven to extreme levels. These properties are usually located in less desirable areas of the city.

If not located in less desirable areas, the building itself may appear less attractive. Often such buildings have been cut up into smaller apartments, thereby providing more rental units but appealing to a less discriminating clientele. Most likely the owners have provided little in the way of modernizing through the years; the new owner, therefore, can expect older bathroom fixtures and kitchen facilities. Plaster walls will typically be patched and heavily painted, and the wood trim may have layer upon layer of paint covering it. A rental property that generates positive cash flow, in short, will usually be a property that appeals to a low-income clientele. While this can be problematic, the fact is that, if managed well, such a property can return a healthy profit year after year.

In Summary

Profit-producing buildings are difficult to find and difficult to manage because, for one reason or another, such buildings are less desirable to the general investing public. Real estate prices have experienced a long period of inflation, a price spiral that was established early on by three influences: condominium conversions, the tax code, and inflation, and which was fed more recently by intense speculation. Following the bull market in real estate, however, has come the inevitable price fall, which shows signs of producing a more realistic price structure for rental buildings. In the mean time, though, properties can still be found that produce positive cash flow. The kinds of properties and the locations may be less desirable, but beauty, as they say—as well as desirability— is in the eye of the beholder.

Eleven

■ ■ ■ ■ ■

Conducting Market Analysis:
How to Cruise the Neighborhoods

In This Chapter

People of like interests and similar backgrounds tend to group together. People of similar financial means and socio-economic tendencies seem to seek each other out and form little communities within the context of the larger town and city. These communities become neighborhoods. The kind of neighborhood one invests in will often determine how profitable the investment will be. The kind of neighborhood also determines how successful the acquisition will be. It isn't enough to know whether a property is in a "good" area or a "bad" area. To be successful with rental properties, one needs to know the character of the neighborhood.

The best way to learn about the neighborhoods is to get out and drive through them; there are any number of characteristics one can glean about a neighborhood and its inhabitants by paying particular attention to certain specific elements one finds there. By becoming acquainted with the residents of a neighborhood, one is actually performing market analysis to determine who the prospective customers are for any building one might purchase in the area. Picking the right neighborhood is as critical as picking the right building, which is why one must know the neighborhoods.

How to Know the Neighborhoods

Author's Note: Several years ago, I sat in on a philosophy class in which the assignment was to define the word neighborhood. Thirty graduate students spent more than 50 minutes wrangling over a task that seemed so simple when first presented. Although they narrowed the concept considerably, the class was unable to accomplish the assignment. They could not define a neighborhood.

This chapter will not attempt what 30 graduate students failed to accomplish. A neighborhood, after all, is an intuitive concept. If you were asked to identify the neighborhood you grew up in, chances are you would have little trouble doing so. Likewise, you probably know a great deal about the neighborhood in which you now live. And from personal experience you can probably identify several other neighborhoods in the area. Although *neighborhood* might defy definition, it is not difficult to know a neighborhood.

Every city, town, and rural area has its neighborhoods. In a densely populated city, a neighborhood may be as small as one or two blocks. In a sparsely populated rural area, a neighborhood might encompass several square miles. Regardless of the size, each neighborhood has one distinguishing factor: the people who live there tend to hold the same values; they tend to share similar goals and ambitions. The people who live there and the people who want to live there know intuitively what those values are. When you buy a property in their neighborhood, they become your potential customers. To be successful, you must also know their values.

Most books on real estate investment treat each individual building as an entity independent of the neighborhood surrounding it. While giving lip service to the concept of area, they rarely deal with the issue of the neighborhood. But a real estate purchase is more than just a lot of brick and concrete. It is more than a set of numbers. As with any business, a rental property will succeed or fail on its ability to draw paying customers. That is why you have to know the neighborhoods.

Market Analysis

American business is known for its market research and analysis. Often, before a product is brought to market, millions of dollars will have been spent testing whether that product will sell. One of the buzzwords in market analysis is demographics: what type of person in what section of the country in what age group and which gender is most likely to buy this product? To answer these simple questions, hundreds of hours are spent with surveys, test groups, test markets, and so on. After all the data has been collected and analyzed, a marketing strategy is developed.

Knowing the neighborhoods is your way of doing market research and analysis, but without surveys or complicated statistical formulae; you will get to know the neighborhoods by going out and experiencing them first hand. Most of the properties you will look at are located in lower income neighborhoods: neighborhoods that are comprised primarily of people from lower socio-economic groups. But not all lower income neighborhoods are the same. Some are safe, others are risky. Some are clean, others are dirty. Some are hard-working, others are primarily welfare. *Picking the right neighborhood is as critical as picking the right building.*

There are different ways to learn about neighborhoods. The most intimate way, of course, is to visit the neighborhood and spend time there talking with tenants and neighbors of buildings that appeal to you. One can also study the back issues of local newspapers, which generally cover neighborhood activities in their human interest sections. Talk with old-timers from the neighborhood who can accurately chronicle the local history and point out the critical dividing lines that define the neighborhood. And, finally, talk with real estate professionals who know the neighborhoods and their history, preferably seeking out someone who has been around the neighborhood awhile. Agents who work their own neighborhoods are usually quite knowledgeable.

Using the Newspaper

When searching for property in a large metropolitan area, the newspaper—particularly the Sunday edition—is an invaluable tool. Most large Sunday papers include a section devoted entirely to real estate. Along with the listings of property for sale and for rent can often be found one or more articles devoted to real estate issues. Often the lead article will focus on a particular area or neighborhood. Keep a file of these articles. Refer back to them from time to time as you drive through the areas. Spend a day at the library looking through back issues. Compare what was being said a few years ago with the current stories.

Keep in mind, however, that the newspaper is not necessarily a good source for investment advice. Remember the stock market axiom: what you read in the paper is already factored into the market. It is the same with real estate. When the paper covers a hot area it usually means that whatever opportunities were offered by that neighborhood are long gone. Or at least the nature of the opportunity is now different—that an investment in that neighborhood will now require much larger sums of money and will return much smaller profits. The reason is clear: by the time a reporter for the Sunday paper hears about the changes in a neighborhood, they are so far along as to be virtually irreversible, which reduces the perceived risk factor for most investors. Reduced perceptions of risk in turn reduce potential profits. It's the old risk/reward ratio all over again.

Driving through the Neighborhoods

Successful real estate investing involves an almost intuitive understanding of buildings, tenants, and neighborhoods. Intuition, of course, is nothing more than a heightened sense of awareness, an awareness that can begin to be cultivated right now. Learning the neighborhoods can commence long before a search for a suitable property. In fact, knowing the neighborhoods is an on-going activity that may prove both exciting and interesting. While out driving, for whatever purpose, keep one eye on the neighborhoods you are driving through. Constantly be aware. Rather than daydreaming or listening to the radio, keep an eye on the street, on the sidewalks, on the houses and buildings. Notice who is walking, notice what the houses look like, observe the changes over time.

To enhance your growing understanding of the neighborhoods, start now to develop another important habit: on Saturdays or Sundays take a drive. Each week, drive through a different neighborhood. Don't stick to the main arteries; drive the residential streets as well. Drive slowly and take in the details. Make notes about what you see. When possible, take someone along who is also perceptive. Ask for their impressions. Most important, don't discount anything in the neighborhood. Pay attention to the details and what those details say about the people who live there. Keep in mind that the people who live in the neighborhood will be your tenants—your customers. You will need to know how they live and what is important to them.

Neighborhoods change. In real estate, change often provides the best opportunities, which is a good reason to stay current on the neighborhoods. But change, of course, is not always for the good. A neighborhood that seemed solid might be changing for the worse, increasing the degree of investment risk. It is important to be able to recognize the signs of change and know how to judge the degree of risk. That is the importance of driving the neighborhoods with a keen eye.

Traveling the Neighborhoods With a Native

Occasionally, you might be fortunate enough to locate someone—a real estate agent is ideal because he or she has a stake in helping you—who is native to a particular neighborhood. An afternoon spent touring the area with this person can prove invaluable. You learn the history of the area and the present status of the neighborhood. Block by block, they can point out the changes that are occurring, and often they are keenly aware of the implications of those changes. They know the local politics and the community dirt. They are not necessarily particularly astute investors, so beware of any investment advice they might offer; and remember, the real estate agent's interest is in selling a piece of property, not in finding the best investment. But don't discount any information they provide regarding the neighborhood. It will work to your advantage later.

What to Look For in the Neighborhood

Use Figure 11.1 as a guide for evaluating a neighborhood. Be observant, and check off each item as you encounter that particular characteristic. When you are finished, you can rate a neighborhood as a Class I—the best, a Class II, or a Class III—the most difficult.

Buildings: When you go into the neighborhood, notice first the buildings. What age are the existing structures? Are they primarily newer, less than 30 years old? Are they primarily older? If the buildings are primarily older structures, have newer structures been built among them, which would indicate a healthy regeneration of the neighborhood, or are the buildings all of the same era and showing their age? What is the condition of the existing structures; are there signs of deterioration? Do you see any indications that some of the buildings are being rehabilitated? Are there new windows in any of the buildings, new paint, new fences? Are there boarded up buildings in the area and vacant lots where buildings once stood? Or, do most of the buildings seem to be inhabited. Do you see gang graffiti, trash, broken cars, or are the lawns well kept and the streets clean?

The condition of the buildings in the neighborhood can indicate where the neighborhood falls in the cycle of deterioration and renewal. Try to determine whether the area is getting better, getting worse, or has stabilized at the bottom or the top of the cycle. If the buildings do not reveal such secrets, investigate further. But first, gather as many clues as possible in order to draw your own conclusions.

After surveying the buildings, it is time to scrutinize the more subtle indicators of the neighborhood. The condition of the buildings can mask the true nature of the residents, and the purpose of your neighborhood cruise is to discover all you can about your prospective customers—the local residents.

Windows: Windows reveal a great deal about the people who live inside, so look carefully at the windows in the neighborhood. Are there curtains in the windows, or old bedsheets? This alone is indicative of the economic status of the residents. Are there shades? Are the shades clean and white or torn and dirty? Shades are the responsibility of the landlord, but the condition of the window shades reveals a great deal about the attitude of the landlord and the tenant. A tenant who cares will pressure a landlord for good shades. A landlord who cares will provide nice shades. Are there blinds instead of shades? This could indicate a younger population of tenants. Do you see newspapers covering the panes of glass? Are there broken panes? If in the summer, are there screens in the windows, or are the curtains blowing through open windows? This is one of the most revealing characteristics of the quality of a neighborhood. When you see a building with the curtains blowing, beware of the tenants inside.

Grass: Lawns need not be the manicured variety that one finds in many suburban neighborhoods to reveal a caring attitude. Nevertheless, the condition of the lawns in the area is another indicator of the quality of the residents. Notice: are there grassy yards and parkways? Or do you see only dirt? If there is grass, is it well kept or shaggy and overgrown with weeds? Does trash litter the front yards, the parkways, the back yards?

Alleys: Most city neighborhoods have alleys. Of all the characteristics to be observed, alleys are the most reliable indicators of the general character of the neighborhood. Building facades might look similar from block to block, and a certain amount of trash is inevitable on city streets. Parkways are tough to keep nice in the city, and the most well-meaning home owner might not have the skills or equipment to keep the lawn looking perfect. But a glance in the alley tells the real story.

Does each building have adequate trash containers? Is there trash overflowing onto the pavement. What about old sofas and mattresses? And what about the ubiquitous throw-away diaper? Some alleys seem to attract cast off belongings, while others remain clean and free of debris. The rule of thumb is, if the alley looks like a land-fill, avoid the neighborhood. But if the alley is clean, the neighborhood is probably alright.

Figure 11.1   Neighborhood Rating Form

NEIGHBORHOOD RATING FORM

OBJECTIVE: This form is used to establish the strengths and weaknesses of a specific neighborhood. Rate each of the 11 characteristics on a scale of 0 to 5, then total the ratings to determine whether the neighborhood is Class I, Class II, or Class III. This rating is important because it becomes one of the indicators of the desirability of a specific building. It is also used to estimate such variables as vacancy rate.

Name of the neighborhood:_____
What are the four boundaries—streets, other neighborhoods, landmarks?
_____
_____

1. TYPES OF BUILDINGS IN THE NEIGHBORHOOD:
   The best neighborhoods for rental properties provide a good mix of residential and commercial buildings, with enough re-tail stores to serve the community and a good mix of multi-family and single-family housing. If industrial buildings exist in the neighborhood, they should not overwhelm the residential nature of the area nor should they blight the area.

   First establish the approximate percentage of each type of building in the neighborhood, then rate the neighborhood accord-ing to the mix of buildings.

   ___% Commercial: ___% Industrial   SIZE:___% Single-story
                     ___% Stores and shops   ___% Two- and three-story
   ___% Residential: ___% Single-family   ___% Over three-story
                     ___% Multi-family   ___% High-rise

Rating #1:   POOR MIX OF BLDG TYPES   **0 1 2 3 4 5**   EXCELLENT MIX OF BLDG TYPES

2. CONDITION OF BUILDINGS IN THE NEIGHBORHOOD:
   The best neighborhoods for rental properties do not have a run-down look, even if the buildings are older. If the neighbor-hood is aging, then look for signs that buildings are being maintained, with here and there some new construction or major rehabilitation of existing structures.

   First establish the age of the buildings in the neighborhood and the average condition of the buildings. Then rate the neigh-borhood according to the condition of the buildings that exist there.

       Age: ___% 1-10 years old   Condition: ___% Excellent condition
               ___% 10-30 years old   ___% Good condition
               ___% 30-70 years old   ___% Fair condition
               ___% Over 70 years   ___% Poor condition

Rating #2:   POOR CONDITION   **0 1 2 3 4 5**   EXCELLENT CONDITION

3. DENSITY:
   An area that is primarily multi-family tends to have a high density of people, which translates into more problems, more noise, more trash, etc. Rate this neighborhood according to density.

Rating #3:   PRIMARILY MULTI-FAMILY   **0 1 2 3 4 5**   PRIMARILY SINGLE FAMILY

4. AVAILABILITY OF PARKING:
   If on-street parking is difficult to find, many of the better tenants will find other areas to live in. If off-street parking is available, that will alleviate some of the problem, but not all because of the extra cost to park in a private lot. Rate this neighborhood on the ease of finding parking.

   Is on-street parking: ___ Impossible ___ Difficult ___ Easy ___ Not allowed overnight
   Is off-street parking available: ___ Yes ___ No

Rating #4:   PARKING IS IMPOSSIBLE   **0 1 2 3 4 5**   PARKING IS EASY

Figure 11.1   Neighborhood Rating Form *(continued)*

---

5. AVAILABILITY OF PUBLIC TRANSPORTATION:
Public transportation is also an important consideration. Rate the neighborhood on the availability of both bus and/or train service.

Is the neighborhood served by major bus-lines: ___ Yes   ___ No
Is the neighborhood served by train lines: ___ Yes   ___ No

| Rating #5:   BUS OR TRAIN UNAVAILABLE   0 1 2 3 4 5   BUS OR TRAIN ACCESSIBLE |

6. DOES THE CONDITION OF NEIGHBORHOOD SEEM TO BE IMPROVING OR WORSENING?
A neighborhood that is improving will attract increasing numbers of good tenants, while a neighborhood that is worsening will steadily lose the best tenants. First note any conditions that exist in the neighborhood, then estimate from all you have learned about this neighborhood whether conditions are getting better or becoming worse.

Negative indicators:
___ Trash and garbage in the streets	___ Boarded up buildings	___ Residents loitering
___ Trash and garbage on the sidewalks	___ Junk cars	___ Uncared for buildings
___ Trash and garbage in the alleys	___ Graffiti	___ Children in the streets
___ Unattractive windows	___ Empty stores	___ Very few banks
___ Ill-kept lawns	___ Old, uncared for school buildings	___ Residents are disheveled
___ Signs of rodents present	___ Stray dogs	

Positive indicators:
___ Rehabbed buildings in the area	___ Repaved streets	___ Well-kept school buildings
___ Attractive windows	___ Sewer construction	___ Residents neatly dressed
___ Clean streets	___ Healthy trees	___ Block clubs
___ Clean sidewalks	___ Well-kept lawns	___ Healthy commercial strip
___ Clean alleys	___ Flowers, shrubs	___ Banks

| Rating #6:   AREA IS WORSENING   0 1 2 3 4 5   AREA IS IMPROVING |

7. CRIME RATE:
A high crime rate will deter the better tenants. Estimate the crime rate in the neighborhood from information derived from the newspaper, from talking with residents and from talking with other investors and individuals familiar with the area.

| Rating #7:   HIGH CRIME RATE   0 1 2 3 4 5   LOW CRIME RATE |

8. SUPPORT SYSTEMS:
Regardless of the other characteristics of a neighborhood, the existence of strong social and economic support systems is a real advantage. From information derived from your sources, indicate which, if any, are available, then rate the neighborhood according to the availability of such support systems.

Are low-interest rehab loans available in the area: ___ Yes   ___ No
Are there any high-profile social service agencies in the neighborhood: ___ Yes   ___ No
Is there a strong local political organization: ___ Yes   ___ No
Is there a strong local community action group: ___ Yes   ___ No
Are there strong block clubs operating in the area: ___ Yes   ___ No

| Rating #8:   SUPPORT SYSTEMS UNAVAILABLE   0 1 2 3 4 5   SUPPORT SYSTEMS AVAILABLE |

9. REPUTATION:
A neighborhood's reputation will determine how easy it is to attract the best tenants. Discuss what is being said about the neighborhood in the newspapers, in the real estate offices, in the local stores, in the local bars: _____

| Rating #9:   BAD REPUTATION   0 1 2 3 4 5   EXCELLENT REPUTATION |

Figure 11.1   Neighborhood Rating Form *(continued)*

---

10. SOCIO-ECONOMIC CONDITIONS:
   The lower the socio-economic conditions in a neighborhood, the more problems there will be. Estimate the type of socio-economic conditions that exist in the area.

Most residents are:	___ Very poor	___ Poor	___ Middle Class	___ Upper Middle	___ Wealthy
Most of the homes in the area are:		___ Small	___ Medium	___ Large	
Property values in the area are:		___ Low	___ Medium	___ High	

Rating #10: LOW SOCIO-ECONOMIC AREA   0 1 2 3 4 5   HIGH SOCIO-ECONOMIC AREA

11. PREDICTORS OF IMPROVING CONDITIONS:
   Other factors may be rated low, but there is reason to believe the neighborhood might improve. If so, this is a positive indicator. First indicate some of the reasons why the area could improve, then rate the neighborhood on such expectations.

Area borders an obviously improving area:	___ Yes	___ No
Area is close to expressway:	___ Yes	___ No
Area has architecturally significant buildings:	___ Yes	___ No
Major public construction is planned for the area (New stadium, new airport, etc.):	___ Yes	___ No
Area has some other reason to predict improving conditions:_____		

Rating #11: NO IMPROVEMENT EXPECTED   0 1 2 3 4 5   IMPROVEMENT EXPECTED

RATING SUMMARY

Rating #1 Mix of buildings in the neighborhood	___
Rating #2 Condition of buildings in the neighborhood	___
Rating #3 Density	___
Rating #4 Availability of parking	___
Rating #5 Availability of public transportation	___
Rating #6 Conditions are improving or worsening	___
Rating #7 Crime rate	___
Rating #8 Support systems	___
Rating #9 Reputation	___
Rating #10 Socio-economic conditions	___
Rating #11 Is improvement expected	___
Total	___

NEIGHBORHOOD RATING:

41 - 55 points = CLASS I   ___
21 - 40 points = CLASS II   ___
 0 - 20 points = CLASS III ___

Schools: Drive past a neighborhood school at playground time or while the children are walking to or from school, just to see how they dress, how well groomed they are, and to observe their general behavior patterns. Are they neat and clean or a little scruffy? The children will also give you a good idea of the racial and ethnic make-up of the neighborhood. If you purchase in the neighborhood, the cultural and ethnic values as well as possible language differences will impact on the ease or difficulty of managing the building successfully.

Grocery stores: Take time to stop and go into one of the little shops in the area. Buy a can of pop and watch the patrons. Listen to their conversations. Ask the shopkeeper about the neighborhood. Make small talk with the person next to you at the counter. Find out what's going on in the neighborhood.

Neighborhood bars: Walk across the street to a local bar and stop in for a soda. Listen to the bar talk. These are the neighborhood people. These are your potential customers. Find out who they are and what is important to them.

Block clubs: In many of the inner city neighborhoods of Chicago, local residents have banded together to establish rules of behavior for their particular block, and they enforce these rules. The presence of these block clubs reveals just the kinds of tenants you are looking for: those who want to be safe, clean, and comfortable. When the residents are looking out for each other, you can feel confident that vandalism and break-ins are less likely to occur, and that the neighbors feel the pressure to keep their homes and lots looking nice.

Transportation: Many city tenants don't own a car and depend on public transportation to get around. An apartment several blocks from a bus stop or train stop won't be very attractive for them. Look for the bus routes and the train stops.

Density: What kinds of buildings predominate in the area? Are most of the structures single family homes and small apartment buildings, or is the area dominated by large apartment buildings? If the neighborhood is primarily comprised of larger apartment buildings, this can create multiple problems. First, competition from other buildings in the area creates a difficult renting environment even when the market is strong, and when the rental market is weak, competition for available tenants can create unacceptably high vacancy rates. Second, a high density neighborhood is simply less desirable because of noise, cars, lack of parking, lack of trees and grass, and all the amenities that make a neighborhood feel good. Consequently, it will be more difficult to attract and hold the high caliber tenant you want.

Parking: Notice whether the streets are lined with parked cars. Because more desirable tenants often own a nice car as well and don't want to park several blocks away from home, they won't be attracted to an apartment in an area where parking is difficult.

Safe, Clean, and Quiet

Most people share three common desires when it comes to their homes: they want to be *safe*, they want to be *clean*, and they want their home to be *quiet*. Your job is to find buildings that offer those three essentials. They can be found in most neighborhoods, but the search might be more difficult in some areas than in others. To draw an analogy from an old cliche, the pearl diver must inspect thousands of oysters in search of a few pearls. To carry the analogy further, a seasoned pearl diver has learned to differentiate among oysters. He can tell which oyster is more likely to contain a pearl by observing subtle characteristics. To the observer, a successful pearl diver may seem intuitive. The truth is, however, that experience has taught the pearl diver certain skills of observation which, however automatic, nevertheless may be identified and taught to another. So it is with your search for the perfect property. Driving through the neighborhoods you will learn to look for the subtle characteristics that lead you to opportunity.

Tenants as Customers

This is the most important rule to keep in mind as you cruise the neighborhoods: *you are not looking for a place for yourself to live; you are looking for a place to make an investment*. The residents of the neighborhood are potential customers. The building you acquire is the product they will buy. If you keep that important relationship in mind, you can avoid some of the worst characteristics of the Social Worker, the Rehabber, or the Urban Pioneer. In a general sense, you are looking for a neighborhood in which you can safely operate a well-managed building for the benefit of those local residents who most care about living in a clean, safe, quiet environment.

Author's Note: Many characteristics of a neighborhood are not obvious, but the subtle indicators are often the most important. They are important because of what they say about the people who live there.

Your first trip into an area will provide an impression, but first impressions can be misleading. One of my best investments was made in a neighborhood that to most people is nothing short of daunting. The first impression was that of a wasteland—a scene from the movie Road Warriors ten years later; there seemed to be more vacant lots than structures. Most of the stores and commercial structures were gone or boarded up. There were no banks in the area. And yet in the middle of all that stood this vintage sixty-unit brick building, clean, well-kept, well managed, and always full of tenants who mostly paid their rent on time and took good care of the building and their apartments. Even in the most uninviting of locales, some pearls can be found.

In Summary

Knowing the neighborhoods is just like doing market research, but without the use of surveys or complicated statistical formulae. The best way to get to know the neighborhoods is by going out and experiencing them first hand. Most of the properties you will look at are located in lower income neighborhoods: neighborhoods that are comprised primarily of people from lower socio-economic groups. There are many subtle and several not-so-subtle signs to look for in a neighborhood to determine whether that area is safe and whether a building located there can attract good tenants. When looking through the neighborhoods, it is important to remember two things: you are not looking for a place for yourself to live, and all tenants want to be safe and comfortable in their homes.

Twelve

■ ■ ■ ■ ■

How to Begin the Search

In This Chapter

Most real estate books and advisors give generous advice about what kinds of properties to look for, how to leverage a real estate portfolio, and other such ivory tower recommendations. Very few, however, explain how to search for such properties, even though the process itself might mean the difference between success and failure. Most potential real estate investors have no idea where to start or how to proceed and therefore take the most obvious route—contacting a real estate broker. Although that strategy might work, it is not the most effective.

The best strategy begins with the Sunday newspaper. There, among the listings, lurks the sought-after property. The key to finding the critical ad is learning how to skim the ads productively, looking for advantageous prices and favorable gross multipliers.

How to Lead the Search for the Right Property

This is where we get into the real mechanics of finding the right property. Much of this chapter may seem rather elementary, but in fact most potential real estate investors have no idea where to start or how to proceed. As novices, they often assume that the first step is to find a real estate broker who will work with them. Although that strategy might work, it is not the most effective.

The search that you are about to begin has one goal: to unearth a gem of a building—a difficult task under the best of conditions. But a broker hoping for a quick sale can often make the task more difficult. How? By trying to convince a buyer that a poor investment property is actually a good investment property. Rather than working with an agent, the best strategy is to lead the search yourself, and the place to start is the local newspaper.

Start With the Sunday Paper

Unless you live in a rural area, the local Sunday paper should be a reliable source for good rental properties. In Chicago, Realtors place ads in the Sunday edition, whether or not they advertise through the week. The unwritten rule is that the majority of buyers and sellers find each other in the Sunday *Tribune*. Your local paper might be different; if it is, find out how it works, but use the newspaper as your *primary* source of information early in the search. Get to know the real estate section intimately, and be faithful in looking through the ads every Sunday. Here is how to use the newspaper most effectively: the first few times reading through the ads look at every ad carefully to get a feel for how the agents write the ads, what kind of information is contained in the ads, and what kinds of phrases are used to attract attention and make the property seem attractive. Reading the ads carefully will help you develop a feel for the various neighborhoods—what kinds of properties are there, what the prices are, what the gross multipliers are—and thereby can develop a basis for comparing prices later on.

Skim the Ads

After two or three weeks of carefully studying the ads, you will begin to develop a strategy for skimming the ads quickly. Most real estate listings are by type of property. In the larger papers, the types will also be broken down by area of the city. Go directly to the type of property—apartment buildings or investment property—then to the section that covers the appropriate area of the city, then skim the ads.

Rule #1: Ignore an ad that does not list either the price or the gross multiplier: if one or the other is not listed the property is usually overpriced and not worth pursuing. Conversely, if the price is listed in the ad it will usually be a competitive price. The logic is simple—an agent preparing an ad will typically list the information that is most likely to attract a buyer. If the price is attractive, it will appear in the ad; if not, it will be omitted. *Author's Note: You will probably want to verify this conclusion by calling about a few ads that omit the price. When you do, your experience will most likely be the same as mine, but it doesn't hurt to check.*

Rule #2: Look for prices within a range based on the amount of investment money available. As a rule of thumb, multiply the cash down payment you can afford (you calculated this in Chapter 5) by 10 to determine the maximum amount that can be spent for a property. (This assumes a property can be bought with a 10% down payment.) Use that amount as a rough upper limit for price. For example, if in Chapter 5 it was determined that $25,000 is available for investment capital, look for properties with a maximum price of $250,000 to $275,000.

Rule #3: Skim the ads for properties in which the number of units falls within a targeted range. The lower limit should be six units, because fewer than six units will rarely generate positive cash flow. The upper limit on size is usually determined by the upper limit on price, which in turn is determined by the amount of cash available for a down payment. As a general rule, however, a building should not exceed 50 or 60 units, for two reasons: *diversification* (if you can afford to purchase a building with more than 60 units, buy two smaller buildings in different neighborhoods) and *management* (a 60-unit building can be managed with one resident manager and one janitor; larger buildings often require more personnel, which complicates the management and increases the demands on your time).

The Gross Multiplier

Author's Note: The quickest formula for assessing whether a property will show positive cash flow is the gross multiplier. Used for years, this simple formula is often disparaged by agents who are convinced of its obsolescence. Such agents will attempt to confuse a buyer with all kinds of formulas and questionable figures, yet the gross multiplier remains the quickest and one of the most reliable of indicators. Only two figures are needed: the gross annual income and the asking price. Divide the price by the gross income to obtain the gross multiplier.

$$\text{GROSS MULTIPLIER} = \text{PRICE} \div \text{GROSS ANNUAL INCOME}$$

If the gross multiplier is 2 or less, the property will probably show cash flow, if all other conditions are right. If the multiplier is 3, the property might show cash flow. If the multiplier is 4 or more, the property will probably not show cash flow.

Generally, the most desirable neighborhoods will produce gross multipliers in the range of 6 to 7, sometimes even as high as 10, which translates into a substantial negative cash flow (the building will lose money every month). Solid low-middle income neighborhoods will range from 4 to 5, while low income neighborhoods will routinely show gross multipliers of 2 to 4. In the ad, the gross multiplier will appear in this simple form: 3x, meaning it is a 3 times building, or the price is 3 times the gross income. Some buyers will not look at a property unless the multiplier is 2x or less.

Skimming the Ads: A Summary

The reason for skimming ads is two-fold: to save time by quickly going to those properties that meet certain basic criteria and to eliminate properties that obviously will not generate positive cash flow. These are the criteria:

1. Size: *At least six units; no more than 60 units.* (You will learn quickly the maximum size you can afford in your area based on the maximum price you can pay. If you can afford more than 60 units, buy two smaller properties.)

2. Price: *Maximum price is approximately 10 times the available down payment.* If you have $15,000 to invest, maximum price is $150,000 to $175,000.

3. Gross multiplier: *Price is no more than four times gross annual income; two times is preferable.* (If the gross multiplier is not given in the ad, you will nevertheless develop, with experience, a feel for estimating the gross multiplier. For example: if you know a ten-flat in a certain neighborhood probably generates rents in the following range: 1 bedroom, $400; 2 bedroom, $500, the building should generate a maximum income of $4,000 to $5,000 per month, or $48,000 to $60,000 per year. The maximum price for this property, therefore, should be $120,000 if the multiplier is 2 times and $240,000 if the multiplier is 4 times.)

In Summary

Knowing how to search for a property is an essential but a rarely taught element in a successful investment plan. Avoid the obvious strategy of calling a broker; working with only one agent is too confining. Use the newspaper ads to begin the search—most good deals will appear there. Learn how to skim the ads productively, looking for favorable prices and gross multipliers on buildings that fit your criteria for size.

Thirteen

■ ■ ■ ■ ■

When You Call About a Property, Know the Questions to Ask

In This Chapter

After circling (or high-lighting) a few likely properties in the newspaper, the next step is to call for information. When calling about the property, certain specific information must be obtained before deciding whether to drive past, so be prepared with the appropriate questions. Pursuing the newspaper ads, of course, soon stirs up a turmoil of activity with real estate agents, who are a necessary part of the process. By leading the search, however, the potential buyer has the opportunity to control the activities of such agents.

Calling About the Property

Be prepared: every real estate ad in the newspaper, other than those for sale by owner (always call "for sale by owner" ads—they are a very likely source of bargains), is designed with one purpose in mind—to develop a list of potential leads for the sales agent. He or she will be happy to share information on the property but will also want to know as much about the caller as possible—what kind of property is being sought, the price range, how much you want to invest, etc.—so as to search for other properties that might be suitable. One good ad will draw several phone calls, and no good salesperson wants to be limited to one property when there are several potential buyers available. The next chapter teaches you how to deal with agents, but for now be aware of the strategy a good agent will employ. Be prepared also for the agent with an arrogant attitude, who will sometimes become downright insulting when you explain what you have in mind. Just remember that if this agent were so smart, he or she would be the buyer, not the agent.

When calling about the property, certain specific information must be obtained before deciding whether to drive past, so be prepared with the appropriate questions. Figure 13.1, a quick income/expense form that functions well as an initial inquiry form, is a handy outline to have available when placing the call. Using such a form gives one control of the conversation by establishing exactly which questions to ask. Find out the exact address, the overall condition of the building, the price (if it hasn't been listed), and the income and expenses. This is where the income/expense form comes in handy—by the end of the conversation, be certain that each blank has been filled in.

In addition to gathering information over the telephone, request that the agent mail a copy of the listing sheet. It is always good to have an original copy as the listing sheet includes information that might not otherwise be given over the phone. Also, many listing sheets include a picture of the building, which can help in the decision whether to drive past. An alternative is to use a fax machine. Most real estate offices can fax immediately a complete copy of the listing sheet. *Author's Note: If you don't have a fax machine, consider buying one soon. I have found them to be a valuable time saver.* The faxed listing sheet will have all the information that otherwise would have been copied onto Figure 13.1. Ordinarily, the agent will fax not only that listing sheet but several others that he or she feels are similar.

Using the Information

Once the income and expense figures have been gathered, the next step is to calculate whether the property will generate positive cash flow. Chapter 18 shows the technique. Don't waste time driving past a building that does not generate positive cash flow unless you are trying to get a better feel for the market, i.e., what kinds of buildings are priced in what range.

If the numbers on a property don't work out, keep the address and the information in the back of a folder. When in the neighborhood, take a drive by and check out the building. This will help develop a feel for the prices in the area. If the building looks particularly good, it might be wise to put in a

Figure 13.1   Initial Inquiry Form

INCOME/EXPENSE FORM

ADDRESS_____ PRICE_____
BROKER_____ PHONE_____
AGENT_____ PHONE_____
OWNER_____ PHONE_____

RENTS:		EXPENSES:	ANNUAL	MONTHLY
___ x ___ rms @	$_____	Taxes	_____	_____
___ x ___ rms @	$_____	Fuel	_____	_____
___ x ___ rms @	$_____	Electric	_____	_____
___ x ___ rms @	$_____	Water	_____	_____
___ x ___ rms @	$_____	Janitor	_____	_____
___ x ___ rms @	$_____	Scavenger	_____	_____
___ x ___ rms @	$_____	Rep & Maint	_____	_____
Annual Income	$_____	Insurance	_____	_____
Monthly Income	$_____	Elevator	_____	_____
___ % Vacancy	$(_____)	Misc	_____	_____
Net Monthly	$_____	TOTAL	_____	_____
Less Expenses	$(_____)	Mortgage		_____
CASH FLOW	$_____	TOTAL MONTHLY		_____

NOTES:_____
_____
_____
_____
_____

much lower offer at a price that will generate cash flow. Alternatively, the owner might lower the price in a month or so. In that case a familiarity with the building can be very helpful.

At this early stage in the search, do everything possible to become educated about the market so that when a good prospect materializes it will be recognized immediately. It might be helpful, in fact, to look through a few properties that do not make sense economically just to develop a basis for comparison. This will also help to develop an intuitive feel for price and condition that will facilitate quick decisions later.

Dealing with the Avalanche

The first few calls will create an avalanche of activity. The pebbles set in motion by placing a few calls will dislodge larger rocks and stones as agents search their listings and call back with other rental properties. The more calls that have been made, the greater the avalanche. Some of this activity is unavoidable; agents will be aggressive in trying to obtain sales. Fortunately, however, some controls can be placed on the amount of follow-up activity that must be dealt with by being assertive from the first. The following chapter is devoted to various strategies to use with real estate agents. After starting the avalanche, plan to spend the next two or three days answering the phone, talking with agents, repeating the criteria, receiving faxes, filling in income and expense information, reviewing listing sheets, and doing the numbers. All of this happens before going out to look at any properties.

Organization

As the avalanche of information continues to grow, a great deal of paperwork will be generated. It is best to get organized early so as not to be buried under the papers. A three-ring binder is particularly helpful in this regard. Organize the binder by type of building or by area, whichever makes most sense, and then insert the information as it is received. A listing sheet can be taped to a sheet of notebook paper and inserted, allowing room at the bottom to write in comments, questions, etc. Alternatively, make copies of the initial inquiry form (Figure 13.1) on notebook paper so it can easily be inserted into or removed from the binder.

Just Like Prospecting

Searching for the right rental property is a lot like panning for gold. While others can point out the most likely spots to a novice prospector, ultimately the most lucrative gold strikes are made by those who find their own way. While searching for the large nuggets, a prospector may spend weeks or months patiently sifting the gravel, searching each panful for the few specks of bright color that indicate the presence of gold. The most successful find that following their own intuition—and perhaps the instructions of those few old-timers who have been around long enough to sort out myth from reality—is the best strategy.

Like panning for gold, real estate investing requires patience and the confidence to strike out on one's own. To be hasty at this point could be the most costly mistake you could make. It does not take long to discover that many experts' advice may be misleading. By avoiding such advice and patiently pursuing a solid investment strategy, however, a clever novice can outperform most of the "experts." And unlike panning for gold, searching for the right rental property is much more likely to pay off in the end.

In Summary

Calling about properties will unleash a fury of activity by agents eager to cash in on a prospective buyer. Resist their overtures by being prepared. Use the income/expense form to structure questions, request that agents mail or fax copies of the listing sheet, and develop a plan for organizing all the information that soon will come flooding in.

Fourteen

■■ ■ ■ ■

How to Use the
Multiple Listing Service

In This Chapter

A secondary source of potential properties is the multiple listing service (MLS). In its simplest form an MLS is a cooperative organization of real estate brokers in which members agree to make their listings available to all other brokers in the association. Most MLS organizations use a computer to maintain a data bank of listings. While this data bank can be helpful, the real bargains are still found by slogging through the MLS book, which can be found in any member broker's office. A morning or an afternoon spent with the MLS listing book can sometimes uncover one or two hidden precious gems, or it may produce nothing except additional experience looking at prices and locations. Either way, the time spent with the MLS book is of value.

The Ubiquitous Multiple Listing Service

It won't take long for you to come into contact with the MLS. Almost every agent you contact will want to send listings gleaned from the MLS data bank. In years past the MLS book was the only source of information on listed properties, and a search through the listings tended to take longer and was done much less frequently by agents. In recent years, however, the MLS has become more of a computer data bank than a publisher of listing books. The result is quicker access to the information and an improved ability to locate specific types of properties. Rather than wade through the listings visually an agent can simply type in specific parameters and let the computer scan the listings in the data bank. A few minutes later the computer spits out a typewritten list of appropriate properties. The book itself, however—a collection of all properties that have been listed for sale by member brokers—is still available and can prove to be exceedingly useful.

Agents and Subagents

Despite appearances, the MLS is more than simply a classified section for brokers. Association with the MLS establishes a clear sub-agency relationship. When a seller lists a property with a broker, that broker becomes an agent for that seller. When the listing is added to the MLS data bank, the broker enters into an agreement with all other brokers who are members of the MLS, giving them an automatic right to show the property and offer it for sale. This agreement, in effect, is a blanket offer of sub-agency to other member brokers. If a member broker sells the property, the sales commission is divided between the listing broker and the selling broker. It is important to remember this relationship.

Because of the MLS, an agent whose loyalty belongs to the seller may at times appear to be working for a buyer. He or she might offer to help locate a suitable property for purchase and in doing so may grant a buyer access to browse through the MLS book, may go along to look at a number of properties, may help write an offer. Regardless of how cozy the relationship becomes, however, the agent remains an agent of the seller. Don't be confused about these loyalties. As the agent's commission will be paid by the seller, his or her loyalty must be to the seller.

How to Use the MLS Book

A buyer's first contact with the MLS will occur soon after the search for a property begins: each real estate agent who is contacted through a newspaper ad will want to present several other listings from the MLS data bank, although probably none will be a good investment. The MLS data bank is a good potential source of properties, however, and obtaining direct access to the MLS book is important. Contact an agent who seems particularly congenial and competent and ask for permission to come into the office to look through the MLS book. Sensing a potential sale, most agents will gladly grant this request. When the request is approved, block off an entire morning or afternoon, polish your glasses, sharpen your pencils, dig out your calculator, and prepare for several hours of hard work.

There are rules governing the MLS book. Brokers spend a substantial annual fee to belong to the MLS and therefore do not want copies of the book floating out of the office. In practice, however, most agents will allow a serious buyer to take past issues of the book out of the office. The current issue, however, typically must remain at the real estate office.

Why work with the book when the entire data bank can be scanned much more quickly by computer? First, the reason for searching the MLS files is to locate a hidden gem, a rare bargain. Such properties seem to lurk around the fringes of the book, easily overlooked and more easily dismissed. It is entirely possible that a computer search of the data will, for one reason or another, miss such a bargain. Second, the MLS book includes pictures of the buildings, which can be helpful in identifying properties of interest. Third, working alone with the book separates the buyer from an overly helpful agent and eliminates the need to explain why one property after another is not suitable.

Why the MLS Book Might Contain Some Bargains

With such quick and easy access to the MLS data bank, it would be easy to assume that a search through the MLS book would be futile—that all the good deals have been identified and snapped up early and only the clunkers linger. It is, in fact, quite easy for a good property to be passed over, to lie buried in the MLS files. Due to unfortunate timing, an overly lengthy listing period, an uncooperative owner, a distressed neighborhood, a broken contract, or an unrealistic listing price, a property might not have received the attention it deserves and now remains in the files virtually ignored.

Unfortunate timing. There are times when a good property hits the market at a slow season or at a time when there are no buyers for that particular kind of property. After working the listing for a while, the agent grows weary of trying to locate a buyer for the building and moves on to other properties that are more likely to sell.

Uncooperative owner. Perhaps the property is excellent but the owner has made if difficult for the agent to show the building to prospective buyers by refusing to allow them to go through the apartments, not providing keys to the agent, limiting the hours that showings can occur, or just being out of town and generally unavailable. Under such circumstances an agent under-standably will give up trying to work that listing and give attention to others that display fewer road-blocks.

Overly lengthy listing period. Six months or more is a long time for an exclusive listing period. Generally, a transaction should occur within 90 days. If a broker has negotiated a lengthy listing period but generated little response after working the property for a while, it is not uncommon to let it lie there without advertising, waiting for the listing period to expire.

Distressed neighborhood. Some neighborhoods are not particularly de-sirable and consequently draw few buyers, even though the property itself might be an excellent investment.

Broken contract. It is not uncommon for a property to generate an offer, go under contract, then end up back on the market months later when the deal falls through. Discouraged, a broker may be less inclined to work the property as hard as before. Such properties can be real sleepers.

Unrealistic listing price. Perhaps the owner originally listed a property for an unrealistic price. After a few weeks, the owner agrees to reduce the price but the broker, reluctant to invest additional time and money to advertise the property, allows it to sit quietly among the listings waiting to be discov-ered.

Become Familiar With the Organization of the Book

For all the above reasons, and perhaps a few more, it is possible for a hidden bargain to be uncovered among the pages of the MLS book. Only patient and determined searching, however, will do the job. Begin by becoming familiar with the book's structure. The MLS book is normally divided by sections of the city, and each section is identified by code. Look in the front of the book to determine the code, then turn to the appropriate section. Within sections, properties are normally organized by type, e.g., 2 to 4 units, over 4 units, etc. Within type, properties are usually organized by price, the least expensive first, the most expensive last. After locating the right section and the right type of property, begin browsing. With some experience each listing can be scanned quickly to determine whether the property is of interest. Early on, however, spend extra time with each listing, carefully searching for the hidden bargains.

What to Look For in the MLS Book

Chapter 18 covers several different rule-of-thumb formulas for determining the rough value of a property. Knowledge of those formulas will be helpful when scanning the MLS listings. Rule of thumb formulas like the gross multiplier and the cost per unit are quick screening devices to determine whether a property should be analyzed more closely. If a property survives the screening, then a more involved analysis of income and expense should be done following a drive-by inspection to assess the physical characteristics of the building.

Rents.   Are the rents abnormally low for the area and the type of building? If so, quickly figure a revised income based on realistic rents and then determine the gross multiplier. There is probably a good reason why the rents are low, but it is possible that the owner has simply neglected to keep up with market rents.

Income/Expense Figures.   For each property that survives the initial screening, check whether the income and expense figures on the listing sheet seem realistic (Chapter 20). If so, run a quick calculation to determine whether the property has the potential to generate positive cash flow. If the figures seem to be incorrect, plug in more realistic figures and calculate cash flow.

Hype.   Brokers spend a lot of energy designing listing sheets. They use catchy phrases to grab the buyer's attention. Ignore the hype. Focus entirely on price, gross multiplier, and cost per unit. Remember that this is a business. If the building will not show a profit, it should not be bought.

What to Do When You Locate an Interesting Property

Make a list of the property addresses that look interesting. For each one, carefully copy the income and expense figures. Use Form 13.1, the income/expense form, to keep the information consistent and to save time. An even quicker alternative is to photocopy each of the listings or ask the broker to print the listings from the computer data-base. For each of the properties that have been identified, do a drive-by inspection (Chapter 19). If the results of the drive-by are positive, carefully work the numbers for each property (Chapter 20). If the numbers work, arrange for a walk-through with the broker (Chapter 21).

Be Fair to the Broker

When an interesting property is discovered as a result of the MLS search, it is only fair to make all further arrangements with the broker or agent who originally granted access to the MLS book. By according this favor, the agent has earned the right to participate in the commission in the event the property is purchased.

Be Patient

The MLS book is quite thick, particularly in large metropolitan areas. Each page contains several listings; even a quick scan will take time. The unavoidable fact is that most of the properties in the MLS book will not work; but don't go to sleep, and don't take short-cuts. There will be a tendency to become discouraged, to pay insufficient attention, to let the mind wander. During the inevitable periods when that happens take a break and come back later. This might seem like obvious and unnecessary advice, but the obvious can often be the most easily overlooked.

An MLS Search That Worked

Author's Note: Although I truly enjoy browsing through the MLS listing book, I realize that not everyone will share my joy. The truth is that looking through MLS books for a hidden gem can be tedious, thankless work—until the right property is found. Then all the tiresome hours of monotony suddenly prove their worth. To illustrate, several years ago a close friend finally chose to use the MLS book after first spending weeks of fruitless searching with Realtor after Realtor. At the broker's office one afternoon, he spent several hours looking at one listing after another. As the hours dragged by, each promising property proved disappointing when he worked the numbers. Finally, after more than six hours of tedious searching, and nearly exhausted, he decided to quit for the day. He just could not look at one more listing. None of them worked anyway, and he felt he was wasting his time with the effort.

Then suddenly, as he calculated the income and expense figures on the last listing for the day, the numbers burst through the malaise that had gathered around him from the long hours of disappointment. The results were so good that he had to go back and check them again. The second time they looked as good as the first. No other property came close to matching the cash flow that his figures indicated was possible with this property!

He assumed that something must be wrong. The date of the listing indicated the building had been on the market for more than six months, which confirmed his assumption. How could any building not sell when it returned that much cash flow on such a small investment? There must be something wrong. But he wrote down the address and decided to drive past the building that day.

The neighborhood looked okay: a marginal area but not a slum. The building looked sound. When he arrived home he immediately called the agent and arranged a showing. Upon closer inspection, he discovered that the building needed some minor repairs and routine maintenance, but otherwise was solid. The tenants were all immigrants who paid their rent on time and looked after the building. The price: $18,000. He offered $15,000 and bought the property. One year later, after pulling a steady cash flow from the building and after some relatively minor painting and repair work, he sold the property for $30,000.

Such properties do not pop up every day in the MLS, but this particular success story illustrates the potential value of the MLS book.

In Summary

The MLS data bank is a good source for acquiring properties, and the MLS book in particular is an excellent way to access that information. Despite what one may assume, the MLS often contains bargain properties for several reasons: unfortunate timing of the listing, an uncooperative owner, a lengthy listing period, a distressed neighborhood, a broken contract, or an unrealistic original listing price.

As with newspaper ads, learning to scan the MLS listings quickly is important. Indicators of value include the gross multiplier and the cost per unit. Using the MLS book, however, requires extreme patience and forbearance.

Fifteen

■ ■ ■ ■ ■

Real Estate Agents Can Be Necessary But Irritating Accomplices

In This Chapter

The real estate brokerage business is a difficult one. Real estate agents are generally competent and honest; but licensing and training are not uniform throughout the United States, with the result that some agents lack the skills to perform their jobs adequately. Others are simply dishonest and always stand ready to profit from a buyer's inexperience or insecurity. Many are starry-eyed young agents hoping to cash in on the fortunes they have heard about. Usually such unrealistic expectations lead to a short, futile career. Such agents will often try to hide their inexperience and lack of fundamental understanding with bravado and aggressiveness.

It is possible to find a real estate agent who is both honest and helpful. Short of a lucky encounter, however, a buyer must work carefully to identify such agents. The most important thing to remember is that the buyer's goals and the agent's goals are in direct conflict. With that understanding, it is possible to co-opt an agent for your mutual benefit, always remaining wary of the agent's bag of tricks.

How to Establish a Mutually Satisfactory Relationship with a Real Estate Agent

Author's Note: I have developed a simple strategy for dealing with real estate agents. I begin by viewing them as necessary irritants in the process of acquiring real estate: necessary because most properties offered for sale are listed with real estate agents; irritants because a real estate agent has no concept of my investment strategy or my criteria for a good property. Through the years I have exhausted, aggravated, and matched wits with hundreds of real estate agents. Only a few were wise enough (or maybe just patient enough) to sell me a building.

A good real estate agent is one who finds the property the buyer is looking for—no more, no less. Age is no indication—I work with one agent who has been successful since before World War II and another who can still count his professional years on one hand. I usually work with whichever agent I encounter in the course of searching through newspaper ads, and like cream in freshly produced milk, the good ones simply rise to the top.

Understand That the Agent's Goals are Different From Your Own

Always remember that the buyer's goals and those of the real estate agent are in direct conflict. The agent's goal is to sell a property; the buyer's goal is to find a rare property that meets rigid criteria. Although most agents will not blatantly pass on incorrect information, the majority of agents are intelligent enough to cast the best light on any property they represent. Unfortunately, this forces a buyer not only to examine each property carefully, but also to fend off efforts on the part of the agent to prove the buyer's analysis faulty.

To illustrate how dissimilar the goals are between an agent and a buyer, here is a list of characteristics that one broker looks for in a prospective real estate agent. The list is taken from a personal interview form that the broker uses to screen applicants for sales positions in his firm. Notice that *honesty* and *integrity* appear eighth on the list, with *personal ownership of real estate* next to the bottom. The broker who uses this list to hire real estate agents has determined that personality, ambition, speaking ability, and aggressiveness rate higher than integrity in an agent, and experience as an owner of real estate is virtually unimportant.

Figure 15.1
Rating Form for Applicants for Real Estate Sales Positions

Rate each characteristic on the following scale:
(1 = highest rating; 10 = lowest rating)

	1	2	3	4	5	6	7	8	9	10
1. Personality	1	2	3	4	5	6	7	8	9	10
2. Ambition	1	2	3	4	5	6	7	8	9	10
3. Speaking ability	1	2	3	4	5	6	7	8	9	10
4. Aggressiveness	1	2	3	4	5	6	7	8	9	10
5. Judgment	1	2	3	4	5	6	7	8	9	10
6. Courtesy	1	2	3	4	5	6	7	8	9	10
7. Appearance	1	2	3	4	5	6	7	8	9	10
8. Honesty and integrity	1	2	3	4	5	6	7	8	9	10
9. Sales experience	1	2	3	4	5	6	7	8	9	10
10. Age	1	2	3	4	5	6	7	8	9	10
11. Automobile	1	2	3	4	5	6	7	8	9	10
12. Economic stability	1	2	3	4	5	6	7	8	9	10
13. Personal ownership of real estate	1	2	3	4	5	6	7	8	9	10
14. Availability	1	2	3	4	5	6	7	8	9	10

No wonder so many agents seem truly ignorant of the important aspects of real estate investing! No wonder they aggressively debunk the best efforts of a buyer to analyze a property.

Co-opt the Agent For Your Own Purposes

In spite of the divergence between buyers' goals and agents' goals, some agents nevertheless can become valuable allies. But they must be shown the way. Here is a strategy that not only will throw agents a bit off-stride but also will give them the opportunity to work for your interests as well as their own.

Tactic #1: Find an agent by first finding a property, not the other way around. Many new investors, unsure where to start, mistakenly contact an agent to ask for assistance in locating a property. This is a mistake because,

---

What is the Difference Between a Real Estate Broker, a Real Estate Salesperson, and a Realtor®?

All three are agents. Although there is a distinction between a real estate broker and a real estate salesperson, they are both referred to as *agent* throughout this book. The distinction is this: a *real estate broker* is licensed to act as an agent for the seller of a property, while a real estate salesperson is licensed to work for a real estate broker. A real estate broker may work alone or with other real estate brokers and salespersons; a salesperson must work under the direct supervision of a real estate broker. The term *Realtor®*, while often used generically, is a registered trademark of the National Association of Realtors. The trademark may be used only by members of the Association who are also licensed real estate brokers, although salespersons may join the Association as Associate Realtors.

---

as we said, the agent's goals are different from the buyer's. Most promising investment properties are advertised in the local newspaper. Rather than seeking out an agent, scan the newspaper ads using the strategies outlined in the previous chapter. If a property seems attractive, call the listing agent. If the property turns out to be wrong but the agent is truly helpful, continue to work with that agent, but only as long as the relationship is focused on appropriate goals—yours.

Tactic #2: Deal with the issue of loyalty immediately.   In many subtle and some not-so-subtle ways, real estate agents will attempt to foster a feeling of loyalty in their customers. From the beginning it is important to clarify the basis upon which an agent may expect such loyalty. The process begins with the first phone call in response to a newspaper ad.

As with any form of marketing, the function of a newspaper ad is primarily to bring in sales leads, secondarily to sell a particular property. A person responding to an ad automatically becomes a sales lead for the agent. Every agent worth his salt will try diligently to sell something to every person who calls. Thus, along with giving the specific information requested, one of the first questions the agent will ask is the Question: "What kind of property are you looking for?" The agent knows that the more properties he or she can present the more likely a customer is to buy something. The Question is designed to trigger a flow of property listings for the customer to peruse, the vast majority of which will be poor investments.

When an agent asks the Question, answer this way:

"I'm interested in properties located in areas like (name the neighborhoods). I'm looking for a property with at least ___ units but no larger than ___ units, and I don't want to pay more than $_____. Most important, I am only interested in looking at properties that generate actual cash flow every month, and I'll use my own figures to determine that."

"If you have listings of properties like that, or if you come across such a property, please call me. If you don't have what I want, please don't waste your time or mine by calling me about a property that does not meet these criteria. If you want to search for the kind of property that meets this criteria it would be greatly appreciated. I also appreciate your willingness to look, but I'm not loyal to any one agent. The first one to find a property that meets my criteria has the sale."

Most real estate agents will take kindly to this straight-forward approach. An aggressive real estate agent, of course, will not give up easily. He or she will attempt to present something even if it does not meet the criteria. But as they do, the best ones learn quickly what will and what will not pass muster. From then on, the best agents will keep in mind what you want, they will know you are a buyer, and if something comes along they will call.

Author's Note: One agent that I have worked with through the years was smart enough to learn early what kind of properties I would buy. He rarely calls, but when something does come along, I can count on a call from George. I also know that when George calls, it is about property that I should look at seriously. As a result, I have purchased two of the properties that George has presented, and have made offers on several others. At the age of 82, it seems that George has learned to ration his time and energies by focusing on the most productive activity. Other agents, much younger, seem to find it difficult to concentrate their efforts on activities that will lead to a successful deal.

Tactic #3: Never assume that the agent is the expert on investment properties. Few real estate agents are successful investors. Many will laud their investments in an attempt to build credibility, but upon further investigation their holdings are often limited to a two- or three-flat, most of which lose money. Perhaps they have ventured into something a little larger, but rarely at the level of success that you demand of your properties. The reason: sales agents who also try to invest often believe what they tell their clients. When an agent purchases a property, the decision likely is based on the same information that the agent presents to a buyer. Using such faulty or incomplete information can lead to poor investment decisions and mediocre performance.

Author's Note: A real estate expert, in my opinion, is someone who actually owns property and who is making money doing it. I have met only two real estate agents who fulfill that criteria. There is good reason for that: real estate sales is a demanding career; likewise, successful real estate investing is a demanding career. Both are worthy pursuits, but the demands of one would seem to preclude success in the other.

Tactic #4: Assert yourself as the expert investor.   All negotiations include elements of self-assertion and intimidation. Many agents are prepared to intimidate a buyer in subtle and in not-so-subtle ways. A confident, self-assured investor who can arrive at an independent decision based on sound reasoning and careful analysis, however, assumes a strong position in the negotiations. This does not mean that the relationship between buyer and agent must be adversarial. In most cases, in fact, the relationship can remain friendly and will even improve as the agent gains respect for the buyer's skills and wisdom. After completing this book you will know how to assess the investment potential of any rental property. That makes *you* the expert. Use that expertise to your benefit.

First, after obtaining the income and expense numbers from the agent, gently let him or her know that you will analyze the figures and soon make a decision whether or not to drive past the property. This action quickly serves notice that you are leading the charge, not the agent, and that you know what you want.

Second, after driving past the property point out any problems with the building. Share with the agent an appraisal of the neighborhood. Along with reinforcing an image of competence and independence, this action is advantageous because it begins to build a case to support a purchase offer if one should be made later. When it comes time to submit an offer the agent will, if you choose, present the offer to the owner. If the rationale for the offer has been clearly communicated, the agent is more likely to represent the buyer's interests at the presentation.

Author's Note: One agent told me, after I had shared with him my impressions of a particular property, "I told the owner that we are dealing with a clever business-

woman." Coming from some agents, this comment could be dismissed as just so much flattery, with an element of sexism attached. This time, however, I recognized the sincerity of the compliment as well as the negotiating advantage it gave me. Several months later, that same agent called with just the right property to bail me out of a tight deadline for completing a tax-deferred exchange. It was then I realized one of the intangible benefits of developing a professional relationship based on mutual respect for each other's skills.

Tactic #5: Beware of smoke and mirrors (otherwise known as B.S.). Chapter 18 explains several rule-of-thumb formulas for assessing cash flow. Chapter 20 follows up with more detailed analysis strategies. Typically, the results of that analysis will be significantly different from the claims made by the agent who will, nevertheless, support his or her figures with impressive formulas and mathematics that border on wizardry. Often, however, that is all the numbers amount to: wizardry. Dare to question the agent's figures, however, and be prepared for a withering look that exceeds even your own mother's most effective look of disdain. But stand your ground; your numbers are the correct ones. And remember that a building either makes money or it doesn't. No amount of smoke and mirrors will change that.

Author's Note: My personal favorite claim by a real estate agent is, "This building makes money every month." Then begins the magic show: a pencil rapidly creates numbers on a sheet of paper while the agent rattles off formulas and percentages and expenses and income, all designed to grab my attention and intimidate me into believing that this particular parcel of real estate is unquestionably the best deal of the decade. At that point, I usually ask in all candor, "If it's that good, why aren't you buying the property yourself?"

In Summary

Use your first contact with a real estate agent to establish the basis for the relationship. A real estate agent works for the seller, not the buyer. No matter how sincere an agent may appear, his or her goals are always opposed to the buyer's. Agents can become valuable allies, but they must be shown the way by an assertive and confident buyer. Establish early in the relationship that you are the expert and that the agent is to follow your lead, and that you are loyal to no agent except the one who finds the property.

Sixteen

■ ■ ■ ■ ■

How to Make the Best Use of a Real Estate Agent through Each Step of the Acquisition Process

In This Chapter

The process of acquiring a rental property progresses through several identifiable steps, each of which involves the agent: the initial inquiry, the walk-through, developing an offer, presenting the offer, negotiating with the seller, financing the property, and closing the deal. Most agents are eager to be of service to a potential buyer. Therefore, knowing how to make the best use of an agent through each step of the real estate transaction is important.

The Steps in Acquiring a Rental Property

Step 1: The inquiry. When first inquiring about a property, follow the procedures from Chapter 13: gather the income and expense figures over the phone using the income/expense form (Figure 13.1), and request that a copy of the listing sheet be mailed. Alternatively, ask that a copy be faxed. Beware of the agent, however, who refuses to divulge information without first meeting face to face. Realizing that buyers are notoriously disloyal, such agents believe that the only way they can assure loyalty is through a personal meeting. Don't allow an agent to talk you into going through a building before doing the numbers and driving past the property. Explain to this agent that you do not want to waste his or her time—or yours, but that you never make an appointment without first calculating the cash flow and driving by the property. Then assure the agent that he or she definitely will be called if you decide to pursue the property further. Throughout your association with the agent, it is essential that you set the tone, establish the ground rules and decide which activities will take place. Otherwise, you will waste a lot of time, and just might get sucked into a property that you shouldn't have purchased.

Step 2: The walk-through. When an analysis of a property indicates possible cash flow (Chapter 18), and after you have done an initial drive-by, contact the agent for an appointment to go inside the building. Normally, the agent will make arrangements with the janitor, the owner, or a tenant to gain access to a few apartments and the common areas of the building. Refer to Chapter 21 for the procedures to follow during a walk-through.

Step 3: The offer. After the walk-through the agent will often think it appropriate to make an offer on the property. He or she may propose going back to the office immediately to do the paperwork. (Salespeople are trained to refer to contracts and offers to buy as "paperwork." This term, they are taught, has less emotional impact on the novice buyer.) Don't go! And never allow the agent to fill in the contract! The agent knows that by completing the contract quickly he or she can facilitate the sale and avoid the potential deal-breaking clauses that attorneys often insist on inserting. But those clauses are the parts of the contract that protect the buyer's interests; they must be included. Don't expect the agent to put them in. See Chapter 22 for the steps to follow when submitting an offer; often, a simple letter of intent is preferable to a contract. Whichever is decided, your attorney must be involved from this point forward. The agent, however well intentioned, now has a singular purpose—to complete this transaction and collect the commission.

Step 4: Time out. Now it is time to go home and study the deal one more time. Here is where you must separate fantasy from reality, optimism from realism. Contact your attorney, sketch the broad outlines of the offer and let the attorney put together a contract.

Step 5: The presentation.   After the attorney has completed the contract (or the letter of intent), take it back to the agent for presentation to the owner. As suggested in Chapter 22, you might want to insist on meeting the owner. Whatever is decided, you set the tone, establish your expectations, tell the agent what you want, and assert your interests. Otherwise, expect to be intimidated into a time-wasting situation, and one that could cost you money if the best terms are not struck.

Step 6: The negotiations.   Throughout the negotiations that ensue after the initial offer, the agent's job is to facilitate. Often this means hand-carrying the contract back and forth for offers and counter-offers until the deal is established.

Step 7: Financing.   If a deal is struck the agent can assist in locating financing, if desired. Although the agent might be helpful, your interests probably will be best served by searching on your own for the best financing package. See Chapter 23 for a discussion of financing techniques.

Step 8: Closing the deal.   Often a real estate transaction can appear to be headed nowhere, with no end in sight. Remember that the agent's interest is in closing the deal in the shortest possible time: closing day is payday. So the agent's concern can work in your favor as the agent pushes and prods the various parties to pick up the pace. The agent's prodding can also be a potential liability, however, as he or she pushes for shortcuts that violate your interests, shortcuts that involve avoiding your attorney at key steps in the negotiations or accepting financing terms that will cost thousands of dollars in additional interest payments in the future. Don't be bullied into skipping important steps in the process.

In Summary

The process of searching for a suitable rental property includes a series of identifiable steps, each of which can be facilitated by a good real estate agent. After establishing the basis for a mutually beneficial relationship during the initial inquiry, make certain the agent follows through at each successive step: the walk-through, drafting the offer, presenting the offer, negotiating the sale, locating financing, and closing the deal. Whatever you do, don't allow the agent either to skip or to abbreviate any of the steps.

Seventeen

■ ■ ■ ■ ■

How to Recognize the Most Common Tactics Employed by Unscrupulous Real Estate Agents

In This Chapter

Despite your best efforts, unfortunately, you will encounter a few unscrupulous real estate agents who slip through your first lines of defense. Interested only in completing the sale at hand, they resort to using some common sales tricks that can be very effective with the unwary buyer. A buyer who recognizes those tricks, fortunately, is in a position to take action at the first sign of such high pressure tactics.

A Question of Loyalty

Many agents are masters at creating a feeling of indebtedness on the part of the buyer. Occasionally they may bring up the number of buildings that have been shown or they may casually grumble about the expenses involved in being a real estate agent—the cost of owning a large new car, their office expenses, the cost of gasoline, the time they often spend with clients that end with no sale. This is all designed to make the buyer feel guilty and to create a feeling that some loyalty is due for the services they have provided. A sensitive buyer, realizing that an agent receives no compensation unless a sale occurs, falls easily into this guilt trap. There is, however, no rational basis for such feelings.

The agent works for the seller, both legally and ethically. To use an obscure legal term, the agent acts in a fiduciary capacity to the seller, which means that the agent must act in the seller's behalf, for the seller's best interests, and *under the seller's control.* There are times, however, when these relationships might be confusing, particularly when the agent who is working with the buyer is not the listing agent for the properties being shown.

When a real estate agent assists a buyer in locating properties that some other broker has listed, it becomes easy to think of this person as the buyer's agent and the listing broker as the seller's agent. The agent might spend time with the buyer searching the MLS files, driving the buyer to see a few properties, phoning listing brokers for information, and generally acting as a representative of the buyer. No matter how he or she might act, however, the agent is always working for the seller.

Fortunately there is a simple test question, the answer to which clearly determines who a real estate agent represents: Who is paying the commission? In most situations it's the *seller.* Even an agent from a different office who locates a property for a buyer is nevertheless working as an agent for the seller. Why? Because the seller is paying a commission to the listing broker who, under the multiple listing agreement, will share that commission with the agent who brought in the buyer. In nearly every situation, therefore, unless you have agreed to pay the agent a commission, you will find yourself working with an agent whose *loyalties lie with the seller.*

If an agent fails to show you, the buyer, the kind of property that you wish to purchase, that agent has not earned a commission and deserves nothing for the time and expense invested. In fact, an agent who wastes two or three days of your time showing properties that do not meet your criteria is in your debt. In sales, the reward comes only with the sale, not with the effort.

High Pressure Tactics

In an attempt to close a sale, it is not uncommon for an agent to resort to rather unscrupulous tactics. Some of the more common techniques are presented here so that you might recognize them when an agent pulls them out. When the pressure begins, it's time to locate another agent, or at least to be very assertive in telling the agent that such tactics have no place in your relationship and that if they continue you will find another agent.

The "kidnapper" technique. This technique is designed to wear a buyer down. First the agent insists on driving the buyer to see a few buildings, regardless of whether they meet the buyer's criteria. When none does, the agent "finds" one more that the buyer "has to see." The line is "I think this one might have sold already, but let's drive over there just in case it hasn't." If that property is not what the buyer is looking for, there is one more that might be seen, and so on until the buyer, in exhaustion, is unable to think rationally. The "kidnapper agent" often has a cellular phone in the car, which he or she uses to obtain information on other listings that were not originally brought. Once the buyer's resistance has been beaten down, the agent will suggest submitting an offer on one of the properties that came closest to meeting the criteria, perhaps one about which the buyer was ambivalent. The weary buyer's response, of course, should always be, "Take me back to my car, it's time to go home. I will talk with you about it tomorrow."

The easiest way to avoid being kidnapped is always to drive to the building and meet the agent there; only ride with an agent who has earned your trust. The second way to avoid this tactic is to screen each listing prior to driving past the property. Why waste time driving around looking at properties that will probably lose money?

The "last chance" technique. The set up for this strategy begins when the agent shows a listing to the buyer. The agent will say something like, "This one is way underpriced, and there are several interested buyers. I think an offer is coming in this afternoon. But let's go see it, and if you like it, maybe I can get your offer in first."

An alternative is to take the buyer to three or four properties that come close to meeting the criteria but miss the target in some significant way. Then, just as the buyer is ready to return to the office disappointed, the agent says something like, "Just a second. There's one more here you might want to see. I thought it was sold already, but here's the listing, so maybe it's still available. There was a lot of activity on this, so I'll be surprised if it hasn't sold. But, since it's on the way, why don't we run over there right now." On the way, the agent extolls the virtues of the building, using the buyer's criteria, of course, and reminding the buyer in several different ways that he or she will need to act quickly to get it. Once at the building, the agent will say something like, "This is so close to what you want, and you have seen several already that weren't even close. Why don't we put in an offer just to see what happens. Otherwise, it might be gone tomorrow."

The buyer's response, of course, is, "Give me a copy of the listing sheet and I'll study it tonight. If the numbers work, I'll call you tomorrow and we can go through it." In the meantime, if the property does in fact sell, simply move on to the next one with no regrets. Better to lose several good properties through patience and forbearance than to acquire one "dog" through impatience and impulsiveness.

The closer.   Every agent will try to "close" a buyer. Simply put, this means that the agent will go through a series of predictable steps to get the buyer to sign a sales contract and submit a deposit. Most of the time the property the agent will try to close on is only second best when compared with the buyer's strict criteria. Inevitably, however, the buyer will be tempted to submit the offer, either because so many properties will have been seen that are totally wrong or the buyer will have seen very few properties with which to compare the present property.

Closing begins the moment the two meet, when the agent starts by trying to impress the buyer with his or her knowledge of real estate investing. The agent builds toward the close the entire time they are together by pointing out particular features of a building, by establishing a sense of urgency (I think an offer is coming in on this one today, but we might be able to beat it), by probing for criteria and by emphasizing the ways in which this or that property meets those criteria. By the end of the tour, the agent will ask something like, "Which one did you like the best?" followed by "Why don't we submit an offer and see what happens?"

If the buyer is not ready to make an offer, the agent will pursue the close by asking something like, "What don't you like about it?" This question is designed to elicit specific objections that the salesperson can work to overcome. This is when the real selling begins—after the buyer has said no and begins to voice objections. If the objection is that there is no cash flow, the salesperson will attempt to demonstrate, often with a smoke and mirror performance, that there is indeed a substantial cash flow. If the objection is the price, the salesperson may reply, "What do you think is a fair price?" If the buyer reveals a price, the salesperson might respond in a manner designed to make the buyer feel foolish or naive for even thinking that this property could be bought for such a price. Or the salesperson might reply, "With properties appreciating at the rate they have been in this area, this property will be worth $50,000 more by next year. Isn't it worth spending a little extra now so you can enjoy that much profit next year?" And so it goes.

Good closers already know most of the objections that people typically raise, and they have prepared a ready supply of answers and practiced their responses. Often these responses can make a buyer feel foolish for even asking, and when the buyer finally runs out of objections, each one having been answered with a response that sounded quite reasonable, the salesperson will move in for the close. "If you don't have any more objections, I'll start preparing the offer." And unless the buyer stops the agent, the offer will be drafted and the buyer will be asked to sign. When the buyer asks for some time to think it over, the agent will put the buyer off guard by apparently agreeing to grant that time: "Sure, take your time and think it over. A decision of this magnitude needs careful thought." This is designed to put the buyer at ease.

Just then, however, the agent will follow up by asking, "By the way, just to clarify things for me, what is it that you still need to think about? Is it . . ." And now the agent will go back over each of the objections that were raised originally, one by one, asking whether it is still a problem. Of course, each objection has been answered so the buyer has to agree they are no longer a problem. At this point, then, the agent will say something like, "What else is there to think about, then? You really like this building, don't you? So why take a chance on losing it by waiting another day?"

A truly persistent sales agent will continue this game for a long time, asking for objections, minimizing them one by one, then asking for the close. Be sure there are more closing strategies than a buyer has reasons to say no, and the experienced sales agent knows and has practiced every one of them until they seem totally fresh and spontaneous. The buyer's job is to remain firm and insist on thinking about it overnight. Then the buyer must go home, run the numbers again, consider every one of the criteria carefully, weigh each of the building's shortcomings against the buyer's goals, then make the decision, away from the probing questions and the slick answers.

Author's Note: When I feel the pressure being turned up for a close, I always explain to the agent in a firm, conclusive tone that it is my practice always to go home and think about the deal before submitting an offer. This gives me a chance to organize things clearly in my mind before submitting an offer, and allows me the opportunity to review all aspects of the deal so that I can continue with confidence.

Remember, for the agent, making the sale is the conclusion of his or her association with this building. For the buyer, the relationship has just begun and he or she will live with the consequences of that decision for a long time.

It is Possible to Build a Long-Term Relationship

There are a few real estate agents, fortunately, who have survived the tough years, maintained their integrity, and become seasoned professionals. Determined to be the best, they have developed a strategy that has led to continuing success without the need to resort to high pressure tactics. If you have the good fortune to encounter such an agent, attempt to build an understanding that will lead to a long-term relationship. Such an arrangement can be mutually beneficial. By knowing just what kind of property you are looking for, the agent will call when something appropriate becomes available. You, on the other hand, now have someone who is watching out for the right kind of property and who will not waste your time with buildings that fail to meet your criteria.

After a few years, you may have developed a relationship with a dozen or more agents who know the kind of property that will interest you. This leads to the added benefit of receiving an occasional call on a property that has just been listed or that is ready to be listed, and provides the inside track on many properties that might otherwise have been sold long before being discovered through normal channels. This kind of relationship can flourish only when both parties—the buyer and the agent—are professionals—with a professional's understanding of the business. No matter how cozy the relationship becomes, however, it is wise always to keep in mind that the agent's interest is substantially different from your own, and it is up to you to watch out for your own interests.

In Summary

Many real estate agents are masters at persuasion. By wearing down a buyer's defenses, by creating a sense of urgency, or simply through persistence, such agents are sometimes able to persuade an unwary buyer to purchase a particular property that is not a good investment. When an agent turns on the heat, find another agent. All investment decisions should be made without pressure, and only after carefully analyzing all aspects of the property.

It is possible to build a long-term mutually rewarding relationship with a real estate agent, one who respects your criteria and your expertise and only presents those properties that are clearly appropriate. The knowledge gained from this book will help to develop those relationships because you will outrank the majority of real estate agents in terms of skill, knowledge, and wisdom, and you will have gained the self-confidence to stand up to their efforts at intimidation.

Section III

■■■■■

How to Acquire the Right Property

Eighteen

■ ■ ■ ■ ■

How to Do the Numbers: Rule-of-Thumb Formulas for Calculating Cash Flow

In This Chapter

The most important characteristic of any property is whether it will generate a profit. Therefore, *the first step in evaluating a potential acquisition is to determine whether the building will generate positive cash flow.* Driving out to see a building takes time; driving past a lot of buildings takes a lot of time. Save time by calculating cash flow *before driving past a property.* This chapter introduces some simple formulas—the Gross Multiplier, the Expense Formula, the Monthly Net Income Multiplier, and the Capitalization Rate—to determine quickly whether a building has the potential to make money. Only if these formulas indicate that cash flow is possible should a buyer go to see the building itself. The more detailed calculations presented in Chapter 20—which are used to compute cash flow more precisely—should be performed only after a visit to the building has confirmed that it meets the other criteria of a good investment.

When the time comes to calculate whether a particular rental property will make money, it is time to set aside all passion. Searching for a suitable rental property, after all, can be an exciting process, for real estate is appealing in many ways: it can fulfill a need for security or it can slake a thirst for adventure. It can be aesthetically appealing or it can lure the handy-man. Rental properties hold the promise of self-employment and independence. The process of real estate investing can excite passions: it can produce anxiety or lift one to heights of ecstasy; it can induce a flow of adrenaline and provoke feelings of great accomplishment. But all of that passion serves for naught unless a buyer, like a skilled surgeon wielding a sharp scalpel, is coldly efficient at doing the numbers.

The Rule-of-Thumb Formulas

In any business, rules of thumb are nothing more than shortcuts that have been developed by experienced practitioners to make the job easier. So it is with the formulas in this chapter. Each has been developed over many years of evaluating properties by many thousands of real estate investors. Often the formulas are used simply to verify what the veteran investor already knows intuitively: whether a property makes any economic sense at all.

Four different formulas are presented here. An experienced buyer may use all four or any combination of the four, depending on the answers that are being sought. As you gain more experience you will learn which, if any, of the formulas work for you. You might even develop some rule-of-thumb formulas of your own. In the meantime, however, practice with each of these formulas until you become conversant with them all. Then choose which ones to use in your evaluation of potential properties. You will learn, as have many investors before you, that these formulas save untold hours of time in the search for the right property.

What Numbers Do You Need?

Working the formulas in this chapter will require three figures that can be taken directly from the listing sheet: gross income, total expenses, and the selling price.

1. *Gross income.* To obtain the gross income, total the monthly rents and subtract a reasonable amount to allow for vacancies. This is important, because different neighborhoods will produce differing vacancy rates. Rule of thumb is to subtract 20% for a Class III neighborhood, 15% for

a Class II neighborhood, and 10% for a Class I neighborhood. (Rate the neighborhood using the Neighborhood Rating Form, Figure 11.1.)

To obtain the gross *annual* income, multiply the *monthly* income by 12.

2. *Expenses* are the utilities, taxes, insurance, repairs, maintenance, and all other expenses *except the mortgage payment.*

3. *The selling price* is the listed price—or it can be a price you believe is more realistic for this property. Generally, the best procedure is to calculate the formulas first using the listed price; then, if that price produces unfavorable results plug in lower prices to determine at what price the property does make sense.

For the examples to follow, assume two properties each with the following numbers:

Property #1:

Price:	$350,000		
Gross monthly income:	$13,750	Gross annual income:	$165,000
Monthly expenses:	$6,613	Annual expenses:	$79,358
Net monthly income:	$7,137	Net annual income:	$85,642

Property #2

Price:	$350,000		
Gross monthly income:	$8,196	Gross annual income:	$98,350
Monthly expenses:	$6,613	Annual expenses:	$79,358
Net monthly income:	$1,583	Net annual income:	$18,992

Formula #1: The Gross Multiplier

This formula was introduced in Chapter 12, but is presented again here as a reminder of its importance and to define its role within the overall process of determining profit potential.

The formula is quite simple: Divide the price by the gross annual income. The formula produces a number that represents the relationship between the income produced by the property and the price. With most properties, the price will be approximately 5 to 7 times the annual income.

Price ÷ Annual Income = Gross Multiplier

Example A (Property #1): A building is selling for $350,000. The listing sheet indicates that the gross income is $165,000.

$$
\begin{array}{ccc}
& \text{Annual} & \text{Gross} \\
\text{Price} \div & \text{Income} = & \text{Multiplier} \\
\$350,000 & \$165,000 & 2.12
\end{array}
$$

In this example, the gross multiplier is 2.12, which is very low and therefore would indicate that the property will likely produce a positive cash flow.

Example B (Property #2): A building is selling for $350,000. The gross income is $98,350.

$$
\begin{array}{ccc}
& \text{Annual} & \text{Gross} \\
\text{Price} \div & \text{Income} = & \text{Multiplier} \\
\$350,000 & \$98,350 & 3.56
\end{array}
$$

Now the gross multiplier is 3.56, which would predict that positive cash flow may be possible, but unlikely.

Rule of thumb: When calculating the Gross Multiplier, if the result is in a range from 1 to 3, pursue the property. If the result is in a range from 3 to 5, analyze the figures more closely to determine whether positive cash flow is possible. If the result is in a range from 5 to 7 or higher, the property will most likely show negative cash flow. Before giving up, however, analyze the rents: when were they last raised? Are they under market rents for the area? Can they be raised? If the rents can be raised, recalculate the Gross Multiplier using the higher annual income figure.

Formula #2: Expense Formula

This formula is also quick and simple. Total the annual expenses from the listing sheet. Do not include mortgage payments. If the total expenses are between 50% and 75% of the gross income, the property has a chance of making money. If the figure is over 75% the building probably will not work. Conversely, if the total is less than 50% something is wrong with the figures; the owner most likely has understated the annual expenses.

Annual Expense ÷ Gross Annual Income = Expense Indicator

Example A (Property #1): From the listing sheet, total the *annual* costs for utilities, taxes, insurance, repairs, maintenance, etc., everything except the mortgage payment. The total is $79,358. The gross income for the building is $165,000.

Annual Expenses	÷	Annual Income	=	Expense Indicator
$79,358		$165,000		48%

The listed expenses are probably understated; expect to pay more than that if the property is purchased. Nevertheless, the building is likely to produce a positive cash flow.

Example B (Property #2): Total annual expenses equal $79,358, but the gross income equals only $98,350.

Annual Expenses	÷	Annual Income	=	Expense Indicator
$79,358		$98,350		81%

With expenses eating up 81% of the annual income from this property, there won't be enough left over to pay the mortgage and still produce a positive cash flow. Before eliminating the property, however, look at the rents. Are they below market? Can they be raised? What is the estimated annual income if the rents are raised to market levels? Now do the calculation again.

Formula #3: Monthly Net Income Multiplier

An alternative to the gross annual income multiplier, the monthly net income multiplier can also produce a reasonable indication of value. Think of the Monthly Net Income Multiplier as a number on a rating scale from 0 to 200. Above 100 indicates an unlikely investment; below 100 indicates a likely investment.

First obtain the monthly net income by totaling the monthly expenses (utilities, repairs, maintenance, taxes, insurance, etc.—everything except the mortgage payment) and subtracting this figure from the gross monthly income. The result is the *net monthly income*.

Gross Monthly Income – Monthly Expenses = Net Monthly Income

The *Net Income Multiplier* is obtained by dividing the price by the net monthly income.

Price ÷ Net Monthly Income = Net Income Multiplier

Example A (Property #1): To obtain the net monthly income, subtract the monthly expenses ($6,613) from the gross monthly income ($13,750). That figure, $7,137, is the net monthly income.

Gross Monthly Income	Monthly − Expenses =	Net Monthly Income
$13,750	$6,613	$7,137

Now divide the selling price by that amount.

Price ÷	Net Monthly Income	Net Income = Multiplier
$350,000	$7,137	49.04

What does this mean? Literally, it means that the price is approximately 50 times the net monthly income. Is this good or bad? On a scale of 0 to 200, a rating of 50 is excellent. Many investors figure that the net income multiplier should be between 110 and 120. Using those guidelines, a multiplier less than 50 is ideal or, said differently, a price that is only 50 times the net monthly income is an excellent price.

Example B (Property #2): If the monthly expenses are $6,613 but the monthly rent is only $8,196, the net income multiplier will be quite different.

Gross Monthly Income	Monthly − Expenses =	Net Monthly Income
$8,196	$6,613	$1,583

Price ÷	Net Monthly Income	Net Income = Multiplier
$350,000	$1,583	221

If 50 is an excellent multiplier, and 110 to 120 is considered good, then a multiplier of 221 is very high. Said differently, if the price is 221 times the net monthly income the price is too high—the income produced by this building won't support such a high price. A better price would be 110 times the net monthly income of $1,583, or approximately $174,000. To compare with Property #1, the multiplier should be 50, producing an ideal price of $79,150.

Rule of thumb: Many investors figure that the net income multiplier should be between 110 and 120. At that level, however, the property may not produce cash flow. As the multiplier sinks below 100, cash flow becomes more likely. A multiplier of 50 is excellent. If the multiplier goes over 100 (if the price is more than 100 times the net monthly income), however, the property probably will not carry itself.

Formula #4: Capitalization Rate

The rule-of-thumb capitalization rate ("cap rate") is a very rough formula that uses two values, the selling price and the net annual income, to determine the rate of capitalization. The cap rate can be likened to an interest rate, or a rate of return on investment. The formula determines how much simple interest is being earned (net annual income) on the investment, which is represented by the selling price, even though most of the money will be borrowed.

Net Annual Income ÷ Selling Price = Cap Rate

True capitalization formulas become quite complex, because they must deal with mortgage rates, tax rates, and equity growth, all of which affect total return on actual investment. As used here, however, the cap rate is designed to produce a quick indicator of value for a property that is being considered.

Example A (Property #1): If the price is $350,000, and the net annual income (gross annual income minus expenses, before mortgage payment) is $85,642, the cap rate is .24 (24%).

Net Annual Income		Selling Price		Capitalization Rate
	÷		=	
$85,642		$350,000		24%

This indicates that if one paid full price in cash for the property ($350,000), the return on investment (from income only) would be 24% per year in simple interest.

Example B (Property #2): If the price is $350,000 but the net annual income is only $18,992, the cap rate is now .05 (5%).

Net Annual Income	÷	Selling Price	=	Capitalization Rate
$18,992		$350,000		5%

This indicates a rate of return of only 5%. Most banks pay at least that much on certificates of deposit, which represent no risk and are completely liquid. Why take the risk on a rental property for such a small return?

Rule of thumb: A cap rate over 20% is good. Between 10% and 20%, remain interested, but look at the figures closely. Under 10%, the property is probably over-priced and likely will not produce cash flow.

A Recap of the Two Properties

If each of the sample properties were analyzed using all four formulas, here is what the results would look like. As you can see, each formula produces a slightly different perspective of the property. Together, they provide a comprehensive picture of the cash flow potential of each building as well as a good indication of whether the selling price is reasonable.

Property #1:

Formula	Specific Results	Ideal Results	Is This A Good Investment?
Gross Income Multiplier	2.12	1 to 3	yes
Expense Indicator	48%	50% to 75%	yes
Net Monthly Income Multiplier	49.04	less than 100	yes
Capitalization (Cap) Rate	24%	over 20%	yes

Property #2:

Formula	Specific Results	Ideal Results	Is This A Good Investment?
Gross Income Multiplier	3.56	1 to 3	marginal
Expense Indicator	81%	50% to 75%	no
Net Monthly Income Multiplier	221	less than 100	no
Capitalization (Cap) Rate	5%	over 20%	no

Analysis

Building #1 should be pursued. The numbers look good at this point, although a more precise analysis of the income and expense figures (Chapter 18) might later reveal some problems. The next step is to drive past the building to see how it looks.

Building #2, on the other hand, seems to be a very poor investment. Overpriced, it will produce a negative cash flow. The best plan is to cease consideration of this building and continue to look for other properties that will produce positive cash flow.

In Summary

Cash flow should be calculated at two different times, in two different ways: the first time before driving past a building; the second time after a drive-by has confirmed that a building meets the other investment criteria. To assess cash flow quickly, use one or more of the rule-of-thumb formulas. These old but reliable indicators will suggest whether to proceed or whether the property is a waste of time. The Gross Multiplier is a quick indicator of value based on the annual income produced by the building. If the Gross Multiplier is under 3, the building has real possibilities.

The Expense Indicator measures how much of the gross income produced by the building must go to cover expenses. If expenses consume more than 75% of a building's income, very little is left over to pay the mortgage and provide profits for the owner.

The Monthly Net Income Multiplier, which evaluates price on the basis of net monthly income, is a little more complex and not as easy to understand as the other formulas. Ideally, the multiplier should be less than 100 (the price is less than 100 times the net monthly income).

The Cap Rate is an indicator of return on investment; more than 20% is good.

Next Steps

If the rule-of-thumb indicators are positive, take a drive past the building (Chapter 19). If, during the drive-by, the neighborhood and the building look good, go back home and complete a more thorough examination of the income/expense figures (Chapter 20). If those figures look promising, arrange to walk through the building (Chapter 21). If everything checks out at each step of the process, submit an offer for the property (Chapter 22). Don't skip any of the steps. Following these procedures will avoid many time-wasting trips to visit buildings that might be exciting in various ways but would drain the pockets of anyone so foolish as to invest.

Nineteen

■ ■ ■ ■ ■

How to Do a Drive-by Inspection

In This Chapter

When a building appears to generate positive cash flow, the next step is to drive past the building to see what it looks like. The agent, eager to move the sale ahead, will want to set up an appointment immediately to see the interior of the building, but a walk-through is premature at this point. Driving past the property first will reveal whether a walk-through is justified. If the drive-by is disappointing no further action is necessary and a great deal of time will have been saved.

The purpose of a drive-by is to establish the following:

1. The quality of the tenants.

2. The quality of the immediate neighborhood.

3. The general condition of the building.

If the neighborhood is already well-known, limit the drive-by to the immediate area of the building. If the neighborhood is unfamiliar, follow the procedures outlined in Chapter 11 to become acquainted with the area.

How Thorough Should a Drive-by Inspection Be?

In the same way that the rule-of-thumb cash-flow formulas (Chapter 18) produce a quick snapshot of a building's financial potential, so a drive-by inspection produces a quick snapshot of the building's physical potential. In both cases the question to be answered is, "Should I continue to be interested in this building?"—not whether the building should be bought.

Both activities—rule-of-thumb formulas and drive-by inspections—are designed to save time by screening out properties that obviously do not meet your investment criteria. Neither activity will deliver the final decision regarding whether to buy the building. For that reason, a drive-by can be accomplished in a relatively short time; the goal is simply to obtain a quick impression of the property. On the other hand, a drive-by should not be so brief that it fails to reveal significant information. The goal is to be thorough but efficient. There are many buildings to consider, only a few of which are good investments, so make good use of the time available.

Safe, Clean, Quiet? Use the Check-off Form

No matter where a rental property is located, three criteria will attract good tenants:

1.   Is it a *safe* building to live in?

2.   Is it a *clean* building to live in?

3.   Is it a *quiet* building to live in?

Figure 19.1 is a simple rating form that can be used during a drive-by inspection. A total score of 40 or better indicates a good building. A score of 30 to 40 indicates that a walk-through is probably justified, but there are some problems that will have to be taken into consideration and that should be reflected in the price. A score below 30 should remove a building from consideration.

In addition, if the score in the Safe category falls below 12, regardless of the overall score, the building probably should be scratched. A dirty building can be cleaned up and a noisy building can be quieted, but an unsafe building can hardly ever escape a poor reputation, and good tenants will continue to avoid the building for years after the unsafe conditions have been corrected.

Figure 19.1   Drive-by Inspection Rating Form

DRIVE-BY INSPECTION RATING FORM

This form is designed to be used when first driving past a property that is being considered for purchase. The important considerations are these: Is the building clean? Is the building safe? Is the building quiet? Rate each of the stages of the drive-by inspection by these three criteria, then check off the positive and negative indicators. Use the extra lines to add additional observations.

When the drive-by is complete, the total of the ratings will indicate whether the building should be pursued. A score of 40 or better indicates an excellent building. A score of 30 to 40 indicates that a walk-through inspection is probably justified, but there are some problems. If the score is below 30, the building should be removed from consideration.

STAGE 1: THE FRONT OF THE BUILDING

FRONT ENTRANCE

OVERALL APPEARANCE: ___ Excellent ___ Good ___ Poor
OVERALL CONDITION: ___ Excellent ___ Good ___ Poor

POSITIVE INDICATORS		NEGATIVE INDICATORS	
__ Door closes securely	__ Clean	__ Broken window	__ Scratched and marred
__ Painted	__ Architecturally pleasing	__ Broken door-knob	__ Dirty
__ Well-lighted	_____	__ Door drags	__ Door does not close
_____	_____	__ Door hangs crooked	securely

FRONT YARD

OVERALL APPEARANCE: ___ Excellent ___ Good ___ Poor
OVERALL CONDITION: ___ Excellent ___ Good ___ Poor

POSITIVE INDICATORS		NEGATIVE INDICATORS	
__ Paint good	__ Clean yard	__ Paint peeling	__ Broken fence
__ Grass	__ Trees	__ Broken concrete	__ Bare earth
__ Flowers	__ Fence in good condition	__ Holes in the yard	_____
__ Shrubs	_____	_____	

FRONT FACADE

OVERALL APPEARANCE: ___ Excellent ___ Good ___ Poor
OVERALL CONDITION: ___ Excellent ___ Good ___ Poor
CONSTRUCTION: ___ Brick ___ Frame ___ Other _____

POSITIVE INDICATORS		NEGATIVE INDICATORS	
__ Paint good	__ Clean	__ Paint peeling	__ Cracks in the wall
__ Windows attractive	__ Storms/screens	__ Windows need glazing	_____
	__ Shrubs	__ Windows broken	_____
_____	_____	__ Brick needs tuckpointing	_____

TENANTS

OVERALL APPEARANCE: ___ Excellent ___ Good ___ Poor

POSITIVE INDICATORS		NEGATIVE INDICATORS	
__ Tenants appearance neat	_____	__ People coming and going	__ People loitering
__ Minimal traffic	_____	__ Tenants look disheveled	_____
__ Tenants quiet	_____	__ Lots of children	_____
__ Few children	_____	__ Home during working hours	_____

THE FRONT OF THE BUILDING

IS IT SAFE?	IS IT CLEAN?	IS IT QUIET?
0 1 2 3 4 5	0 1 2 3 4 5	0 1 2 3 4 5

Rating Scale: 0 = lowest rating; 5 = highest rating

Figure 19.1   Drive-by Inspection Rating Form *(continued)*

STAGE 2: THE REAR OF THE BUILDING

THE ALLEY

OVERALL APPEARANCE: __ Excellent __ Good __ Poor
OVERALL CONDITION: __ Excellent __ Good __ Poor

POSITIVE INDICATORS		NEGATIVE INDICATORS	
__ Clean alley	__ Trash containers neat and clean	__ Broken glass	__ Evidence of rodents
__ Adequate trash containers	__ Rodent free	__ Trash all over the alley	_____
__ Well-lighted	_____	__ Broken furniture	_____
__ Parking area for tenants	_____	__ Garages in poor condition	_____

REAR ENTRANCE

OVERALL APPEARANCE: __ Excellent __ Good __ Poor
OVERALL CONDITION: __ Excellent __ Good __ Poor

POSITIVE INDICATORS		NEGATIVE INDICATORS	
__ Door closes securely	__ Trash containers neat and clean	__ Broken windows	__ Door hangs crooked
__ Painted	_____	__ Broken door-knob	__ Dirty
__ Well-lighted	_____	__ Door drags	__ Trash lying around
__ Clean	_____	__ Scratched and marred	_____

REAR FACADE

OVERALL APPEARANCE: __ Excellent __ Good __ Poor
OVERALL CONDITION: __ Excellent __ Good __ Poor

POSITIVE INDICATORS		NEGATIVE INDICATORS	
__ Paint good	__ Storms/screens	__ Brick needs tuckpointing	__ Windows broken
__ Painted	_____	__ Paint peeling	__ Dirty
__ Windows attractive	_____	__ Cracks in the wall	_____
__ Clean	_____	__ Windows need glazing	_____

THE REAR OF THE BUILDING

IS IT SAFE?	IS IT CLEAN?	IS IT QUIET?
0 1 2 3 4 5	0 1 2 3 4 5	0 1 2 3 4 5

Rating Scale: 0 = lowest rating; 5 = highest rating

— NOTES —

Figure 19.1   Drive-by Inspection Rating Form (continued)

STAGE 3: THE NEIGHBORHOOD

THE NEIGHBORS

OVERALL APPEARANCE: ___ Excellent ___ Good ___ Poor

POSITIVE INDICATORS   NEGATIVE INDICATORS

___ Neighbors appearance neat _____   ___ Groups loitering   ___ Lots of children
___ Minimal traffic   _____   ___ Neighbors look disheveled _____
___ Neighbors quiet   _____   ___ Home during working hours _____
_____   _____   ___ People coming and going   _____

THE NEIGHBORHOOD

OVERALL APPEARANCE: ___ Excellent ___ Good ___ Poor
OVERALL CONDITION: ___ Excellent ___ Good ___ Poor

POSITIVE INDICATORS   NEGATIVE INDICATORS

___ Low density   ___ Public transportation nearby   ___ High density   ___ Commercial area
___ Parking not a problem ___ Mostly residential   ___ Parking problems   ___ Dirty
___ Close to trains   ___ Close to buses   ___ Manufacturing area _____
___ Clean   _____   ___ High traffic area   _____

OTHER BUILDINGS IN THE AREA

OVERALL APPEARANCE: ___ Excellent ___ Good ___ Poor
OVERALL CONDITION: ___ Excellent ___ Good ___ Poor
CONSTRUCTION: ___ Brick ___ Frame ___ Other _____

POSITIVE INDICATORS   NEGATIVE INDICATORS

___ Nicely painted   ___ Mostly small buildings   ___ Paint peeling   ___ Mostly commercial
___ In good repair   ___ Mostly residential   ___ No screens on windows ___ Dirty
___ Windows attractive _____   ___ In poor repair   _____
___ Clean   _____   ___ Mostly large buildings _____

IS IT SAFE?   IS IT CLEAN?   IS IT QUIET?
0 1 2 3 4 5   0 1 2 3 4 5   0 1 2 3 4 5

Rating Scale: 0 = lowest rating; 5 = highest rating

RATING SUMMARY

Stage 1: The Front of the Building	___ Safe	___ Clean	___ Quiet
Stage 2: The Rear of the Building	___ Safe	___ Clean	___ Quiet
Stage 3: The Neighborhood	___ Safe	___ Clean	___ Quiet
Total	___ Safe	___ Clean	___ Quiet

What To Look At

A drive-by should be done in three stages. Stage 1 is the front of the building. Stage 2 is the alley and the rear of the building. Stage 3 is the immediate neighborhood—the area within a two-block radius of the building.

Stage 1: The front.   Go to the front of the building first, stop, and look for the following:

The front door: The front door provides a quick insight into the quality of tenants in the building. A door that is standing open indicates an insecure environment in the building. A scratched or dirty door reveals a lot of traffic by abusive tenants. Conversely, a painted, secure front entrance reveals pride and concern on the part of both the tenants and the owner.

Windows: We have said that windows reveal a great deal about the people who live in a building (Chapter 11). The condition of the window coverings indicates both the economic status of the residents as well as their sense of pride.

Grass: Regardless of the neighborhood, a building that is cared for will sport a good lawn. A poor lawn—one that is full of weeds, trash, or just bare earth—is indicative of an owner who does not care. That kind of owner is also likely to be less conscientious about screening tenants and keeping up with maintenance.

Tenants and neighbors: Sit for a while in front of the building and watch who comes and goes: usually the people one sees walking past the front and going in and out of the building will verify the other indicators. Also, look for loiterers, porch sitters, drinkers, and vagrants. Good tenants will be intimidated if a lot of unsavory types hang out around a building.

Overall condition of the building: Scan the front of the building to determine whether the owner has maintained the building properly. Look for peeling paint, cracks in the brick, broken windows, torn screens, graffiti, and other signs of neglect.

Stage 2: The alley. If the front of the building passes muster, drive through the alley and look at the rear. Of all the characteristics to be observed during a drive-by, the alley behind the building is one of the most reliable, as the alley reveals the true story of the building. In the alley look for the following:

Trash in the alley: As a rule of thumb, if the alley looks trashy, avoid the building; a trashy alley is a sure sign of uncaring tenants and neighbors.

Windows: Are the windows in the rear and the sides of the building—away from the public eye—worse than the windows in front?

Door: The rear door is an important key to building security. A tightly fastened, clean and freshly painted rear door indicates a secure building and a caring owner.

General condition: Again look for cracks, peeling paint, loose and chipped mortar, rotted wood, and other signs of neglect. Sometimes an owner will maintain the front facade of a building while allowing the sides and rear to deteriorate.

Stage 3: The immediate neighborhood. If the building still holds your interest after scanning the front and the rear, the next step is to drive around the few blocks surrounding the building and look for the following:

Density: An area dominated by large apartment buildings can create multiple problems. First, competition from other buildings in the area will tend to create a higher vacancy rate even in a strong market. Second, a high density neighborhood is less desirable because of noise, cars, lack of parking, and lack of trees and grass and other amenities. Consequently, it will be more difficult to attract and hold desirable tenants.

Parking: If parking is a problem, the better tenants will go elsewhere.

Transportation: Good tenants can afford to be selective about where they live, and many will choose to be near a bus or train line if they do not drive. If the building is close to such transportation it will help in attracting quality tenants.

Condition of the surrounding buildings: If the building under consideration is in good condition but the buildings in the area are not, it may be difficult to attract good tenants.

The neighbors: Look to see who lives in the neighborhood. Are they the kinds of people who would make desirable tenants?

When to Go

Do a drive-by in the late afternoon or early evening when people are out and about, the children are on their way home from school or at play in the neighborhood, and the tenants are coming home from work. Drive by in the daylight; it will be difficult to pick out the details after dark. If looking during the winter, be aware that you are missing many of the details of the neighborhood that can be observed readily during the warmer months. People stay in during the winter.

In Summary

A drive-by is an essential step in the process of evaluating a building; the purpose of a drive-by is to establish the quality of the tenants, the quality of the immediate neighborhood, and the general condition of the building. An effective drive-by is done in three stages: the front of the building, the alley and the rear of the building, and the immediate neighborhood. At each stage, the three primary considerations are whether the building is *safe, clean,* and *quiet.* If the building passes muster at each stage, the next step is go back home and analyze the income and expense figures in detail.

Twenty

■ ■ ■ ■ ■

How to Do the Real Numbers: Calculating True Income and Expenses

In This Chapter

The goal of every business venture is to generate a profit for the investor. With rental properties, profits occur when the rental income pays all of the operating expenses on the building, plus the mortgage payment, with some money left over for the investor. The concept is so simple as to seem obvious, yet the majority of investors who purchase rental properties seem to ignore this basic principle. To ascertain whether a property will generate profits, one must project accurately the value of the rental income as well as the liability of the operating expenses. If a mistake is made at this stage, the venture will be put at risk.

A common error when calculating income and expenses is to over-estimate the rental income and under-estimate the expenses. An agent eager for a sale often willingly contributes to this error. Because the investor rather than the agent will suffer the consequences from any miscalculation that occurs, it is the investor's job to avoid such errors. It is safe to assume that the income and expense numbers that appear on a listing sheet are designed to cast the property in its best light. Even if the owner and the listing agent are being completely honest, *which is not a safe assumption,* the numbers do not account for worst possible scenarios. Because you want to know what your true risk is, you must be concerned with worst possible scenarios. Therefore, when calculating the income and expenses it is essential to use extremely conservative numbers.

How to Calculate True Rental Income

A listing sheet typically presents both a list of projected income and a list of the expenses. The difference between the two is the net operating income for the building, from which the mortgage payment must be paid. On the income side, the listing sheet enumerates the total number of *potential* sources of income for the building: the number of apartments, stores, and garages in the building. Potential is emphasized because some owners are very *creative* when it comes to listing income sources. Until a space is actually seen, it will not be known whether that space can be rented. The figure also represents only *potential* income because it does not take into account vacancies or true market rents for the area.

Do not believe the rent figures that appear on the listing sheet! Because the price of a rental property is determined primarily by the value of rental income, many sellers attempt to inflate the price of a building by falsely increasing the income figures. There are several commonly used strategies to accomplish this. One method is to charge the tenants a posted rent but refund a portion of it under the table. Another is to offer substantial discounts to attract tenants to a property. A third method is to list vacant apartments at a higher rent than they actually can produce. A fourth method is to fill vacant apartments with non-paying friends and relatives to hide the true vacancy rate. A fifth method is simply to lie about the rental income. In each scenario, unfortunately, the true income and the listed income are significantly different. An unwary investor, unfamiliar with such practices, could easily be snared by such false figures. *The only way to protect yourself from these unscrupulous methods is to calculate the income using realistic numbers.*

Inspect the Building and Check the Rents

The solution to the problem of over-stated income is two-fold. First, make a mental note to inspect the building carefully during the walk-through to verify that each space listed as an income source is in fact rentable. Second,

Figure 20.1 Cooperative Listing Service

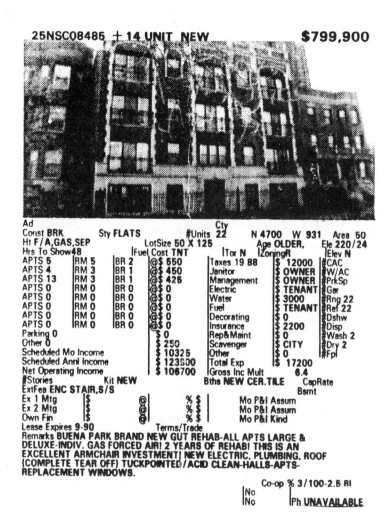

```
25NSC08485  +14 UNIT  NEW                          $799,900
```

```
Ad                                      Cty
Const BRK        Sty FLATS       #Units 22      N 4700   W 931   Area 50
Ht F/A,GAS,SEP          LotSize 50 X 125        Age OLDER,      Ele 220/24
Hrs To Show48           |Fuel Cost TNT     |Tor N  |ZoningR     |Elev N
APTS 5     |RM 5  |BR 2  |@$ 550    |Taxes 19 88   |$ 12000   |#CAC
APTS 4     |RM 3  |BR 1  |@$ 450    |Janitor       |$ OWNER   |#W/AC
APTS 13    |RM 3  |BR 1  |@$ 425    |Management    |$ OWNER   |#PrkSp
APTS 0     |RM 0  |BR 0  |@$ 0      |Electric      |$ TENANT  |#Gar
APTS 0     |RM 0  |BR 0  |@$ 0      |Water         |$ 3000    |#Rng 22
APTS 0     |RM 0  |BR 0  |@$ 0      |Fuel          |$ TENANT  |#Ref 22
APTS 0     |RM 0  |BR 0  |@$ 0      |Decorating    |$ 0       |#Dshw
APTS 0     |RM 0  |BR 0  |@$ 0      |Insurance     |$ 2200    |#Disp
Parking 0                |$ 0       |Rep&Maint     |$ 0       |#Wash 2
Other 0                  |$ 250     |Scavenger     |$ CITY    |#Dry 2
Scheduled Mo Income      |$ 10325   |Other         |$ 0       |#Fpl
Scheduled Annl Income    |$ 123900  |Total Exp     |$ 17200
Net Operating Income     |$ 106700  |Gross Inc Mult   6.4
#Stories        Kit NEW           Bths NEW CER.TILE      CapRate
ExtFea ENC STAIR,S/S                                     Bsmt
Ex 1 Mtg    |$          @      % $ |   Mo P&I Assum
Ex 2 Mtg    |$          @@     % $ |   Mo P&I Assum
Own Fin     |$          @@@    % $ |   Mo P&I Kind
Lease Expires 9-90          Terms/Trade
Remarks BUENA PARK BRAND NEW GUT REHAB-ALL APTS LARGE &
DELUXE-INDIV. GAS FORCED AIR! 2 YEARS OF REHAB! THIS IS AN
EXCELLENT ARMCHAIR INVESTMENT! NEW ELECTRIC, PLUMBING, ROOF
(COMPLETE TEAR OFF) TUCKPOINTED/ACID CLEAN-HALLS-APTS-
REPLACEMENT WINDOWS.
                                    Co-op % 3/100-2.5 BI
                                |No
                                |No       |Ph UNAVAILABLE
```

Listing made subject to errors, omissions, change of price, prior sale and withdrawal without notice.

use your own rent figures to determine gross income, based on an informed opinion regarding the price at which each apartment can actually be rented. This requires some homework. Check the rent levels in the neighborhood where the building is located. The easiest way to do so is to look in the apartment rental section of the newspaper. Try to determine the rent that can be obtained from a comparable apartment in the area. If necessary, travel to the neighborhood and inquire about some apartments; this will soon reveal the true rents that can be expected from apartments in the building under consideration.

Use the Form to Calculate True Gross Income

Figure 20.2 is a form that can be used to calculate the true income for an apartment building. In the example the income was taken from an actual listing sheet (Figure 20.1). The real estate agent who sent this form crowed that it represented an excellent investment because the property showed great cash flow. A glance at the listing sheet seems to verify his claims. The real numbers, however, tell a different story.

Notice that the columns on the the left side of Figure 20.2 provide blank lines for entering the rents and other income as they appear on the listing sheet, while the columns on the right side provide parallel blanks for entering true market rents, if different. This parallel construction allows you to compare the broker's figures with your own.

Line 1:   On the left side of the form, enter the amount of rent for each rental space *according to the listing sheet.* For purposes of calculating income it is acceptable to group units when possible, as in the example. How the apartments are grouped is not important but the amount assigned to each apartment is. If a unit is listed as vacant on the listing sheet, enter an amount that corresponds with other units of similar size in the building.

Author's Note: In the example, the listing sheet reports a total of 22 apartment units: 5 two-bedrooms at $550, 4 one-bedrooms at $450, and 13 one-bedrooms at $425. I entered those figures in the left-hand columns of Figure 20.2.

In the right-hand columns enter the amount of rent each apartment realistically will command, if that amount is different from the listed rent. Be certain that each number is accurate for the neighborhood. If the amount the owner has listed seems low, which can often occur, enter the more accurate rent. If the listed amount is too high, enter a lower figure. If a unit is listed as vacant on the listing sheet enter a realistic rent for the neighborhood.

Figure 20.2   Rental Income Form

PROPERTY ADDRESS									TOTAL APTS 22			

RENTS FROM LISTING SHEET						TRUE RENTAL AMOUNTS					
	NO	SIZE		RENT	TOTAL		NO	SIZE		RENT	TOTAL
1	5	2BR	x	550 =	2,750	1	5	2BR	x	450 =	2,250
2	4	1BR	x	450 =	1,800	2	17	1BR	x	375 =	6,375
3	13	1BR	x	425 =	5,525	3			x	=	
4			x	=		4			x	=	
5			x	=		5			x	=	
6			x	=		6			x	=	
7			x	=		7			x	=	
8			x	=		8			x	=	
9			x	=		9			x	=	
10			x	=		10			x	=	
11	Parking					11	Parking				
12	Other				250	12	Other				250
13	Scheduled Monthly Income				10,325	13	Scheduled Monthly Income				8,875
14	Scheduled Annual Income				123,900	14	Scheduled Annual Income				106,500
15	Less 15% Vacancy Rate				(18,585)	15	Less 15% Vacancy Rate				(15,975)
16	True Gross Income				105,315	16	True Gross Income				90,525
17	Less 6% Management Fee				(6,319)	17	Less 6% Management Fee				(5,431)
18	Total				98,996	18	Total				85,094

Author's Note: My experience with the neighborhood in which this particular building is located suggests that the scheduled rents on the listing sheet are too high (these are tenant-heated apartments). A more realistic figure is $450 for the two-bedrooms and $375 for the one-bedrooms, so I entered those figures in the right-hand columns.

Line 13:   Total the rents to obtain the scheduled monthly income.

Line 14: Multiply the total scheduled rents by 12 months to obtain the scheduled annual income.

Author's Note: In the example, the total scheduled rent is $10,325 per month, which translates to $123,900 per year according to the listing sheet. By entering amounts that represent more realistic rents in the neighborhood, the gross annual income is reduced to $106,500, a difference of $17,400 per year. My figures might be a little low. The owner's figures, I know, are too high.

Calculating the Vacancy Rate

The scheduled monthly income is the amount of income the building would generate if every space were occupied every day by a tenant who paid rent on time. Even in the most desirable neighborhoods, however, there will be times when an apartment is vacant, if only to redecorate after one tenant leaves and before the next moves in. There will also be those tenants who fall behind in their rent and must be evicted. The total loss of income that results from these situations is called the *vacancy rate*.

Line 15: Enter a vacancy rate factor. This is an arbitrary figure based on experience with the area or, if you lack experience with the neighborhood, from extensive research. If the neighborhood is a Class III neighborhood, or if the neighborhood is Class II or Class I but competition for tenants is stiff in the area because of numerous other apartment buildings, enter 20%. If the neighborhood is a Class II neighborhood but competition is not a factor, enter 15%. If the neighborhood is a Class I neighborhood enter 10%, *which is the lowest vacancy factor to use regardless of the neighborhood or the owner's claims.* Above all, be both realistic and conservative when estimating neighborhood rents and vacancy rates. It is far better to enjoy unexpected income later as a result of overly conservative calculations now rather than come up short later because of overly optimistic projections. The best rule of thumb is always to over-state liabilities and under-state income. Now, multiply the scheduled annual income by the vacancy factor and subtract the result to obtain the True Gross Income for the property (Line 16). This figure should be used in all calculations from this point forward.

Subtracting Management Fees

Management firms charge a fee equal to a percentage of the gross receipts each month. Because the fee is not a fixed expense, but a floating expense based on income, it is more accurate to list it here as a deduction against income rather than in the expense column.

Line 17: If you intend to use a professional firm to manage the property, enter on line 17 the percentage they are likely to charge. This fee will range from 5% if the property is in a Class I area and does not present significant management problems to 10% if the property is located in a Class III area. Subtract the fee from the net monthly income, as in the example.

Calculating Expenses

If listing sheets were gospel, nearly all rental properties would generate positive cash flow. Unfortunately, however, most listing sheets fudge the expenses in one way or another. A novice buyer scanning the listed expenses on one of these sheets would easily be misled into believing the property is an excellent investment when in fact the property will deliver consistent negative cash flow. *Do not believe the expense figures from the listing sheet!* Some items, like taxes and insurance, are easily verifiable and therefore usually are accurate. Check the tax figure, however, to determine whether it is for the current year and not one or two years old. (If a property is listed with a broker, the broker's code of ethics requires that he or she verify such expenses.) Other expenses, however, such as repairs and maintenance costs, are not verifiable and therefore are subject to being understated.

Like rents, however, expenses from building to building follow certain patterns, patterns that will become familiar as more properties are reviewed. The more practiced one becomes, therefore, the easier it is to detect fraudulent expense claims and the quicker one becomes at estimating more accurate figures.

Figure 20.3 is an expense form that will be particularly helpful. This form lists each of the typical expenses one encounters with rental properties. By filling in each of the blanks, a buyer can be assured that every potential expense is covered. The key is first to enter expense figures that are completely realistic and second to be certain that any errors made are due to overstating, rather than understating, expenses.

The sample numbers in Figure 20.3 are taken directly from the same listing sheet (Figure 20.1) that produced the income figures in Figure 20.2. Those income figures, it turns out, are significantly over-stated. On the expense side, moreover, it becomes clear that the expenses on the listing sheet are significantly understated, producing a terribly skewed picture of this particular property. Follow along to see how inaccurate a listing sheet really can be. *Remember that these figures were taken from an actual listing sheet sent by a real estate agent who insisted that this property would generate good cash flow.*

Just as with the income form, the expense form provides two sets of columns, the left-hand column for entering expenses directly from the listing sheet, and the right-hand column for entering more accurate expense figures.

Figure 20.3 Expense Form

		LISTED EXPENSES		TRUE EXPENSES	
1	TAXES 1988	$1,000	$12,000	$1,500	$18,000
2	FUEL	TENANT	TENANT	$400	$4,800
3	ELECTRIC	TENANT	TENANT	$200	$2,400
4	WATER	$250	$3,000	$300	$3,600
5	JANITOR	OWNER	OWNER	$1,000	$12,000
6	SCAVENGER	CITY	CITY	$00	$00
7	REPAIRS & MAINTENANCE	$00	$00	$500	$6,000
8	INSURANCE	$183	$2,200	$200	$2,400
9	ELEVATOR	NONE	NONE	NONE	NONE
10	MISCELLANEOUS	$00	$00	$400	$4,800
11	TOTAL	$1,433	$17,196	$4,500	$54,000
12	GROSS INCOME	$10,325	$123,900	$6,891	$82,696
13	NET OPERATING INCOME	$8,892	$106,704	$2,391	$28,696
14	MORTGAGE ($550,000 @ 8%)	$4,037	$48,444	$4,037	$48,444
15	CASH FLOW	$4,855	$58,260	$-1,646	$-19,748

Line 1: Taxes. From the listing sheet, enter the amount for taxes in the column under Listed Expenses. Next, look to see whether this is a current figure. (In the example, the taxes on the listing sheet are from 1988. This means that the listed taxes precede the total rehab that was done. The rehabbed building, because it is worth more money, will also be charged significantly greater taxes.)

If the taxes are current, add at least 10% to account for the likelihood that taxes will rise during the next year, and enter this figure in the column under True Expenses. If the figure on the listing sheet is not current, as in the example, do everything possible to determine a more accurate number. Compare the taxes with similar properties, talk with other owners or, better yet, ask the agent to obtain a copy of the most recent tax bill.

In the example, the taxes on the listing sheet are for 1988. The listing was sent late in 1991. This makes the tax figures at least three years old, with a minimum increase of 10% per year. In addition, the property has just experienced an extensive rehab, thereby increasing the tax liability over the coming years. Taking all of that into consideration, 1992 taxes were entered at a 50% increase, or $18,000.

Line 2: Fuel. In the example, the broker has listed heating gas as the tenant's responsibility, at no expense to the building. Because each of the apartments has been rehabbed and an individual heating unit installed, this seems plausible. The truth is, however, that such a building possibly has a central hot water heater, which will result in some fuel expense. And there is likely a unit for heating the common areas. If, during the walk through, it is determined that neither condition exists then the fuel expense can be eliminated. For now, it is safer to assume there will be some fuel expense. An arbitrary figure of $400 per month has been included, based loosely on experience with similar buildings.

For centrally heated buildings, the cost of fuel is a major expense, particularly during a severe winter. If a building is centrally heated, pay particular attention to the amount listed for heating expenses. Compare it with other buildings of similar size to determine whether the costs seem to be in line. If there seems to be a disparity, call the agent and inquire whether the heating bills were verified and, if so, how. If necessary, verify the heating bills yourself by calling the fuel company. After arriving at a figure that seems realistic, add 10% to allow for increases in usage or price. If the previous winter was particularly mild, moreover, add 10% more to allow for the possibility of a severe winter, which can dramatically increase the heating bill for a large building.

Line 3: Electric. The listing sheet in the example indicates that tenants are responsible for paying their own electric bills. This is a common practice, even in centrally heated buildings. Every building, however, has some common electrical fixtures—hall lights, basement lights, exterior lights, pumps, etc.—which result in an expense to the owner. In the example, an arbitrary figure of $200 per month, again based on experience with similar buildings, has been added for the cost of common electricity.

When the listing sheet includes an amount for common electricity, follow the same procedure as with the heating bills: compare the cost with similar buildings, check with the listing agent to determine how the amount was verified, and add 10% to allow for increased usage or higher prices.

Line 4: Water. Virtually every building is charged for water usage. Unlike heat and electricity, this is not an expense that can be transferred to the tenants. As with the other utilities, do everything possible to determine a realistic amount, then add 10% to allow for increased usage or higher prices.

In the example, the listing sheet indicates that water usage has been costing $250 per month. Adding 10% would increase that to $275 per month. Because the agent indicated that this building suffers presently from a high vacancy rate, however, it is safe to assume that when the building is full the cost for water usage will increase. For that reason, an additional $25 per month has been included.

Line 5: Janitor. In the example, the real estate agent has found a slick way to avoid listing this major expense: he has indicated that the owner is the janitor. Whether true or not, the next owner is unlikely to perform the janitor's duties, and a building of this size requires at least a part-time janitor. The cost for that service, based on experience with similar buildings, will be at least $1,000 per month. When the listing sheet does indicate an expense for a janitor, verify the cost and compare it with similar buildings.

Line 6: Scavenger. Typically, when a building is over 6 units the city will not pick up trash from individual tenants. In such a situation a professional scavenger service must be used—at the owner's expense. In Chicago, a local ordinance allows for city scavenger service for tenant-heated buildings—a curious practice, but one that favors the owner in those circumstances. In the example, therefore, no expense is listed for scavenger service.

When a building requires a commercial scavenger, it is best to verify the expense by calling a couple of companies for a price quote. With a little experience, however, you will become quire familiar with the cost for this service.

Line 7: Repairs and maintenance. Unlike the previous expenses, repairs and maintenance allow the owner a certain degree of discretion: some maintenance and many repairs can be deferred if the money is not available or if the owner chooses not to spend the money. On any listing sheet, therefore, ignore the amount listed for repairs and maintenance; owners notoriously understate this expense. The projected cost for repairs and maintenance depends, to a great extent, on the current age and condition of the building. If the building has been well maintained, costs will be somewhat lower. If, on the other hand, the owner has deferred a great deal of maintenance, the new owner can anticipate rather high costs.

Keep in mind that this line includes the routine costs of painting and decorating apartments, which will be encountered each time an apartment becomes vacant and must be prepared for a new tenant. The cost for such routine painting will range from $350 to $700 or more, depending on the size and condition of the apartment.

To determine the *annual* projected costs for repairs and maintenance, first determine the number of apartments in the building. Next multiply that number by one of the following amounts, depending on the condition of the building and the size of the apartments.

Repairs and maintenance: $500 per apartment, if:

The apartments are primarily *small*—studios with some one- bedrooms—and the condition of the building is *good.*

$750 per apartment, if:

A.   The apartments are primarily *small*—studios with some one-bedrooms—and the condition of the building is *fair,*

or

B.   The apartments are primarily *medium*—one- and two-bedrooms—and the condition of the building is *good.*

$1,000 per apartment, if:

A.   The apartments are primarily *small*—studios with some one- bedrooms—and the condition of the building is *poor,*

or

B.   The apartments are primarily *medium*—one-bedrooms with some two-bedrooms—and the condition of the building is *fair.*

$1,250 per apartment, if:

A.   The apartments are primarily *medium*—one-bedrooms with some two-bedrooms—and the condition of the building is *poor,*

or

B.   The apartments are primarily *large*—mostly five rooms to seven rooms—and the building is *fair* or *good.*

These amounts are meant to serve as rough guides, not hard and fast projections. Through the years inflation will require some modification of the amounts and experience will teach a formula that works well for you.

In the example, the building is a 22-unit walk-up, comprised primarily of medium-sized apartments—one-bedroom units with some two-bedrooms. The condition of the building is excellent, having just been completely rehabbed. Unrealistically, the listing sheet indicates no expense for repairs and maintenance, ignoring completely the routine expenses for decorating as well as the inevitable malfunctions that will occur even with new furnaces, plumbing, and electrical systems. Because a new owner can look forward to significantly reduced costs for repairs and maintenance due to the recent rehab, however, a reduced amount of $275 per apartment, rounded off to $6,000, has been included for repairs and maintenance.

Line 8:   Insurance. The best procedure for calculating insurance is to verify the amount, if possible, and compare it with similar buildings. Then add 10% to allow for probable inflation. The listing sheet in the example indicates $2,200 for insurance. Experience says that this figure is probably close to correct. Adding 10%, the cost for insurance has been increased to $200 per month, or $2,400 per year.

Line 9:   Elevator: If the building has an elevator, it is typical to pay a monthly maintenance fee that covers periodic inspections, routine maintenance, and many routine repairs. If the cost for this routine maintenance is stated, attempt to verify the amount and add 10% to cover inflation.

In the example, the building is a walk-up and therefore has no elevator expense.

Line 10:   Miscellaneous. Every building will incur certain miscellaneous expenses on a random basis, such as advertising and legal fees. Advertising can be a significant expense if the vacancy rate is high; legal fees can be significant if numerous eviction proceedings are anticipated. An eviction can cost as low as $275 or as high as $500 or more. In addition, the building might require the services of an attorney to deal with building code violations and other regulatory issues.

In the example, because the agent has indicated that the building suffers from numerous vacancies, advertising expenses will be rather high until the vacancy problem can be alleviated. Therefore, $400 per month, or

$4,800 annually, has been budgeted for miscellaneous expenses. Advertising costs alone will consume that amount for awhile.

Line 11: Total the expenses.

> *The fudge factor:* *Author's Note: After estimating the expenses, I often add a factor of 10% to the total to allow for unforeseen expenses, errors in estimating some of the items, or just as a fudge factor. The purpose in calculating accurate income and expense figures is to determine, with some degree of reliability, whether the property under consideration is capable of producing a positive cash flow. The best way to do that is to underestimate income and overestimate expenses. Although no fudge factor has been added in the example, I think it is a good idea. Historically I have miscalculated some expenses and suffered reduced income as a result.*

Line 12: Enter the Gross Income from Figure 20.2, Line 16, in the left hand column, and the True Gross Income from Figure 20.2, line 16 in the right hand column.

Line 13: Calculate the Net Operating Income (NOI) by subtracting the expenses (Line 11) from the gross income (Line 12). The listing sheet indicates an NOI of $106,704. A more accurate calculation, however, reveals a true NOI of only $28,696.

Calculating the Mortgage Payment

Line 14: Mortgage payment. After calculating the Net Operating Income (Line 13), the final step is to calculate the mortgage payment. Use the chart below (Figure 20.4) to estimate the mortgage payment for the property under consideration. To use the chart, you will need three figures: (1) The amount of the mortgage; (2) The interest rate; and (3) The term—how many years it will take to pay off the mortgage.

Step 1: Determine the total amount of the mortgage. Typically, the amount to be mortgaged will be approximately 80% to 90% of the selling price. In the example, however, the asking price for the building under consideration is $799,900 but the agent has indicated that the seller is desperate to sell and will let the building go for a price equal to the outstanding mortgage plus enough cash to cover a broker's commission of $20,000: a total of $570,000.

Figure 20.4   Monthly Payment Factors to Amortize a Loan of $1,000

TERM RATE	10 yrs.	15 yrs.	20 yrs.	25 yrs.	30 yrs.	TERM RATE	10 yrs.	15 yrs.	20 yrs.	25 yrs.	30 yrs.
7 %	11.62	8.99	7.76	7.07	6.66	11.0	13.78	11.37	10.33	9.81	9.53
7.1	11.66	9.05	7.82	7.14	6.73	11.1	13.83	11.43	10.39	9.87	9.60
7.2	11.71	9.11	7.88	7.20	6.79	11.2	13.89	11.49	10.46	9.95	9.67
7.25	11.75	9.13	7.91	7.23	6.83	11.25	13.92	11.53	10.50	9.99	9.72
7.3	11.77	9.16	7.94	7.27	6.86	11.3	13.95	11.56	10.53	10.02	9.75
7.4	11.81	9.22	8.00	7.33	6.93	11.4	14.00	11.62	10.60	10.09	9.83
7.5	11.88	9.28	8.06	7.39	7.00	11.5	14.06	11.69	10.67	10.17	9.91
7.6	11.92	9.33	8.12	7.46	7.07	11.6	14.12	11.75	10.73	10.24	9.98
7.7	11.97	9.39	8.18	7.53	7.13	11.7	14.17	11.81	10.80	10.31	10.06
7.75	12.01	9.42	8.21	7.56	7.17	11.75	14.21	11.85	10.84	10.35	10.10
7.8	12.02	9.45	8.25	7.59	7.20	11.8	14.23	11.87	10.87	10.38	10.13
7.9	12.08	9.50	8.31	7.65	7.27	11.9	14.29	11.94	10.94	10.46	10.21
8.0	12.14	9.56	8.37	7.72	7.34	12.0	14.35	12.01	11.02	10.54	10.29
8.1	12.19	9.62	8.43	7.79	7.41	12.1	14.40	12.07	11.08	10.61	10.36
8.2	12.24	9.68	8.49	7.86	7.48	12.2	14.46	12.13	11.15	10.68	10.44
8.25	12.27	9.71	8.53	7.89	7.52	12.25	14.50	12.17	11.19	10.72	10.48
8.3	12.29	9.74	8.56	7.92	7.55	12.3	14.52	12.20	11.22	10.75	10.52
8.4	12.35	9.79	8.62	7.99	7.62	12.4	14.58	12.26	11.29	10.83	10.60
8.5	12.40	9.85	8.68	8.06	7.69	12.5	14.64	12.33	11.37	10.91	10.68
8.6	12.45	9.91	8.75	8.12	7.77	12.6	14.70	12.39	11.43	10.98	10.75
8.7	12.51	9.97	8.81	8.19	7.84	12.7	14.75	12.46	11.50	11.05	10.83
8.75	12.54	10.00	8.84	8.23	7.87	12.75	14.79	12.49	11.54	11.10	10.87
8.8	12.56	10.03	8.87	8.26	7.91	12.8	14.81	12.52	11.57	11.13	10.91
8.9	12.61	10.09	8.94	8.33	7.98	12.9	14.87	12.59	11.64	11.20	10.98
9.0	12.67	10.15	9.00	8.40	8.05	13.0	14.94	12.66	11.72	11.28	11.07
9.1	12.72	10.21	9.07	8.47	8.12	13.1	14.99	12.72	11.79	11.35	11.14
9.2	12.78	10.27	9.13	8.53	8.20	13.2	15.05	12.78	11.86	11.43	11.22
9.25	12.81	10.30	9.16	8.57	8.23	13.25	15.08	12.82	11.90	11.47	11.26
9.3	12.83	10.33	9.20	8.60	8.27	13.3	15.11	12.85	11.93	11.50	11.30
9.4	12.89	10.39	9.26	8.67	8.34	13.4	15.17	12.92	12.00	11.58	11.38
9.5	12.94	10.45	9.33	8.74	8.41	13.5	15.23	12.99	12.08	11.66	11.46
9.6	12.99	10.51	9.39	8.81	8.49	13.6	15.29	13.05	12.15	11.73	11.53
9.7	13.05	10.57	9.46	8.88	8.56	13.7	15.35	13.12	12.22	11.81	11.61
9.75	13.08	10.60	9.49	8.92	8.60	13.75	15.38	13.15	12.26	11.85	11.66
9.8	13.10	10.63	9.52	8.95	8.63	13.8	15.41	13.18	12.29	11.88	11.69
9.9	13.16	10.69	9.59	9.02	8.71	13.9	15.47	13.25	12.36	11.96	11.77
10.0	13.22	10.75	9.66	9.09	8.78	14.0	15.53	13.32	12.44	12.04	11.85
10.1	13.27	10.81	9.72	9.16	8.85	14.1	15.59	13.38	12.51	12.11	11.93
10.2	13.33	10.87	9.78	9.23	8.92	14.2	15.65	13.45	12.58	12.19	12.01
10.25	13.36	10.90	9.82	9.27	8.97	14.25	15.68	13.49	12.62	12.23	12.05
10.3	13.38	10.93	9.85	9.30	9.00	14.3	15.71	13.52	12.65	12.27	12.09
10.4	13.44	10.99	9.92	9.37	9.07	14.4	15.77	13.59	12.73	12.34	12.17
10.5	13.50	11.06	9.99	9.45	9.15	14.5	15.83	13.66	12.80	12.43	12.25
10.6	13.55	11.12	10.05	9.51	9.22	14.6	15.89	13.72	12.87	12.50	12.33
10.7	13.61	11.18	10.12	9.59	9.30	14.7	15.95	13.79	12.95	12.58	12.40
10.75	13.64	11.21	10.16	9.63	9.34	14.75	15.99	13.83	12.99	12.62	12.45
10.8	13.66	11.24	10.19	9.66	9.37	14.8	16.01	13.86	13.02	12.65	12.48
10.9	13.72	11.30	10.25	9.73	9.45	14.9	16.07	13.93	13.09	12.73	12.56

The mortgage, therefore, is $550,000. In this case, the down payment is only 3.5% of the selling price, significantly less than the normal 10% minimum.

Selling Price:	$570,000
Down Payment:	$20,000
Mortgage:	$550,000

Step 2:   Call a few banks or real estate offices to determine current interest rates. At the time of this writing, interest rates were approximately 8% for 30-year fixed rate loans.

Step 3:   Decide on the term of the mortgage—the typical term is 30 years, but a shorter term might be preferable.

Step 4: Locate on the chart the monthly payment factor (this number represents the monthly payment required to amortize a loan of $1,000). From the chart, the monthly payment factor for 8%, 30-year mortgages is $7.34 per thousand.

Step 5: Divide the amount to be mortgaged ($550,000) by $1,000 and multiply the result by the monthly payment factor (7.34).

$550,000 *(mortgage amount)* ÷ $1,000 = 550 *(the number of 1,000s in 550,000)*

550 x $7.34 *(the monthly payment factor)* = $4,037 *(monthly mortgage payment)*

The mortgage payment for this particular property is $4,037 per month.

Rule of thumb: To obtain a quick estimate of the mortgage payment when using one of the rule-of-thumb formulas in Chapter 15, use a monthly mortgage factor of 8. This factor gives a fairly good estimate for interest rates ranging from approximately 10% to as low as 7%. Example: Using a factor of 8, the estimated monthly payment for a mortgage of $550,000 equals 550 x 8 = $4,400. This figure is close to the actual figure ($4,037) and good enough for an initial assessment of cash flow.

Another suggestion: Obtain a copy of a "Mortgage Payment Book" from a stationery or office supply store. Easy to use, this small book can produce accurate mortgage payments in seconds.

Does This Building Generate Positive Cash Flow?

Line 15: Cash flow. According to the listing sheet, the Net Operating Income is $106,704, or $8,892 per month, which allows plenty of room for a mortgage payment of $4,037 and leaves a cash flow of $4,855 per month. These are impressive figures, indeed! Using realistic figures, however, the picture is entirely different. By plugging in more accurate income and expense numbers, it can be seen that the building will likely lose $1,646 per month, or $19,748 per year. If the building were bought for cash, with no mortgage, the profits each month would be $2,391, or $28,696 per year, for a cap rate of 5% (the interest earned on investment would be only 5%). Wouldn't a savings account make more sense?

What About the Hype?

The listing sheet (Figure 20.1) from which the figures were taken for the above example includes the following comments:

> "BUENA PARK BRAND NEW GUT REHAB!ALL APTS LARGE & DELUXE-!INDIV. GAS FORCED AIR! 2 YEARS OF REHAB! *THIS IS AN EXCELLENT ARMCHAIR INVESTMENT!* (emphasis added). NEW ELECTRIC, PLUMBING, ROOF (COMPLETE TEAR OFF) TUCKPOINTED/ACID CLEAN-HALLS-APTS-REPLACEMENT WINDOWS."

Is this an *excellent armchair investment?* Only if the investor is prepared to lose nearly $20,000 per year!

In Summary

The best rule of thumb to follow when calculating income and expenses is: Don't believe the listing sheet. Calculate true income by knowing what the realistic rents and vacancy rates are in the neighborhood, and verify that all listed rental units are rentable. Calculate true expenses by verifying fixed expenses like utilities and taxes and using realistic figures for variable expenses like repairs and maintenance. The result is a true picture of a building's cash flow.

Twenty-One

■ ■ ■ ■ ■

Is This a Good Building or Not? Here Is How to Do a Walk-through

In This Chapter

When you reach the point that you are ready to walk through a building, you have already completed several critical steps in the process of shopping. You have done the numbers and know that the building meets your criteria for positive cash flow. You have assessed the neighborhood and feel comfortable. You are confident that the building is compatible with the neighborhood and that the building can attract a steady supply of qualified tenants. Now it is time to assess the building itself to determine whether it will do the job you have in mind. As you walk through the building, evaluate its suitability on three levels:

1. How does the building feel?

2. Are there basic faults with the structure?

3. What about deferred maintenance?

To accomplish an effective walk-through, you need an attitude that will seem to others to be almost intuitive. You need to tune your senses to the subtle things you see and hear and experience around you. During the walk-through you will be dealing with observable criteria, but much of what you observe will have meaning only to you. At the same time, you will notice basic construction details and items of deferred maintenance—the commonplace characteristics that, although important, will not tell you the real story of the building. Although this approach may seem almost metaphysical, be assured that the process is based on conventional powers of observation. You will learn to look past the basic construction, the deferred maintenance, the housekeeping, and the decoration. Instead, you will notice the important things—the characteristics that give you a feel for what goes on in this building.

Taking a Walk Through a Building

Author's Note: A few years ago I was in the final stages of acquiring a new property. I had located several buildings, all belonging to the same owner, all situated within a few blocks of each other, that showed excellent cash flow potential. I had driven the neighborhood; I knew the blocks that were good and the blocks to avoid. I had driven past each of the properties; observed the tenants coming and going; noted the location, the general appearance of each building, the proximity to public transportation and shopping; and, one by one, had eliminated most of them. Step by step, the search had narrowed until finally only two buildings were left to choose from. And now it was time to walk through each of the final two.

Both the owner and the agent had identified these two buildings as being nearly identical, and indeed in many respects they were. Both had a facade that spoke of an earlier, more gracious era: graystone front, small steeples framing a formal wooden entry, small balconies with french doors overlooking the sidewalk. Both buildings were situated on a main thoroughfare in a blighted neighborhood. Each was a long, narrow corridor-style elevator building. A half block separated them, and the casual observer could assume that one was the twin of the other.

On paper also they were nearly identical: the number of apartments, the size of the apartments, the gross income, the expenses, the cash flow. But there was a difference, and the difference was critical. As I entered the first building, I had a strong feeling that this was not a property I would want to own. In spite of my initial misgivings, however, I completed the tour, checking off all the standard criteria as I went. Determined to base my decision on objective criteria rather than subjective feelings, I forced myself to spend time analyzing the property thoroughly.

After an hour or more in the first building, our small party—the real estate agent, the management agent, and I—proceeded north across a narrow side street past a huge vacant lot where once had stood a majestic apartment building, now littered with trash and broken glass and the hulks of ten or more automobiles obviously in the last stages of their usefulness, some with hoods up with backyard mechanics rattling around inside with pliers and socket wrenches. But as we turned in toward the scarred wooden entrance of the second building I noticed, in the few little patches of earth not interred in concrete, beautiful, healthy flowers. An hour later, I emerged from this "twin" convinced that this was the building I would own. What did I see, what did I experience, that caused me to reject the first building without hesitation and to embrace the second just as readily?

Much of what will be covered in this chapter will seem pretty obvious. But don't be mistaken. Obvious or not, each item should be noted carefully on the Evaluation Check Sheet (Figure 21.1). Do not discount anything that is seen or felt. Some buyers tend to discount some of the more obvious problems of a building, viewing them as unimportant or repairable. These are the kinds of mistakes that can lead to failure. Rather, be certain that each item on the check sheet is granted full attention. Often it is only when all of the items are taken in their aggregate that one has a true picture of a building.

Like a drive-by, the walk-through proceeds through several stages. Stage 1 is the exterior front of the building. Stage 2 is the interior—the lobby, the halls, the stairs. Stage 3 is the basement and furnace room. Stage 4 is the inside of the apartments. Stage 5 is the roof. Stage 6 is the back entrance, the rear of the building and the alley. At each stage, the building will be evaluated according to how it feels, whether there is any structural damage, and how much deferred maintenance exists.

Stage 1: Approaching the Building

A walk-through begins as you approach the front of the building. Before entering the building, stop for a few minutes and note these things.

The Feel of the Building. Is It Cared For?   No matter what the neighborhood, a building can be cared for in many little ways, and good tenants will either be attracted to the building or repulsed by little things they see. Stand a few minutes and experience how the building feels. Does it feel neglected or cared for?

The front yard: Is there a front yard? If so, has grass been planted and tended? Have flowers been planted? Are there weeds and bare earth; are trash and broken glass strewn about? Is the sidewalk swept clean? If there is no grass or flowers, is there evidence of care on the part of the janitor or the owner? Does the area in front of the building seem to convey a feeling

Figure 21.1 Walk-Through Evaluation Check Sheet

WALK-THROUGH EVALUATION CHECK SHEET

This form is designed to be used during a walk-through inspection, as a guide for evaluating how the building feels, whether there is deferred maintenance that will need to be addressed and whether any major structural defects exist. After completing the form, the buyer will have a good idea whether to pursue the purchase of the property.

If any part of the building does not feel safe, the property probably should be dropped from consideration, unless the buyer is confident that the conditions can be rectified. If there are structural problems, the buyer should obtain professional estimates of the cost of repairing such defects. If unrepairable, how seriously will such defects impair the operation or effect the future resale of the building? In the case of deferred maintenance (peeling paint, cracks in the walls, etc.) the buyer should obtain cost estimates from professional contractors to determine how such problems will impact on the cash flow from the building.

This form is organized to allow the buyer first to observe the front of the building, then to enter the building and observe the interior components, and finally to step out the back entrance and observe the rear of the building. Each building is different, and the form might be used in some other order for some buildings. The important consideration, of course, is to address each component thoroughly.

STAGE 1: EXTERIOR FRONT

THE FEEL OF THE BUILDING: __ Cared for   __ Safe   __ Quiet   __ Clean
                                                   __ Neglected   __ Unsafe   __ Noisy   __ Dirty

STRUCTURAL DEFECTS: DEFERRED MAINTENANCE:

FRONT AREA:

Concrete: __ STRUCTURALLY SOUND   __ WELL MAINTAINED
                __ Concrete tipped   __ Large cracks   __ Cracks forming   __ Rough surfaces
                __ Cracks where concrete meets foundation   _____   _____

                Comments: _____   Comments: _____

Fence: Type: __ Wrought iron   __ Wood   __ Chain link   __ Other

                __ STRUCTURALLY SOUND   __ WELL MAINTAINED
                __ Reset posts   __ Replace sections   __ Fence needs paint   __ Needs minor repairs
                __ Fence needs to be replaced   __ Gate needs repairs   _____

                Comments: _____   Comments: _____

Landscaping: Describe general condition, potential for improvement and general observations regarding lawn, flowers, shrubs,
                trees, trash, litter: _____
                _____
                _____

Porch: Type: __ Wood   __ Concrete   __ Steel   __ Other _____

                __ STRUCTURALLY SOUND   __ WELL MAINTAINED
                __ Sagging   __ Tilted   __ Needs paint   __ Parts need repair
                __ Evidence of rotted beams, posts, flooring   _____   _____

                Comments: _____   Comments: _____

EXTERIOR WALLS: Type: __ Brick   __ Wood siding   __ Vinyl siding   __ Aluminum siding   __ Stone   __ Masonry   __ Other

Walls: __ STRUCTURALLY SOUND   __ WELL MAINTAINED
                __ Cracks in the walls   __ Evidence of settling   __ Siding needs paint   __ Wood trim needs paint
                __ Bulges in walls   __ Windows out of square   __ Siding needs repair   __ Wood trim needs repair
                _____   _____   _____   __ Brick needs tuckpointing _____

                Comments: _____   Comments: _____

Windows: Type: __ Wood   __ Aluminum   __ Vinyl   __ Storms/Screens   __ Double pane __ Single pane __ Other _____

                __ STRUCTURALLY SOUND   __ WELL MAINTAINED
                __ Windows loose   __ Evidence of rotted frames   __ Frames need paint   __ Windows need glazing
                __ Bulges in wall under windows   __ Frames need repair   __ Broken windows

                Comments: _____   Comments: _____

Figure 21.1 Walk-Through Evaluation Check Sheet *(continued)*

Gutters and
downspouts: __ STRUCTURALLY SOUND
    __ Parts of the gutter system missing
    __ Evidence of major rust and deterioration

    Comments: _____

    __ WELL MAINTAINED
    __ Gutters need paint   __ Parts need replaced
    __ Some repair needed   _____

    Comments: _____

FRONT ENTRANCE:

Front door: __ STRUCTURALLY SOUND

    __ Frame out of square   __ Evidence of rotting wood
    __ Door needs replaced
    _____   _____

    Comments: _____

    __ WELL MAINTAINED

    __ Broken window   __ Needs better lighting
    __ Broken door-knob   __ Needs paint
    __ Door hangs crooked   __ Door drags

    Comments: _____

Mailboxes: __ STRUCTURALLY SOUND
    __ Need replaced

    Comments: _____

    __ WELL MAINTAINED
    __ Need minor repairs

    Comments: _____

Intercom: __ STRUCTURALLY SOUND
    __ Needs major reconstruction/replacement

    Comments: _____

    __ WELL MAINTAINED
    __ Needs minor repairs

    Comments: _____

— NOTES —

Figure 21.1   Walk-Through Evaluation Check Sheet *(continued)*

STAGE 2: INTERIOR HALLS, LOBBY AND STAIRS
(Also known as the Common Areas)

THE FEEL OF THE INTERIOR: __ Cared for   __ Safe   __ Quiet   __ Clean
                             __ Neglected   __ Unsafe   __ Noisy   __ Dirty

                    STRUCTURAL DEFECTS: DEFERRED MAINTENANCE:

LOBBY: Describe general condition: Is the lobby well-lighted, clean, inviting? Is it dark, dingy, foreboding? How does it smell?

_____

_____

Walls: __ STRUCTURALLY SOUND   __ WELL MAINTAINED
          __ Cracks indicate settling __ Doorframes out of square   __ Need to be cleaned   __ Need to be painted
          __ Old plaster needs replaced   __ Plaster needs repairs   __ Minor cracks

          Comments: _____   Comments: _____

Floor: Type: __ Wood   __ Vinyl tile   __ Carpet   __ Linoleum   __ Concrete   __ Ceramic tile   __ Other _____
          __ STRUCTURALLY SOUND   __ WELL MAINTAINED
          __ Floors slope, sag   __ Floors creak loudly   __ Carpet worn out   __ Covering needs replaced
          __ Floors sway   __ Dirty—needs cleaned   _____

          Comments: _____   Comments: _____

Ceiling: Type: __ Plaster   __ Plaster board   __ Acoustic tile   __ Suspended __ Other
          __ STRUCTURALLY SOUND   __ WELL MAINTAINED
          __ Ceiling needs replaced _____   __ Plaster needs repair   __ Ceiling tiles broken
          _____   __ Needs paint   _____

          Comments: _____   Comments: _____

Lighting: Type: __ Fluorescent __ Incandescent fixtures   __ Bare bulbs   __ Other _____
          __ STRUCTURALLY SOUND   __ WELL MAINTAINED
          __ Evidence that fixtures will need to be rewired   __ Bulbs missing   __ Bulbs burned out
          __ Needs new fixtures   __ Fixtures broken   __ Lights dirty

          Comments: _____   Comments: _____

STAIRS: Type: __ Wood   __ Concrete   __ Steel   __   __ Evidence of water damage__ Ceiling needs paint
          __ STRUCTURALLY SOUND   __ WELL MAINTAINED
          __ Stairs weak, loose   __ Railings loose, broken   __ Dirty—needs cleaned   __ Stair treads need replaced
          _____   _____   __ Carpet needs replaced   __ Treads loose, broken

          Comments: _____   Comments: _____

HALLS:

Walls: __ STRUCTURALLY SOUND   __ WELL MAINTAINED
          __ Cracks indicate settling __ Doorframes out of square   __ Need to be cleaned   __ Need to be painted
          __ Old plaster needs replaced   __ Plaster needs repairs   __ Minor cracks

          Comments: _____   Comments: _____

Floor: Type: __ Wood   __ Vinyl tile   __ Carpet   __ Linoleum   __ Concrete   __ Ceramic tile   __ Other _____
          __ STRUCTURALLY SOUND   __ WELL MAINTAINED
          __ Floors slope, sag   __ Floors creak loudly   __ Carpet worn out   __ Covering needs replaced
          __ Floors sway   __ Dirty—needs cleaned   __ Wood needs refinishing

          Comments: _____   Comments: _____

Ceiling: Type: __ Plaster   __ Plaster board   __ Acoustic tile   __ Suspended __ Other _____
          __ STRUCTURALLY SOUND   __ WELL MAINTAINED
          __ Ceiling needs replaced _____   __ Plaster needs repair   __ Ceiling tiles broken
          _____   __ Needs paint   _____

          Comments: _____   Comments: _____

Figure 21.1   Walk-Through Evaluation Check Sheet *(continued)*

Lighting: Type: __ Fluorescent __ Incandescent fixtures __ Bare bulbs __ Other _____

    __ STRUCTURALLY SOUND   __ WELL MAINTAINED
    __ Evidence that fixtures will need to be rewired   __ Bulbs missing   __ Bulbs burned out
    __ Needs new fixtures   __ Fixtures broken   __ Lights dirty

    Comments: _____   Comments: _____

Doors: __ STRUCTURALLY SOUND   __ WELL MAINTAINED
    __ Doorframes out of square __ Doors need to be replaced   __ Hinges loose   __ Knobs loose/missing
    __ Doorframes cracked and broken   __ Need to be painted   __ Locks need repair
    Comments: _____   Comments _____

Windows: __ STRUCTURALLY SOUND   __ WELL MAINTAINED
    __ Frames out of square   __ Frames rotted, coming apart   __ Loose glass   __ Frames need paint
    __ Water damage under windows   __ Broken glass   __ Dirty
    Comments: _____   Comments: _____

— NOTES —

Figure 21.1   Walk-Through Evaluation Check Sheet *(continued)*

STAGE 3: BASEMENT AND FURNACE ROOM

THE FEEL OF THE BASEMENT: __ Cared for   __ Safe   __ Quiet   __ Clean
__ Neglected   __ Unsafe   __ Noisy   __ Dirty

BASEMENT: Describe general condition: Is the basement well-lighted, clean, orderly? Is it dark, dingy, cluttered? How does it smell?_____

STRUCTURAL DEFECTS: DEFERRED MAINTENANCE:

Floor: Type: __ Concrete   __ Wood   __ Bare dirt   __ Brick   __ Other _____

__ STRUCTURALLY SOUND   __ WELL MAINTAINED
__ Cracks in the concrete   __ Evidence of rotted wood   __ Needs to be painted   __ Needs to be cleaned
__ Uneven floor, indicating freezing and heaving   _____   _____

Comments: _____   Comments: _____

Comment on whether water is standing anywhere on the floor. Is there evidence of prior flooding (water marks on the walls, etc.) Is there a sump pump; is it working? _____

Walls: Type: __ Concrete block   __ Wood   __ Brick   __ Plaster   __ Other _____

__ STRUCTURALLY SOUND   __ WELL MAINTAINED
__ Cracks indicate settling __ Doorframes out of square   __ Need to be cleaned   __ Need to be painted
__ Furnace room walls not fireproof   __ Plaster needs repairs   _____

Comments: _____   Comments: _____

Ceiling: Type: __ Plaster   __ Plaster board   __ Concrete   __ Other _____

__ STRUCTURALLY SOUND   __ WELL MAINTAINED
__ Ceiling needs replaced   __ Beams are sagging   __ Plaster needs repair   __ Ceiling tiles broken
__ Furnace room ceiling not fireproof   __ Needs paint   _____

Comments: _____   Comments: _____

Furnace: Type: __ Gas boiler (steam)   __ Gas hot water   __ Gas forced air   __ Other _____

__ STRUCTURALLY SOUND   __ WELL MAINTAINED
__ Very old   __ Evidence of water leaks   __ Insulation torn   __ Dirty, grimey
__ Rusty pipes   __ Doors not snug   __ Evidence of having been worked on recently
Comments: _____   Comments: _____

Electric: Type: __Fuses   __ Circuit breakers   __ Individually metered   __ Wires enclosed in conduit
Comment on age of electric service, amperage, number of circuits per apartment: _____
_____
_____

__ STRUCTURALLY SOUND   __ WELL MAINTAINED
__ Service needs replaced   __ Deteriorating wires   __ Meter area dirty   __ Some wires hanging
__ Wires improperly installed   __ Very old wires   __ Conduit not secure   _____

Comments: _____   Comments: _____

Pipes: __ STRUCTURALLY SOUND   __ WELL MAINTAINED
__ Pipes are very old   __ Evidence of water leaks   __ Insulation torn   __ Dirty, grimey
__ Rusty pipes   __ Old rusty valves   __ Evidence of having been worked on recently
Comments: _____   Comments: _____

Figure 21.1   Walk-Through Evaluation Check Sheet *(continued)*

STAGE 4: INSIDE THE APARTMENTS

THE FEEL OF THE APARTMENTS: __ Cared for   __ Safe   __ Quiet   __ Clean
__ Neglected   __ Unsafe   __ Noisy   __ Dirty

STRUCTURAL DEFECTS: DEFERRED MAINTENANCE:

LIVING ROOM:

Walls:
__ STRUCTURALLY SOUND
__ Cracks indicate settling __ Doorframes out of square
__ Old plaster needs replaced
Comments: _____

__ WELL MAINTAINED
__ Need to be cleaned   __ Need to be painted
__ Plaster needs repairs   __ Minor cracks
Comments: _____

Floor: Type: __ Wood   __ Vinyl tile   __ Carpet   __ Linoleum   __ Concrete   __ Ceramic tile   __ Other _____

__ STRUCTURALLY SOUND
__ Floors slope, sag   __ Floors creak loudly
__ Floors sway   _____
Comments: _____

__ WELL MAINTAINED
__ Carpet worn out   __ Covering needs replaced
__ Dirty—needs cleaned   __ Wood needs refinishing
Comments: _____

Ceiling: Type: __ Plaster   __ Plaster board   __ Acoustic tile   __ Suspended   __ Other

__ STRUCTURALLY SOUND
__ Ceiling needs replaced   __ Water stains
__ Water damange
Comments: _____

__ WELL MAINTAINED
__ Plaster needs repair   __ Ceiling tiles broken
__ Needs paint   _____
Comments: _____

Lighting: Type: __ Fluorescent   __ Incandescent fixtures   __ Bare bulbs   __ Other _____

__ STRUCTURALLY SOUND
__ Evidence that fixtures will need to be rewired
__ Needs new fixtures   __ Pull-chain fixtures
Comments: _____

__ WELL MAINTAINED
__ Bulbs missing   __ Bulbs burned out
__ Fixtures broken   __ Lights dirty
Comments: _____

Doors:
__ STRUCTURALLY SOUND
__ Doorframes out of square __ Doors need to be replaced
__ Doorframes cracked and broken
Comments: _____

__ WELL MAINTAINED
__ Hinges loose   __ Knobs loose/missing
__ Need to be painted   __ Locks need repair
Comments: _____

Windows:
__ STRUCTURALLY SOUND
__ Frames out of square   __ Frames rotted, coming apart
__ Water damage under windows
Comments: _____

__ WELL MAINTAINED
__ Loose glass   __ Frames need paint
__ Broken glass   __ Dirty
Comments: _____

Electric:
__ STRUCTURALLY SOUND
__ Not enough outlets   __ Two-prong outlets
__ Lots of extension cords __ Will need new wiring
Comments: _____

__ WELL MAINTAINED
__ Broken switches, outlets _____
_____   _____
Comments: _____

BEDROOM:

Walls:
__ STRUCTURALLY SOUND
__ Cracks indicate settling __ Doorframes out of square
__ Old plaster needs replaced
Comments: _____

__ WELL MAINTAINED
__ Need to be cleaned   __ Need to be painted
__ Plaster needs repairs   __ Minor cracks
Comments: _____

Floor: Type: __ Wood   __ Vinyl tile   __ Carpet   __ Linoleum   __ Concrete   __ Ceramic tile   __ Other _____

__ STRUCTURALLY SOUND
__ Floors slope, sag   __ Floors creak loudly
__ Floors sway   _____
Comments: _____

__ WELL MAINTAINED
__ Carpet worn out   __ Covering needs replaced
__ Dirty—needs cleaned   __ Wood needs refinishing
Comments: _____

Figure 21.1   Walk-Through Evaluation Check Sheet *(continued)*

Ceiling: Type: __ Plaster   __ Plaster board   __ Acoustic tile   __ Suspended   __ Other _____

__ STRUCTURALLY SOUND   __ WELL MAINTAINED
__ Ceiling needs replaced   __ Water stains   __ Plaster needs repair   __ Ceiling tiles broken
__ Water damange   __ Needs paint

Comments: _____   Comments: _____

Lighting: Type: __ Fluorescent __ Incandescent fixtures   __ Bare bulbs   __ Other _____

__ STRUCTURALLY SOUND   __ WELL MAINTAINED
__ Evidence that fixtures will need to be rewired   __ Bulbs missing   __ Bulbs burned out
__ Needs new fixtures   __ Pull-chain fixtures   __ Fixtures broken   __ Lights dirty

Comments: _____   Comments: _____

Doors: __ STRUCTURALLY SOUND   __ WELL MAINTAINED
__ Doorframes out of square __ Doors need to be replaced   __ Hinges loose   __ Knobs loose/missing
__ Doorframes cracked and broken   __ Need to be painted   __ Locks need repair
Comments: _____   Comments: _____

Windows: __ STRUCTURALLY SOUND   __ WELL MAINTAINED
__ Frames out of square   __ Frames rotted, coming apart   __ Loose glass   __ Frames need paint
__ Water damage under windows   __ Broken glass   __ Dirty

Comments: _____   Comments: _____

Electric: __ STRUCTURALLY SOUND   __ WELL MAINTAINED
__ Not enough outlets   __ Two-prong outlets   __ Broken switches, outlets _____
__ Lots of extension cords   __ Will need new wiring

Comments: _____   Comments: _____

KITCHEN: Describe general condition: Is the kitchen well-lighted, clean, modern? Is it dark, greasy? How does it smell? Is the
sink old and worn-out? Are there cabinets? A pantry? What condition are the stove and refrigerator? _____

_____

_____

_____

Walls: Type: __ Plaster   __ Tile   __ Wallpaper   __ Plaster board   __ Other _____

__ STRUCTURALLY SOUND   __ WELL MAINTAINED
__ Cracks indicate settling __ Doorframes out of square   __ Need to be cleaned   __ Need to be painted
__ Plaster needs replaced   __ Water damange   __ Plaster needs repairs   __ Broken tiles

Comments: _____   Comments: _____

Floor: Type: __ Wood   __ Vinyl tile   __ Carpet   __ Linoleum   __ Concrete   __ Ceramic tile   __ Other _____

__ STRUCTURALLY SOUND   __ WELL MAINTAINED
__ Floors slope, sag   __ Floors creak loudly   __ Carpet worn out   __ Covering needs replaced
__ Floors sway   __ Dirty—needs cleaned   __ Wood needs refinishing

Comments: _____   Comments: _____

Ceiling: Type: __ Plaster   __ Plaster board   __ Acoustic tile   __ Suspended __ Other _____

__ STRUCTURALLY SOUND   __ WELL MAINTAINED
__ Ceiling needs replaced   __ Water stains   __ Plaster needs repair   __ Ceiling tiles broken
__ Water damange   __ Needs paint

Comments: _____   Comments: _____

Lighting: Type: __ Fluorescent __ Incandescent fixtures   __ Bare bulbs   __ Other

__ STRUCTURALLY SOUND   __ WELL MAINTAINED
__ Evidence that fixtures will need to be rewired   __ Bulbs missing   __ Bulbs burned out
__ Needs new fixtures   __ Pull-chain fixtures   __ Fixtures broken   __ Lights dirty

Comments: _____   Comments: _____

Figure 21.1   Walk-Through Evaluation Check Sheet (continued)

Doors:	__ STRUCTURALLY SOUND __ Doorframes out of square __ Doors need to be replaced __ Doorframes cracked and broken Comments: _____	__ WELL MAINTAINED __ Hinges loose __ Knobs loose/missing __ Need to be painted __ Locks need repair Comments: _____
Windows:	__ STRUCTURALLY SOUND __ Frames out of square __ Frames rotted, coming apart __ Water damage under windows Comments: _____	__ WELL MAINTAINED __ Loose glass __ Frames need paint __ Broken glass __ Dirty Comments: _____
Electric:	__ STRUCTURALLY SOUND __ Not enough outlets __ Two-prong outlets __ Lots of extension cords __ Will need new wiring Comments: _____	__ WELL MAINTAINED __ Broken switches, outlets _____ _____ _____ Comments: _____
Plumbing:	__ STRUCTURALLY SOUND __ Low water pressure __ Old sink and faucets __ Chipped, discolored sink Comments: _____	__ WELL MAINTAINED __ Leaky faucets __ Leaky drains Comments: _____
Cabinets:	__ STRUCTURALLY SOUND __ Inadequate cabinets _____ __ Worn-out, will need replacing Comments: _____	__ WELL MAINTAINED __ Need to be painted __ Need repairs to doors __ Need repairs to drawers __ Counter stained, chipped Comments: _____
Appliances:	__ STRUCTURALLY SOUND __ Stove old, worn-out __ Refrigerator old, worn-out _____ _____ Comments: _____	__ WELL MAINTAINED __ Stove greasey, dirty __ Refrigerator dirty Comments: _____
BATHROOM:	Describe general condition: Is the bathroom well-lighted, clean, inviting? Is it dark, damp, foreboding? How does it smell? Are the fixtures old and worn-out? Is there a vanity? A tub-on-legs? _____ _____	
Walls:	Type: __ Plaster __ Tile __ Wallpaper __ Plaster board __ Waterproof board __ Other _____	
	__ STRUCTURALLY SOUND __ Cracks indicate settling __ Doorframes out of square __ Plaster needs replaced __ Water damange Comments: _____	__ WELL MAINTAINED __ Need to be cleaned __ Need to be painted __ Plaster needs repairs __ Broken tiles Comments: _____
Floor:	Type: __ Wood __ Vinyl tile __ Carpet __ Linoleum __ Concrete __ Ceramic tile __ Other _____	
	__ STRUCTURALLY SOUND __ Floors slope, sag __ Floors creak loudly __ Floors sway Comments: _____	__ WELL MAINTAINED __ Carpet worn out __ Covering needs replaced __ Dirty—needs cleaned __ Wood needs refinishing Comments: _____
Ceiling:	Type: __ Plaster __ Plaster board __ Acoustic tile __ Suspended __ Other _____	
	__ STRUCTURALLY SOUND __ Ceiling needs replaced __ Water stains __ Water damange Comments: _____	__ WELL MAINTAINED __ Plaster needs repair __ Ceiling tiles broken __ Needs paint Comments: _____
Lighting:	Type: __ Fluorescent __ Incandescent fixtures __ Bare bulbs __ Other _____	
	__ STRUCTURALLY SOUND __ Evidence that fixtures will need to be rewired __ Needs new fixtures __ Pull-chain fixtures Comments: _____	__ WELL MAINTAINED __ Bulbs missing __ Bulbs burned out __ Fixtures broken __ Lights dirty Comments: _____

Figure 21.1   Walk-Through Evaluation Check Sheet *(continued)*

Door: __ STRUCTURALLY SOUND   __ WELL MAINTAINED
              __ Doorframes out of square __ Doors need to be replaced __ Hinges loose   __ Knobs loose/missing
              __ Doorframes cracked and broken   __ Need to be painted   __ Locks need repair

              Comments: _____   Comments:_____

Window: __ STRUCTURALLY SOUND   __ WELL MAINTAINED
              __ Frames out of square   __ Frames rotted, coming apart __ Loose glass   __ Frames need paint
              __ Water damage under windows   __ Broken glass   __ Dirty

              Comments: _____   Comments:_____

Electric: __ STRUCTURALLY SOUND   __ WELL MAINTAINED
              __ Two-prong outlets   __ Will need new wiring   __ Broken switches, outlets_____
              __ Lots of extension cords _____   _____   _____

              Comments: _____   Comments:_____

Plumbing: __ STRUCTURALLY SOUND   __ WELL MAINTAINED
              __ Low water pressure   __ Old fixtures and faucets __ Leaky faucets   __ Leaky drains
              __ Chipped, discolored, cracked fixtures   _____   _____

              Comments: _____   Comments:_____

Vanity/Sink: __ STRUCTURALLY SOUND   __ WELL MAINTAINED
              __ Worn-out, will need replacing   __ Needs to be painted   __ Needs repairs to doors
              _____   _____   __ Needs repairs to drawers __ Counter stained, chipped

              Comments: _____   Comments:_____

— NOTES —

Figure 21.1   Walk-Through Evaluation Check Sheet *(continued)*

STAGE 5: THE ROOF

THE FEEL OF THE ROOF: __ Cared for   __ Safe   __ Quiet   __ Clean
                             __ Neglected   __ Unsafe   __ Noisy   __ Dirty

STRUCTURAL DEFECTS: DEFERRED MAINTENANCE:

ROOF: Type: __ Flat   __ Pitched

Describe general condition: Does the roof appear to be very old or relatively new? Has it been patched? Are the patches recent? If flat, is it coated with aluminum coating? Are there several layers of roof material? _____
_____
_____

Flat roof: __ STRUCTURALLY SOUND   __ WELL MAINTAINED
               __ Extreme alligatoring   __ Deep cracks in surface   __ Surface dried out   __ Evidence of alligatoring
               __ Roof will need to be replaced soon   __ Flashings pulled away from chimney, pipes, walls
               Comments: _____   Comments: _____

Parapets: __ STRUCTURALLY SOUND   __ WELL MAINTAINED
               __ Brick is crumbling   __ Tile are broken and missing   __ Brick needs tuckpointed __ Tile are loose
               __ Parapet needs rebuilding _____   __ Flashing pulled away   _____
               Comments: _____   Comments: _____

Chimney: __ STRUCTURALLY SOUND   __ WELL MAINTAINED
               __ Brick is crumbling   __ Chimney needs rebuilding   __ Brick needs tuckpointed __ Flashing pulled away
               __ Some brick are missing _____   _____ _____
               Comments: _____   Comments: _____

Pitched roof: __ STRUCTURALLY SOUND   __ WELL MAINTAINED
               __ Roof has sway or sag   __ Shingles curling up   __ Some shingles missing or broken
               __ Roof will need to be replaced soon   __ Flashings are pulling away from chimney, pipes
               Comments: _____   Comments: _____

Soffit, facia: __ STRUCTURALLY SOUND   __ WELL MAINTAINED
               __ Soffit, facia rotted   __ Soffit, facia broken   __ Soffit, facia need paint __ Soffit, facia need caulk
               __ Soffit and facia need to be replaced   _____ _____
               Comments: _____   Comments: _____

— NOTES —

Figure 21.1   Walk-Through Evaluation Check Sheet *(continued)*

STAGE 6: EXTERIOR REAR
(Including rear entrance, alley, and exterior walls, both side and rear)

THE FEEL OF THE REAR AREA: __ Cared for   __ Safe   __ Quiet   `__ Clean
__ Neglected   __ Unsafe   __ Noisy   __ Dirty

STRUCTURAL DEFECTS: DEFERRED MAINTENANCE:

REAR ENTRANCE:

Rear door: __ STRUCTURALLY SOUND   __ WELL MAINTAINED
__ Frame out of square   __ Evidence of rotting wood   __ Broken window   __ Needs better lighting
__ Door needs replaced   __ Broken door-knob   __ Needs paint
                                                         __ Door hangs crooked   __ Door drags

Comments: _____   Comments: _____

EXTERIOR WALLS: Type: __ Brick   __ Wood siding   __ Vinyl siding   __ Aluminum siding   __ Stone   __ Masonry   __ Other

Walls: __ STRUCTURALLY SOUND   __ WELL MAINTAINED
__ Cracks in the walls   __ Evidence of settling   __ Siding needs paint   __ Wood trim needs paint
__ Bulges in walls   __ Windows out of square   __ Siding needs repair   __ Wood trim needs repair
                                                     __ Brick needs tuckpointing_____

Comments: _____   Comments: _____

Windows: Type: __ Wood   __ Aluminum   __ Vinyl   __ Storms/Screens   __ Double pane __ Single pane __ Other _____

__ STRUCTURALLY SOUND   __ WELL MAINTAINED
__ Windows loose   __ Evidence of rotted frames   __ Frames need paint   __ Windows need glazing
__ Bulges in wall under windows   __ Frames need repair   __ Broken windows

Comments: _____   Comments: _____

Gutters and
downspouts: __ STRUCTURALLY SOUND   __ WELL MAINTAINED
__ Parts of the gutter system missing   __ Gutters need paint   __ Parts need replaced
__ Evidence of major rust and deterioration   __ Some repair needed

Comments: _____   Comments: _____

ALLEY: Describe general condition, potential for improvement and general observations regarding trash, litter: _____

_____

_____

Trash
containers: Describe general condition, adequacy of containers—both size and number, trash and litter lying around, containers
overflowing, etc.: _____

_____

_____

FIRE ESCAPE: Type: __ Wood   __ Steel

__ STRUCTURALLY SOUND   __ WELL MAINTAINED
__ Pulling away from wall   __ Evidence of rotted wood   __ Needs paint   __ Parts need repair
__ Pieces missing

Comments: _____   Comments: _____

REAR PORCH: Type: __ Wood   __ Concrete   __ Steel   __ Other _____

__ STRUCTURALLY SOUND   __ WELL MAINTAINED
__ Sagging   __ Tilted   __ Needs paint   __ Parts need repair
__ Evidence of rotted beams, posts, flooring   __ Loose treads   __ Loose railings

Comments: _____   Comments: _____

Figure 21.1   Walk-Through Evaluation Check Sheet *(continued)*

QUESTIONS TO ASK TENANTS

How much is your rent?_____

Have you received a rent concession? (i.e., first month's rent free, special rebate, etc.)_____

Is the apartment warm enough?_____

Has the heat been interrupted during this past year?_____

Do you blow fuses or circuit breakers very often?_____

Is the water pressure adequate?_____

Does the roof leak?_____

Does your ceiling leak from the bathroom or kitchen above you?_____

Does the basement flood?_____

Do your stove and refrigerator work well?_____

Do your kitchen and bathroom drains work?_____

Are the laundry facilities adequate?_____

Are there insects or rodents in the building?_____

Does the owner exterminate regularly?_____

Are you satisfied with the manager's performance?_____

Are there any tenants you wish would move?_____

Is there a problem with crime in the building?_____

Is there a problem with crime in the neighborhood?_____

Are there any problems with parking?_____

What about trash and snow removal?_____

Is the area noisy?_____

Does the intercom and door buzzer work?_____

Do you intend to renew your lease?_____

of home? Or does it tell of transient, uncaring tenants who trample the grass, abuse the front door and throw trash about?

The front of the building: Look at the apartment windows. Specifically look for window shades. Are they dirty or clean? Are they uniform in their appearance? Many of the better buildings will have shades drawn half-way up during the daytime, giving a uniform, homey appearance. If it is summertime, are windows standing open with no screens? Are there curtains blowing out the windows? This is a sure sign of uncaring tenants. Look at the front door. Is it dirty from people passing through, or has it been kept clean? Even the most heavily used door can be kept clean, painted and inviting.

Structural Defects
Concrete: Look at the concrete sidewalk. Is it cracked? Is it straight? Look closely at the point where the concrete sidewalk meets the foundation of the building, particularly if there is a sidewalk that runs along the side of the building for any distance. Is there a gap? Does the sidewalk tilt toward the building? If so, you may have significant erosion around the foundation of the building, which can cause structural damage or at least result in moisture in the basement.

Exterior walls: If the building is of brick construction, step back and scan the facade. Look particularly at the area underneath each window. Are there cracks in the brick wall or is mortar washed away? Has the mortar been repaired? Has the face of any bricks cracked off? The areas underneath the windows are particularly vulnerable to moisture that seeps into and between the bricks and then freezes, causing cracks to appear and creating some structural problems that can be expensive to repair. If the building is of frame construction, has it been sided with aluminum or vinyl siding? If so, is the siding in good repair? Do you see storm windows? If so, what is the condition of the storm windows? Are the screens in place and in good shape? Have the windows been replaced with newer double pane windows? If so, this is a real advantage. New windows require much less maintenance and significantly reduce the heating bill.

Roof: Look above you at the roof line. If the building has a flat roof, check the parapets (the top-most part of the building) for damage. Are the tiles on the top of the parapet missing or broken? If the building has a pitched roof, note the condition of the shingles. Is it a rolled roof or a shingle roof? Are the edges of the shingles curling up? Does it appear that the roof has been patched extensively? Does the building have gutters? If so, are they rusty or sagging or do they look painted and straight?

Doorway: Look at the entrance doorway. Is it straight, or is there evidence of settling, causing the doorframe to be uneven?

Deferred Maintenance

Paint: Look closely at the painted parts of the building, the window frames, the wood siding, the doors, the trim around the roof: is the paint flaking, peeling, chalky?

Window panes: Do the window panes need to be re-glazed?

Front door: Does the front door swing easily, or is it hanging from loose hinges, causing it to rub the door frame when it closes. Do both inner and outer doors close tightly and hang straight? Do the locks work? Is the automatic door closer in place and working?

Tuckpointing: Is there any evidence that the brick walls need tuckpointing? (Tuckpointing involves replacing mortar that has broken out between the bricks.)

Mailboxes and intercom: Do the mailboxes have working doors and locks? Does the entry buzzer system work? Both are indicative of the level of security provided by the building.

Intuition.   Each building you look at will have its own unique characteristics. They can't all be covered in this chapter. The important thing to remember is: before entering the building, get a feel for whether the building is cared for by the resident manager or janitor. Get a feel for whether there is extensive deferred maintenance. Get a feel for whether the building has structural problems that may be costly to repair. Pay attention to details, and pay no attention to what the real estate agent may be telling you.

By taking time with the exterior of the building you already know, intuitively, a great deal about a property, the tenants who live there, and the person who owns it. Without setting foot inside the building you already can anticipate what the inside will be like. There may be some deferred maintenance. That can be taken care of and should be figured into the price. There may be some structural problems. These too can be repaired, although the extent of the damage must not be underestimated and the expense of doing so should not be discounted and should be reflected in the selling price. But most important is the feel of the building. Does it seem to be a safe, clean, quiet home for caring tenants, or does it reflect an uncaring, callous disregard for tenants' needs?

Author's Note: In the case of the "twin" buildings, both needed paint on the windows, both had been tuckpointed recently, and neither revealed obvious structural problems that could be seen from the front of the building. The door on the first building, however, was dirty from hundreds of hands. Where a lawn should be, there were weeds and small bits of broken glass. In the parkway along the street there was bare earth, a few bottles and some trash. Not a lot of trash—the building didn't have a neglected look; in fact, it was cleaner than many of the buildings in the area. But neither did it have that cared for look. As we approached the second building, I noted there was no broken glass, not even small pieces. No trash, not even gum wrappers. The front area had mostly been paved with concrete, but here and there, where dirt was exposed, grew several varieties of flowers from freshly turned earth. The front door was clean.

Stage 2: The Interior

Now it's time to go inside. As you walk through the front door, get a feel for who lives here and how the building is cared for on the inside. Does the inside confirm what you learned from the exterior?

Ask to talk with the building manager or janitor if they are not conducting the tour. It is important right now to begin to develop a rapport with those who tend the building. If you should buy the property, this person will be a critical factor in whether the building is successful. Either the manager or the janitor can also fill you in on critical details about the building as you walk through, particularly if you have gained their trust.

The Feel of the Building. Is It Cared For?
The lobby: As you walk through the door does the interior feel dark and dingy, or is it well lit and freshly painted? Does the lobby invite tenants inside or is it dark and foreboding? Do you see graffiti on the walls? Good tenants will turn away from a lobby that seems sinister and threatening.

The lobby floor: Look at the floor: is it swept clean or is there litter? Has it been mopped, or is there a layer of dirt and grime? Look at the corners of the floor: are they swept clean or has dirt and grime been allowed to build up?

Walls and ceilings: Are the walls and ceilings clean or is there a collection of dust, dirt, and cobwebs?

Smells: As you first come inside, how does the building smell? Does it smell fresh or dank? Do you smell cats or dogs? Are there other pungent and uninviting odors? Or is there a clean, fresh smell?

Stairs and hallways: As you walk through the halls and up the stairs, continue to check for evidence of an uncaring attitude: unswept halls, a build-up of dirt in the corners, dirt on the ceilings and walls, threadbare carpeting, light fixtures that are dirty and dim.

Light fixtures: Are there bare bulbs in the halls or have bright, attractive light fixtures been installed?

Doorframes: Look at the doorframes. Are they in original condition or have they been repaired? Look closely at the doors and the jambs near the area of the doorknob and lock. Is there evidence of break-ins occurring in the building? If the door-frames have been repaired, what is the quality of the workmanship? Did the workmen attempt to match the original wood or has someone settled for a cheap piece of pine and a quick coat of paint? Is the woodwork varnished or has it been painted? How well has it been painted? Is there a build-up of many coats of paint or have the owners been careful to scrape the older paint before repainting?

Structural Defects
Floors: Be aware of sloping or sagging floors that might indicate major problems with supporting beams and floor joists. The best way to assess such defects is to walk the floors—often a sagging floor can be felt before it can be seen.

Author's Note: *Personally, I tend to stay away from a building whose floors are uneven and sagging. The poor thing probably settled that way years ago, but I know when I try to resell the building it won't be easy.*

Doorframes: Check for doorframes that are out of square. They, too, can reveal major settling, foundation problems, and rotting support beams.

Cracks in the walls: Large cracks that go all the way through the plaster often indicate major structural problems.

Deferred Maintenance

Floors: What shape is the floor covering in? Is it carpet, linoleum, tile, rubber runners, or painted wood? Will the floor need to be recovered, repaired, or replaced?

Walls: Are the walls in need of patching and painting? Will they need extensive repair or minor filling and paint?

Windows: Are the windows clean and painted? Is there evidence that water has been coming in and rotting the wood? Does it come in around the panes of glass, indicating a need for re-glazing, or does it come in around the edges of the window frame itself, indicating a need for caulking or tuckpointing?

Stairs: Are the stair treads loose? Are the railings loose and maybe broken? Are any balusters (spindles) missing?

Author's Note: As I walked into the "twins," I noticed several revealing differences. Whereas the second building was bright and cheerful as I came in, the first had been dark, poorly lit, and in need of paint. The floors in the first were poorly kept, with dirt in the corners, litter here and there, and a poorly installed piece of linoleum running the length of the first floor hall. In the second, the halls, while tiled with very old tile, sparkled under a fresh application of Mop 'N Glo. The freshly painted walls reflected lots of light from the ceiling fixtures, inviting me inside into a clean, safe place.

Stage 3: The Basement and the Furnace Room

The furnace room is at the heart of future potential expenses. Look it over carefully. Boiler repairs are expensive, and inefficient heating systems drive up heating bills. Also, the basement can reveal any significant structural defects in the building.

The Feel of the Building. Is It Cared For?

The furnace room is the janitor's domain. One look at this room reveals volumes about the attitude of the janitor and, by inference, the owner. Most furnace rooms, unfortunately, are not well kept. They become littered and dirty, full of worn-out and useless junk. Dark, foreboding and full of hisses and smells, they often feel like the devil's living room.

They don't have to be that way. Some are well lighted, clean, and orderly. A caring janitor will keep a clean, painted, freshly swept furnace room.

Structural Defects
Basement: Is there evidence of prior flooding? Do you see any cracks in the foundation walls? Look at the beams. Are they sagging? Have they been propped up with new posts?

Floor: Do you see cracks in the concrete floor? Is the floor uneven, indicating that water has seeped under and frozen, raising parts of the floor?

Boiler: To an untrained eye most old boilers will look pretty much alike—resembling an octopus with uncounted arms, each running off in a different direction into the far reaches of the basement. Unfathomable to most novices, the boiler does not easily reveal its structural defects, many of which will be inside and out of sight. There are a few clues to look for, however. Is the boiler new or old? Is there water on the floor in and around the boiler? This can indicate a leak inside the boiler—a leak that will be very expensive to repair.

Electrical: Check the electric boxes. Are there fuses or circuit breakers? Has the electric service been upgraded? Each apartment should have at least three circuits, with at least one 20 amp circuit. Buildings under twelve units should have 200 amp service; over twelve, 400 amps.

Deferred Maintenance
Paint and plaster: Do the walls and ceiling need repair and repainting?

Insulation: Is the insulation around the steam pipes loose and hanging?

General condition of the boiler: Look at the doors on the boiler. Do they shut tightly? Look at the fittings and the pipes. What condition are they in? Are there leaks, are they rusted? Do you see new pipes or fittings, giving evidence of work that has been done to the heating system? If so, ask about it.

Author's Note: In both of the "twins" the boiler rooms had the appearance of being well maintained. Both, of course, had been under the management of the same company. The boiler room in the first building, however, was junky and dirty. In the second building, the floor was clean and junk free. The room was bright and freshly painted—not at all threatening. I felt comfortable being in there, unlike the first building, where I had the feeling that something could fall on me at any minute.

Stage 4: Inside the Apartments

How many apartments should one view on the first walk-through? As a rule of thumb, if there are less than 12 apartments in the building, try to see each one. Typically, several of the apartments will be unavailable for viewing, but you should be able to see the majority. If there are more than twelve apartments in the building, go through at least two apartments on each floor. Later, if you decide to pursue the property, you will want to look at many more of the apartments. But for now, two apartments per floor should be sufficient.

The Feel of the Building. Is It Cared For?

If the tenants are home when you arrive, begin by establishing a rapport with them. After all, you are an intruder in their home. Apologize for the inconvenience and ask whether it is okay to go through. Reassure them that you are looking only for defects in the building, and not at the way they keep house. If possible, say something nice about their apartment, or some item in it. Show interest in them as people—do not just ignore them or act as if it is your right to intrude into their home.

As you look through the apartment, ask the tenant whether they have experienced any problems. If there is an opportunity, get them off to the side, away from the real estate agent or the owner, before asking. Your earlier interest in them should make it more likely that they will confide in you. Ask about the heat: is the apartment warm enough? Ask about the water: is it hot enough; is there sufficient pressure? What about the windows, do they open? are they tight enough in the winter? What about other problems? Keep it open ended and the tenant is likely to give you an ear full. How better to learn about the building?

Security: As you walk into the apartment note the front door. Is there evidence that it has been pried open or kicked in? Has the door jam been repaired? How well was it repaired? Have the locks been changed a lot? All of this is evidence of a building with low security. Good tenants will avoid such a building.

Decoration: Pay no attention to how the apartments are decorated. Remember that you are not looking at this property with an eye toward living in it yourself. You want a building that will attract good tenants and make them feel comfortable. If their decorating tastes happen to be different from yours, that's just fine.

Clean: Note whether the apartments are clean and well kept or dirty and ill cared for. In any building, there will be a few tenants who are not as fastidious as one would like. It is important to note, however, whether the majority of the tenants in the building seem to keep their apartments and their personal possessions clean and in good condition.

Structural Defects
Windows, doors, floors, and walls: Check to see whether the doorframes, the windows and the floors are straight. Or do you find sags, slopes, and cracks? Look at the walls in the corners of the room and over the doorframe. Are there cracks? This can indicate a structural problem. Smaller spider-web cracks around the room simply indicate older plaster and poor maintenance. Larger jagged cracks going into a corner can indicate uneven settling and possibly rotted beams.

Electric: Look at the electrical fixtures. If the room has pull chains, local building codes may require that they be changed to wall switches later. This can be very costly. Pull chains also indicate very old wiring in the building, which may need to be replaced. This too can be very expensive.

Water pressure: Now go into the bathroom. Flush the toilet, then turn on the hot water and the cold water independently, in both the lavatory and the bath-tub. Is there sufficient water pressure when the toilet is filling? Inadequate water pressure may indicate clogged lines, which can be very expensive to replace. Check the pressure in the kitchen faucets as well.

Sewer: Does the water in the toilet go right down? If the toilet does not flush adequately, this can indicate problems with the sewage pipes, which also can be very expensive to repair or replace.

Deferred Maintenance
Leaks: Do any of the faucets leak? Run water into both the kitchen and the bathroom sinks, then look under the sinks: do the drains leak? Look at the ceiling over the bathroom and the kitchen sink area. Is there any indication of water coming through from the apartment above? Leaks from one bathroom to another, which often exist inside the ceiling that separates them, can be the most intractable and costly to repair. Freshly painted ceilings might indicate a quick fix that may be hiding a serious problem. Small bubbles in the fresh paint can be a sign of moisture.

Bathroom: Are the bathroom fixtures chipped and stained, or are they in good shape? Look at the wall around the tub. Is there any evidence that moisture is causing the wall to crumble?

Ceramic tile: If the bathroom walls have been tiled, look for grout that has turned black, which indicates moisture in the wall behind the tile. To repair this condition, the tile must be removed, but the wall material behind the tile also must be removed and replaced with moisture resistant wall board before the tile can be replaced and re-grouted, all of which is very expensive.

Kitchen cabinets: Check the kitchen cabinets. Are the doors loose and ill fitting? Will they need to be repaired or replaced? Is the counter top in good condition?

Floors: Will the kitchen floor need new tile or linoleum? What about the bathroom floor?

Windows: Now go to the windows. Look behind the shades and curtains. Is there evidence of moisture coming through? Are the windows loose and rattling? Are there storms and screens? Look at the window panes and the window sash. Is the wood solid or is it rotting? Are there locks on the windows? Do the window panes need glazing? Look below the window. Any indication that water has been coming in around the window frame may indicate the need for tuckpointing or caulking.

Paint: Does the interior need a coat of paint?

Author's Note: When I walked through the "twins," I found that the apartments were almost identical in size and layout. In both buildings, there was little evidence of severe structural defects. Plumbing problems seemed to have been taken care of promptly in both apartments. The difference was in the feel of the apartments. In the first building, the tenants seemed to take little interest in their living quarters, allowing them to become dirty, unkept and littered. In the second building, however, I found most of the apartments clean, well kept, and indicative of tenants who took personal pride in their homes.

Stage 5: The Roof

Roofs are costly to repair or to replace. And a leaky roof can cause untold damage to the interior of the apartments on the top floor. Check the roof carefully if you want to avoid serious problems later, but on a cold, windy day hang onto your hat!

The Feel of the Building. Is It Cared For?

The first place to begin checking for roof problems is inside the top-floor apartments. Look for the tell-tale signs of water coming through the ceilings: blistered paint, peeling paint, areas where the ceiling has recently been repaired and repainted. Sometimes only a small brown stain on the ceiling tells the story.

Suggestion: when you are in the apartment, ask the tenant whether they have noticed any leaks.

Structural Defects

The second place to check the roof is on the roof itself. (Do this only on flat roofs. Pitched roofs are too dangerous—and produce fewer problems.) Typically, a larger building with a flat roof will have access directly onto the roof, either by a staircase that leads to the roof or through a hatch that can be entered via a small ladder. Take the opportunity to go onto the roof.

Patches: Look for areas that have been freshly patched, particularly if you found freshly patched ceilings in the apartments. The owner might have completed a quick cover-up to make the building more marketable. If the remainder of the roof is worn out, a small patch will be only a temporary solution.

Recoating: Look for evidence that a section of the roof has been recently recovered with hot tar and felt. If the roof was in poor repair, such recoatings can extend the life of the roof for only a few years before problems return.

Aluminum coating: Another way to extend a roof's life for a few more years is to coat it with aluminum roof coat. This coating material, recognizable by its silver color, is superior to hot tar because it reflects heat and sunshine, reducing the expansion and contraction of the roof material. If the roof has been so coated, check the condition of the coating to determine whether further repairs might be needed in the near future.

Alligatoring: Named after the distinctive pattern that erupts after many years in the sun, alligatoring is a sure sign of a worn-out roof. Expansion and contraction have finally worn out the asphalt on the roof, creating a pattern that closely resembles alligator hide and which creates deep cracks in the roof material. Such a roof can be covered with another layer of felt and hot tar, but its days are numbered.

Deferred Maintenance

Flashings: The metal caps that are placed around pipes that protrude through the roof are called flashings. Check several of them to see whether they have pulled loose from the pipe. If so, they need to be resealed with plastic roofing cement.

Parapet walls: Check the walls that extend past the roof. Typically, these walls are constructed of brick and covered with rounded ceramic tile sections that shed the water. Check whether these walls require tuckpointing. (Is the mortar coming loose from between the bricks?) Also check the flashings that attach to the walls. Are they pulled loose? Check whether the tiles on top of the parapet walls are loose.

Chimney: Does the chimney need tuckpointing? What about the flashings around the chimney?

Scuttle holes: The holes in the roof that allow water to drain into the down spouts are called scuttle holes. Check to see whether water can get to these holes, and whether the holes are open so that water can pass through freely.

Author's Note: The roofs on both of the "twin" buildings were in good repair. Neither posed any serious problems.

Stage 6: Rear Entrance, Alley, and Rear Exterior

The rear entrance, the alley, and the rear exterior of the building should be dealt with similarly to the front entrance and hall-ways. Check for cleanliness, security, signs of structural defects, and deferred maintenance. Is the rear of the building consistent with the rest of the property? If this area is significantly darker, dirtier, and less well-kept, the owner might have cleaned up the rest of the building for the showing, covering up some secrets that could cause problems for the new owner.

Rear Porches: Exposed wood porches are very expensive to maintain and replace. Take a walk up the back stairs clear to the top. Check for warped or rotted cornerposts, loose and rotted stair treads and floor boards, loose railings, and evidence of the porch pulling away from the building. Will the porch need paint? That, too, will be expensive. If repairs have been made, was treated wood used?

Fire escapes: If the building has separate fire escapes, check the condition just as you did the porch system.

Trash: Particularly notice how the janitor and the tenants dispose of trash. Are there adequate containers, is there trash littered about or is the area kept clean? Are there trash bags lying on the ground because the containers are full or because tenants are too lazy to throw them into the container?

Author's Note: The rear entrances of the "twin" buildings mirrored my perceptions of the other areas: the entrance door and the alley in back of the first building were dark, unpainted, scarred, with trash littered about and overflowing the container. The second: clear of trash and as clean as the front entrance.

In Summary

A walk-through must be carried out carefully and deliberately, knowing exactly what to look for. It should be done in stages, being careful to observe the feel of the building as well as indications of deferred maintenance and structural defects. Stage 1 is the front of the building, including the yard and walk-way. Stage 2 is the interior—the lobby, the halls, and the stairs. How do they feel? Stage 3 is the Boiler room—the heart of the building and potentially the source of thousands of dollars in expenses. Stage 4 is the interior of the apartments themselves. Look for evidence of caring tenants, not stylish interior decorating. Stage 5 is the roof, and the only way to check it out is to get up there. Stage 6 is the rear entrance, the alley and the rear of the building. Check them out the same way the front was examined. Throughout the examination, the most important characteristic is the feel of the building. Does it feel safe, secure, clean, and quiet? That is the only kind of building that will attract good tenants.

Twenty-Two

■ ■ ■ ■ ■

How to Negotiate the Best Deal

In This Chapter

After working hard to locate just the right investment property, a critical step is still ahead: negotiating the best possible price and conditions for acquiring the property. The negotiations begin when the offer is first submitted; therefore, the form of the offer and the manner in which it is presented are crucial elements in the negotiation strategy.

All the conditions of a sale are negotiable, not just the price. This includes the terms of the sale, the financing (whether the owner might help out with some or all of the financing), the size of the down payment, the amount of earnest money to be given, and even the amount of the agent's commission. To produce a successful outcome, follow these six basic rules for negotiating:

1. Know the seller.

2. Know the property.

3. Don't be intimidated.

4. Be prepared for the tactics that will be used by the agent and the seller.

5. Be persistent.

6. Know when to quit.

How to Present an Offer

Submitting an offer to purchase a property is the first and most important step in negotiating the best possible conditions for the sale. This is your first and best opportunity to establish the groundwork for the negotiations, so be certain that all the important conditions are covered by the initial offer. If the offer is accepted as presented the deal is done; if any items of importance were left out it's then too late to add them to the contract. If the offer is rejected, which is more likely, it nevertheless does not make good sense to add additional conditions when resubmitting the offer later. Be certain everything is included in the contract before it is submitted the first time.

An offer should be presented in one of two forms: a signed purchase and sale contract or a signed letter of intent. There are advantages and drawbacks to each. If a number of offers are being submitted for different properties, letters of intent simplify the process: they are easy to prepare and leave plenty of room to back out if the buyer has a change of mind or if one of the offers is accepted and the others are to be withdrawn. For those same reasons, however, a letter of intent does not convey the same seriousness of purpose as a signed contract and may not elicit a serious response from the seller. Choose the method that best satisfies the conditions of each particular transaction. Either way, of course, an attorney should help draw up the form before submitting it.

Purchase and Sale Contract

The most common procedure for submitting an offer is to draw up a purchase and sale contract, which spells out in detail the conditions of the sale. Most real estate brokers' organizations have a standardized form that can be used. Such "standardized" forms often differ from one another in significant ways, however, and most are biased toward the seller. For those reasons, it is rarely sufficient simply to fill in the blanks on a standardized form and submit it as an offer to purchase. The agent handling the sale, nevertheless, will typically request that you use one of the broker's forms for submitting an offer. Probably the agent will also propose to "write up the offer." Don't allow that to happen. Remember that the agent works for the seller; therefore, the agent is duty-bound to represent the interests of the seller.

When and How to Involve an Attorney

It is imperative that the buyer's interests be protected when the offer is submitted, and the only way to do that is to involve an attorney as early as possible in the transaction. A contract that has been signed by both the seller and the buyer is binding on both parties; no further modifications can be made. The buyer's attorney should therefore help prepare the purchase and sale contract *before it is submitted to the seller*.

When you insist on using your attorney to draft the contract, however, the agent probably will not be happy. In an attempt to present an offer as quickly as possible and to deflect what is viewed as a potential deal-breaker, the agent might suggest drawing up the contract without the attorney and inserting a clause that says, "Subject to attorney's approval." This allows modifications to be made after the seller's signature is affixed to the contract. Psychologically, however, it is better to include all necessary clauses and conditions at the time of the offer rather than coming back later with additional conditions that the seller must approve.

Making a trip to the attorney's office every time an offer is submitted, however, can be unwieldy and time-consuming. There is a simple way to solve this problem: select a standardized purchase and sale form that is acceptable to you and to your attorney—most such forms are adequate—then have the attorney modify the contract to suit your needs. Thereafter use that form as a model to prepare all subsequent offers, being careful, however, to copy each modification word-for-word on each new contract. This usually involves only a paragraph or two.

Letter of Intent

A letter of intent (Figure 22.1) signals a willingness to purchase a property but leaves the details of the contract to a later date. The purpose of a letter of intent is to negotiate a price before going to the effort of preparing an unwieldy contract. If several offers are being submitted for different properties, or if the price being offered is substantially lower than the asking price on a particular property, a letter of intent opens the negotiations without an inordinate investment of time.

The letter of intent commonly specifies the price and the down payment being offered, the financing that is being sought, and any other item that seems appropriate to this deal. The letter also specifies that a suitable

Figure 22.1 Sample Letter of Intent

March 15, 199-

Robert Daniels
1569 W. Honeycutt Lane
Bringham Park, MA 12345

RE: 6980 W. Gulbranson Blvd.
Prospect Hills, MA 12345

Dear Mr. Daniels:

This letter will convey my interest in purchasing the above referenced property. I will complete the purchase under the following terms and conditions:

1. Purchaser: Donald E. Smith

2. Property location: 6980 W. Gulbranson Blvd.
Prospect Hills, MA 12345

3. Purchase price: $125,000, payable as follows: $10,000 cash down.
Seller to hold a second mortgage for $15,000.
Contingent upon obtaining approval of the holder of the present purchase money mortgage to allow transfer of the mortgage in the amount of approximately $100,000 to the purchaser.

4. Earnest deposit: $2,000 check or money order.

This Letter of Intent is further subject to Purchaser and Seller entering into a formal Purchase and Sales Contract acceptable to both Purchaser's and Seller's attorneys within ten (10) days after full execution of this Letter of Intent.

Purchaser to pay real estate sales commission as per listing agreement.

Purchaser	Date	Seller	Date

contract for sale will be executed within a reasonable length of time upon acceptance of the terms of the offer. As with the contract itself, all items in the letter are negotiable. Be willing to make concessions in one area to obtain attractive terms in another.

Negotiable Items

When an offer is submitted, all the conditions of the sale are negotiable, not just the price. Following is a list of the items that must receive attention when a purchase and sale contract is prepared. The final form that each item takes will depend upon the buyer's strategy. The key point, however, is to remember that each item is negotiable, regardless of the language that appears in the standardized form.

1. Price.   The offering price should represent the buyer's best estimate of the value of the property, while *allowing some room to negotiate for a final price.* In other words, the first offer should not be the best offer. If you wish to pay $200,000 for a property, the initial offer should be at least 10% less than that amount. The appropriate price to pay for a property is relatively easy to arrive at, using the rule-of-thumb formulas and the more elaborate calculations learned in Chapters 18 and 20. As an added check, however, ask the agent to provide a list of comparable properties that have sold in the past six months. This list discloses the *selling* price, rather than the *asking* price, of similar buildings. Conditions, of course, play a part in the offer. If the property is highly desirable and other offers are coming in, a good strategy might be to offer full price or, in rare instances, even more than the asking price. Most often, however, there is time to negotiate and the initial offer should not be the best offer.

2. Terms.   The terms of a sale can significantly affect the net price paid for a building. Items such as settlement fees, closing points, etc., typically involve payments of thousands of dollars at closing. Chapter 24 introduces the costs typically associated with the purchase of a property; some are traditionally paid by the seller, others by the buyer. The standardized form used to submit the offer will likely include each of these costs, with reference to which party is responsible for paying them. By assigning some or all of these costs to the seller, a buyer can reduce the net price paid for the property. For example, an offer might be for $190,000, with the seller paying all points, transfer costs, settlement fees, etc.—which might total as much as $5,000. Clever manipulation of the terms of the sale can in effect reduce the price of the property.

3. Financing.   If the offer requires owner financing, it is wise to spell out the terms of the financial agreement at the time the offer is submitted. Minimally, the purchase and sale agreement should make reference to the specific form that will be used to draft the financing agreement. Also include these items (all of which are negotiable):

- Interest rate (keep it low)

- Amortization period

- Any balloon payments being offered and the length of time before the balloon is due

- Whether the financing is to be by articles of agreement for a deed or a purchase money mortgage

- The amount to be financed

- Whether the interest rate is fixed or adjustable

- Whether the financing is secondary to another mortgage

In offering the terms of the financial agreement, draw up an arrangement that will provide maximum advantage but allow room to negotiate if necessary. Also, be ready to negotiate price against the terms of the financing agreement. A higher down payment, for instance, can be offset by a lower interest rate, or the selling price can be higher if the seller agrees to a longer amortization period for the financing.

Outside financing. If a buyer anticipates obtaining a mortgage to purchase the property, the contract should spell out the maximum acceptable terms, including the amount of the loan, the maximum interest rate, the length of amortization, and any other terms appropriate to the transaction. A mortgage contingency, which allows the buyer to exit the contract if those terms are unavailable, is a standard part of any real estate contract.

4. Down payment.   The size of the down payment is a critical part of the negotiation process. A large down payment can signal a serious buyer, and the seller, knowing that the buyer will have little trouble obtaining financing, might then be open to a lower price. On the other hand, a small down payment leverages the deal and preserves capital for other acquisitions. If a small down payment is offered, be ready to make concessions on other items, such as interest rate on owner financing, price, or any other item that seems appropriate.

5. Earnest money.   As the name implies, earnest money is offered at the time an offer is submitted to signal the seriousness of the offer. The tendency is to offer as small an amount as possible. On the other hand, a sizable earnest money check can signal a very serious offer and sway the buyer's attitude toward the price being offered. Some earnest money offers are in the form of a personal promissory note to be redeemed when the offer is accepted.

Other times, the earnest money is in the form of cash or a personal check. The initial earnest money can be small, with the provision that it will be increased to a mutually acceptable amount within a few days of acceptance of the contract. In any event, specify on the contract that all earnest money will be held in an interest bearing account by the broker and will be refunded entirely in the event the sale does not occur, so long as the fault does not lie with the buyer.

Rules for Negotiating

The art of negotiating is a subject for another complete book, and indeed several have been written on the topic over the past few years. To become a first-rate negotiator, one should read these books. In the absence of such formal instruction, however, there are a few important rules that should be followed if the negotiations are to lead to a successful conclusion.

Rule #1:   Know the seller. Learn all you can from the agent about the seller, why he is selling, how long he has owned the property, how many other properties he owns, his age, how involved he is in his business, etc. Structure the offer to appeal to your perceptions of the seller's motivations. If possible, meet the seller face to face before submitting the offer. Talk about the property. Ask him questions, show interest in him as a person, encourage him to talk about the building—about the tenants, how he acquired it, why he has decided to sell. Lead the seller to reveal as much as possible about himself and the building before extending an offer.

Rule #2:   Know the property. You have done the numbers very carefully. You have studied the neighborhood and the building. You know the tenants. You know the risks. Be ready to use this information to justify your offer. But more important, use the information to build an image of a confident, competent investor.

Rule #3:   Don't be intimidated. The agent wants to bring the best possible price to the seller. You, on the other hand, wish to buy at the lowest possible price. The agent will give many reasons why the property is worth a higher price and try to intimidate you in subtle and not-so-subtle ways to offer more. You have done the numbers. You know the value of the property. Stick to your guns. Don't be intimidated into offering more.

Rule #4:   Be prepared for the tactics. All negotiations include a few well-used tactics. When used against the unprepared, these tactics can be very effective. Before making an offer, read a few books on negotiating strategies. This will help in two ways: to recognize the tactics of your adversary and to hone a few strategies of your own.

Rule #5:   Be persistent. A deal is not over 'til it's over.
Author's Note: One of the best properties I have owned was under contract to be sold when I first called about it. Disappointed, I did what most people would do: I thanked the owner and hung up. I was frustrated because I knew intuitively that the price was excellent: the neighborhood was perfect, the building was tenant-heated (a big plus for keeping costs under control), and the building would generate positive cash flow.

I had been looking religiously for months. Nothing I had seen even came close to the performance I anticipated from this building. My disappointment bordered on depression, having come so close to the perfect building only to miss it through bad timing. But after an hour or so of such thoughts, I decided not to throw in the towel so quickly. I picked up the phone, dialed the number again, and when the owner answered I simply asked whether there was any way we could do business. I explained why I was so interested in the building and that I was willing to offer more than the asking price to buy it. He told me he was sorry, but nothing could be done; the contract was signed and the building would be sold. I asked him to take my phone number and to call if anything happened.

One week later, unable to get the building out of my mind, I called again and asked how the deal was going. His response took me completely by surprise. He was, at that very moment, extremely angry at the buyer, who had missed an important appointment. Miffed, he had decided not to sell the building to that kind of individual. I assured him that I was a responsible person who would keep my appointments. Impressed with my tenacity and with my personality, he agreed to meet with me. At that meeting we drew up a contract for a price less than the amount in the original contract.

I owned that building for 12 years. During that time, the cash flow was approximately $1,000 per month. The original down payment: $18,000. The original price: $92,000. After twelve years I reluctantly sold the building for $265,000 and used the proceeds to purchase two larger buildings.

Rule #6:   Know when to quit. If the property cannot be bought for a price that makes good economic sense, in spite of your best negotiating skills, break off the negotiations. The best thing about real estate investing is that there is always another deal just around the corner. The corollary to this rule is "Don't be disappointed." After giving your best effort to the negotiations and failing to buy the property, walk away confident, ready for the next opportunity.

The Process of Negotiating

Real estate agents generally like to follow a traditional negotiating procedure that keeps them in the middle of the dialogue. With this strategy the
buyer and the seller talk only to the agent, never to each other. Often the
buyer and seller never meet prior to the closing. This is how the traditional
negotiating strategy works:

1.   The agent receives an offer from the buyer in the form of a contract or
     a letter of intent.

2.   The agent hand carries the offer to the seller and formally presents the
     offer. At the presentation the agent will make every attempt either to
     obtain the seller's signature or—if the offer is unacceptable—encourage
     the seller to produce a counter-offer.

3.   The seller responds in one of three ways:

     a.   accepts the offer by signing the contract or the letter of intent. The
          deal is now struck;

     b.   rejects the offer; or

     c.   counters the offer by changing the unacceptable items and signing
          the contract or the letter of intent.

4.   If the seller accepts the offer, the agent returns the signed contract to
     the buyer, who begins preparing for a closing.

5.   If the seller counters the offer, the agent returns the contract with each
     change noted and initialed by the seller.

6.   The buyer responds in one of two ways:

     a.   accepts the counter-offer by signing the amended contract or the
          letter of intent, initializing the changes, if any, submitted by the
          seller; or

     b.   counters the counter-offer by noting additional changes on the
          contract and sending it back to the seller.

7.   From here, the process continues until the deal is completed or until
     the negotiations break down.

All such negotiations are handled at arm's length: the buyer and seller never meet and the agent is the only one who knows both parties to the deal.

Try Negotiating Face to Face

There are times when the arm's-length process can be very effective, but other times this anonymous process can be problematic. Many sellers are not sophisticated negotiators. Thinking their price is fair, they often view with anger a faceless outsider submitting an offer that is significantly less than their asking price. The key to negotiating with such a seller is to get to know the person, to learn what his or her needs are, to assess their feelings about the property. Such information gives the buyer a significant advantage in the negotiations.

If you are a good negotiator, or at least an earnest, pleasant kind of person, you might well have a better chance of selling your proposal than the agent has. By developing a rapport, overcoming initial objections, and communicating clearly the reasons for making the offer, a buyer often stands a better chance than the agent, who represents the seller's interests and whose only motivation is to put together a deal.

Getting to know the seller has other advantages as well. A buyer, for example, might wrongly believe that price is the most important consideration to the seller. That is not always the case. The property in the example above was purchased at a price *significantly lower than another offer that had already been accepted.* The reason: the original buyer missed one appointment and the owner decided that he would not sell to someone so inconsiderate.

In Summary

Negotiating the best price and terms of the sale begins when the offer is first submitted. The form that is used is therefore very important. Whether the offer is made on a contract for purchase and sale or a formal letter of intent, an attorney must be involved from the beginning. Most contract forms favor the seller, and the agent's loyalties are with the seller. The buyer, then, needs an attorney to watch out for his or her interests in the transaction.

All the conditions of a sale are negotiable, even those items that are included in the text of the contract form. Often a willingness to be flexible in one area can result in better terms in another.

A real estate agent prefers to follow a traditional negotiating strategy in which the seller and the buyer never meet. Such an anonymous process eliminates the possible effectiveness of a buyer's personality and negotiating skills in obtaining a better deal. When possible, the buyer should meet the seller prior to submitting an offer, for the purpose of learning as much as possible about the seller and to convince the seller of the buyer's own sincerity and honesty.

The basic rules to follow when negotiating a deal are these: 1. Know the seller. 2. Know the property. 3. Don't be intimidated. 4. Be prepared for the tactics. 5. Be persistent. 6. Know when to quit.

Twenty-Three

■ ■ ■ ■ ■

How to Finance Your New Property

In This Chapter

Properties that produce the most cash flow are also often the most difficult to finance. Lenders are reluctant to provide financing for properties they view as risky. Thus, it is important to become familiar with a broad array of financing strategies. The truth is, however, that finding suitable financing often requires the patience of Mother Theresa and the tenacity of Rambo.

Conforming loans—those that meet the requirements of the government-sponsored secondary mortgage market—increase the difficulty associated with obtaining suitable financing for some less desirable or higher risk properties. The answer often lies with owner financing of some or all of the purchase. Such owner financing, in the form of a second mortgage, articles of agreement, or purchase money mortgage, is often the only way a deal can be made on many higher-risk properties.

Traditional Forms of Financing

Long-term mortgages were designed by the Federal Housing Administration (FHA) shortly after the Depression years of the 1920s. Traditionally, monthly payments are amortized over many years, with an accompanying escrow payment to cover taxes and insurance. To assure consistency and the long range soundness of the FHA program—and to avoid abuses—a uniform system of real estate appraisal and borrower credit analysis was also established. This system is now so firmly rooted in the American economy, and long-term mortgages are so ubiquitous, that it hardly seems possible that the entire system is only about 60 years old.

Where to Locate a Source for Financing

There is no one best source for mortgage money—each option has both good and bad points.

Mortgage Brokers.   Mortgage brokers work very much like insurance brokers: they function as a representative for one or more lending companies, assisting the buyer in obtaining suitable financing from those companies. Mortgage brokers can be found advertised in the yellow pages and in newspapers. The right mortgage broker can do a lot of the leg work in locating financing. The draw-back is that brokers work on a commission basis and often over-extend themselves in an attempt to boost their income. Consequently, the mortgage broker who seems so responsive on initial contact often has little time later to respond to phone calls.

Mortgage Bankers.   Mortgage bankers offer the same kinds of loans with the same conditions and terms as mortgage brokers. The difference is that mortgage bankers work with their own funds while mortgage brokers locate financing through other companies.

Savings and Loan Associations.   S&Ls have been around for many years, primarily to provide home mortgages. Some commercial financing can be found through S&Ls, although since the S&L fiasco, funds are increasingly difficult to obtain for any kind of property viewed as risky.

Individual Financiers.   Occasionally it is possible to find, through a newspaper ad or by word of mouth, an individual who wishes to invest in real estate mortgages. Typically, the terms of such financing are quite difficult to meet, but an inquiry might be worth the effort.

Search for the Best Deal

The first place to look for a lender who will offer reasonable investor financing is in the yellow pages. Most sources of mortgage financing will be listed there: mortgage bankers, mortgage brokers, savings and loan associations, individual financiers.

Another place to look for financing is the newspaper: financiers often advertise in the classified section while advertisements for mortgage brokers can usually be found in the real estate and business sections. If your paper has a mortgage watch you may find several lenders listed together in a chart that compares interest rates, types of mortgages, points charged, and other pertinent information.

A third source of information is the real estate broker who is handling the sale of the property. Most real estate brokers have a cozy relationship with one or more lenders.

The best way to gain a familiarity with the entire mortgage market is to start calling. Ask many questions, write down the answers, and compare the various lenders. Use the list of questions on page 209 as a guide.

Alternatives to Fixed Rate Financing

For many years the terms for a conventional mortgage were pretty much the same—30-year declining balance, fixed interest rate for the life of the loan, monthly payments that included principal and interest as well as payments into an escrow account to cover insurance and taxes. One can still obtain this type of mortgage, but the high inflation and corresponding high interest rates of the late 1970s and early 1980s significantly changed the rules for mortgage financing.

Caught between long-term fixed rate mortgages at low interest rates and a highly competitive interest rate market that was forcing savings account rates to exceptionally high levels, the mortgage industry came up with various creative solutions. Two important innovations that have survived that period are the adjustable rate mortgage (ARM) and the balloon payment.

Balloon Payment Loans.   In a balloon mortgage, the buyer pays a reasonable down payment, just as with a conventional mortgage. The mortgage is amortized over a long term—usually 15 to 30 years. But, the loan is actually extended for a much shorter term—often only three to five years—sometimes as long as seven to ten years. At the end of the agreed-upon term, the remaining principal of the loan is to be paid in full (a balloon payment).

The concept of a balloon payment is particularly attractive to lenders who wish to offer lower interest rates but would like to avoid being stuck with such rates for a long term.

There are times when a balloon loan is just the right kind of financing for a particular project—if a property is being purchased with early resale in mind, for instance. But the risks are obvious: what if the property remains unsold and refinancing is unavailable when the balloon payment comes due? An owner might be forced to sell prematurely and take considerably less than the true value; or, in an extreme case, an investor might be forced to default on the loan and watch the property be repossessed by the lender. Balloon loans can play a valuable role in an attempt to finance a desirable property, particularly when traditional sources are unavailable in the amounts required. But they must be undertaken with due caution and with an alternative bail-out plan in mind.

Adjustable Rate Mortgages. Another solution for lenders caught in the grip of volatile interest rates is the adjustable rate mortgage (ARM). As the name implies, the interest rate for this type of mortgage can be adjusted as rates fluctuate. Although it is conceivable to adjust the rate every time interest rates change, the normal practice is to establish anniversary dates for changing the rate.

An ARM involves four variables: the length of time between rate adjustments (one-year, two-year or three-year periods are most common), the maximum rate change that can occur on the anniversary (a cap of two percentage points is common), the maximum rate change that can occur during the life of the loan (a cap of six percentage points is common), and the benchmark rate that will determine the adjusted rate when a change occurs (a common benchmark is the prime rate plus two percentage points). A typical ARM mortgage might be described as follows: "A one-year ARM, with a cap of two and six, prime plus two. In other words, the interest rate is adjusted once a year, and the new rate will be two percentage points above the prime rate on that date, except that the rate will never change more than two percentage points on the anniversary and will never change more than six percentage points during the life of the loan.

When does an ARM make sense? If a property is to be held for only a few years, an ARM can provide significant savings. If the plan is to hold the property for a longer term and interest rates are reasonable, a fixed rate mortgage is probably the best route to take. If interest rates are high, however, an ARM might be the best alternative—with a plan to refinance when rates drop.

Where Does All the Mortgage Money Come From?
The Secondary Mortgage Market

Years ago, the procedure for obtaining a mortgage was fairly simple: a borrower would approach a mortgage banker or a savings and loan association who would take an application, appraise the property, check the borrower's credit rating and make a decision regarding the loan. The availability of a mortgage depended upon the amount of cash the lender had on hand. Such loans were commonly held in the lender's own portfolio until the borrower paid off the loan. The limiting factor in such a system was the amount of money available to lend: when interest rates were favorable and the real estate market was hot, lenders commonly ran out of available mortgage money. Because of this limitation, the secondary mortgage market was established.

The secondary market is comprised primarily of three quasi-government agencies: the Government National Mortgage Association (Ginnie Mae), the Federal National Mortgage Association (Fannie Mae), and the Federal Home Loan Mortgage Corporation (Freddie Mac). These agencies get their money from institutional investors such as pension funds and insurance companies, who are eager to invest in mortgages because of the relatively high interest rates that are charged and the security that mortgage loans provide.

With the money they get from the large investors, Ginnie Mae, Fannie Mae, and Freddie Mac do not actually make mortgages, they buy mortgages that have been made by the direct lenders—mortgage bankers, S&Ls, and lending companies. This system provides an almost limitless supply of mortgage money. As a local lender uses up their own funds, they sell some of their mortgages to one of the three agencies and, presto, they have more funds to lend.

Conforming Loans. Ginnie Mae, Fannie Mae, and Freddie Mac have solved the problem of availability of mortgage funds, but unfortunately they have created other problems: problems that the investor must be aware of and attempt to avoid. To create a market for the buying and selling of mortgages, the three agencies were forced to develop standardized rules for the kinds of loans they would buy. These rules must be followed by the lender granting a mortgage, otherwise the mortgage cannot be sold in the secondary market. The loans that meet the stiff criteria for the secondary market are called *conforming* loans. The rules for obtaining conforming loans for investment financing are both extremely confining and costly. As a result, nearly all investor financing is difficult to obtain and problematic. Not so, of course, with homeowner loans, where low down payments are the rule and the terms are attractive.

There are two primary problems presented by conforming loans for investment financing: prepayment penalties and high down payments. To satisfy the rules of the secondary market, lenders are not allowed to lend more than 70% of the value of an investment property. This means that the buyer must make a 30% down payment to buy a property with a conforming mortgage loan. For a $200,000 property, the required down payment would be $60,000.

But the most difficult aspect of a conforming loan for investment financing is the limit placed on pre-payment: many such loans will allow no pre-payment for an established period of time and, after that time has elapsed, a pre-payment penalty is charged if the mortgage is paid off early. This rule is particularly confining when an investor decides to sell a property and is unable to pay off the existing mortgage at closing. The solution often is for the seller to finance the sale until the exclusionary period has elapsed, when new financing can be arranged—a procedure that is both exasperating and expensive.

Non-conforming Loans.   Some traditional lenders still offer non-conforming loans for investor use. By avoiding the secondary market, these lenders are able to provide 80% loans that require only 20% down payment, as well as much more attractive pre-payment arrangements. Although such non-conforming loans are available, some shopping is required to locate them.

Characteristics of a Mortgage Loan

Mortgage loans have certain peculiarities that are not found with other types of financing. When shopping for a mortgage, you should have at least an acquaintance with these distinctive features.

Points.   Chapter 24 explains the function of points and what they mean. Suffice it to say here that a lender will charge points in addition to the other costs of obtaining a mortgage. A point is 1% of the loan amount. The number of points charged will vary, depending upon the current interest rate market.

Floating Interest Rates.   Because interest rates are rarely stable, the rates charged for a mortgage can change significantly between the time the application is made and the loan is closed, which can often take 60 days or more. Some lenders will lock in the interest rate, which means that at the time of application they will guarantee that a specific rate will be charged, as long as the loan is completed within a specified period—usually 60 days—although they might charge a fee for doing so.

Origination Fee. This fee amounts to approximately 1% of the loan amount. It is just one more way the lender can make money on your mortgage loan.

Loan-to-value (LTV).   This is just a bureaucrat's way of saying how much you can borrow on a property. For a conforming loan, the maximum LTV is 70%, which means the lender is prohibited from loaning more than 70% of the appraised value of the property, which may or may not be the same as the selling price.

Questions to Ask When Shopping for Financing

When calling about financing, these are the questions that should be asked. It will be helpful to have them written down, with room for taking notes.

1.   Do you offer loans for investment properties? If not, can you direct me to a lender who does?

2.   What interest rate do you currently charge for loans on investment properties?

3.   How many points do you currently charge?

4.   How long will it take to process a loan?

5.   When are interest rates locked in: at the time of the application or at the closing?

6.   Can I lock in interest rates by paying an additional fee? How much is the fee and how long does the lock remain in effect?

7.   Do you charge an application fee? How much?

8.   Do you offer both fixed rate and adjustable rate mortgages?

9.   On an adjustable rate mortgage, what is the initial interest rate? How often does the rate change? What index is used to determine future

interest rates? Is there a cap on each rate change? How much? Is there a cap on the life of the mortgage? How much? Can I convert from an ARM to fixed-rate financing?

10.   Can I prepay the loan, in whole or in part, without any penalty? Is this clearly written into the loan agreement?

Short-term Financing and Commercial Banks

If for some reason your needs are for short-term financing rather than a long-term mortgage, a commercial bank might provide the ideal solution. Perhaps the property will need initial rehab work, which will then substantially increase the resale value of the property so that long-term financing can be arranged. Or perhaps your intentions are to hold the property for less than five years. In such cases, mortgage financing can be very expensive because of the costs associated with obtaining and servicing the mortgage. A commercial bank, which avoids such upfront costs as points and origination fees, is a less expensive alternative for shorter term financing.

Dealing with a bank, however, has problems of its own. Unlike mortgage lenders, banks do not typically seek out real estate business. Therefore, the likelihood of walking into a bank and obtaining any kind of financing is remote without a long term relationship with the bank. This typically involves maintaining both personal and business accounts with the bank, obtaining credit cards through the bank, and perhaps even holding a home equity loan from the same bank. Once a relationship has been developed, though, bank financing can be an excellent source of investment funds.

Line of Credit

One way to use bank financing and avoid the lengthy approval process is to obtain a line of credit. A credit line qualifies the borrower for a specific maximum amount of credit that the bank will extend when needed. After the loan has been approved, to get the money the borrower simply writes a check. The cost of obtaining a line of credit is typically an up-front fee of 1% of the entire line of credit, whether the funds are used or not, and a rate that amounts to 1 1/2 to 2 percentage points above the prime interest rate.

If the need to access a line of credit is not immediate, an informal line of credit can be established by submitting the necessary paperwork for review and letting the banker know that he or she will be notified when the credit line is to be used.

Owner Financing

When money is tight or when a property is in a high-risk neighborhood, it may be impossible to find financing from traditional sources. In such cases, the owner might be persuaded to finance the deal. There are several ways this can be done:

1. The seller can finance the entire deal. This would occur if the property is owned free and clear.

2. The seller can finance part of the purchase while the majority of the financing is obtained from traditional sources.

3. The seller can retain the present mortgage and finance part or all of the remainder.

4. The seller can transfer the present mortgage to the buyer and finance part or all of the remainder.

Each method is viable and the type of owner financing should reflect the specific circumstances of the deal, but each method should be approached with extreme caution and all contracts should be prepared and approved by an attorney.

Purchase-Money Mortgages

One method of owner financing is a purchase-money mortgage. Very simply, the present owner holds the mortgage to the property while title to the property passes to the buyer. Typically, such a deal requires a rather large down payment because the owner, who likely owns the property free and clear, wants to leave the table with some cash after paying the realtor's commission and other expenses of closing. Nevertheless, if no other financing is available this is a nice way to purchase a property.

Author's Note: With a purchase-money mortgage all the terms are negotiable—the size of the down payment, the interest rate, the number of years over which the mortgage will be amortized, whether there will be a balloon, whether the rate will be adjustable, and the price. Often, I have been willing to pay a higher price if the terms of the mortgage were attractive. Conversely, if I pay a large down payment, the price should be lower. I have also found that owners holding a mortgage are often willing to accept lower than market interest rates in order to put together a deal.

Typical purchase-money mortgage:

Selling price:	$200,000
Down payment (10%):	$20,000
Mortgage (held by the seller):	$180,000
Interest rate:	10%
Monthly payment:	$1,580

Land Contract (Articles of Agreement)

A land contract can work just like a purchase-money mortgage except that the Articles of Agreement specify that the owner retains title to the property until the contract is paid off. A land contract is often used for short term financing, allowing a buyer to pay down the balance far enough to obtain more conventional financing. It is not uncommon, however, for an owner to hold a land contract for many years. Some entrepreneurs, in fact, use land contracts as an integral part of their investment strategy, purchasing properties at a low price, reselling at a much higher price on a land contract and enjoying the monthly payments, which work very much like an annuity. Like the purchase-money mortgage, everything about a land contract is negotiable.

The question often arises: is it better for the buyer to hold title and allow the seller to hold the mortgage or to allow the seller to hold title and purchase the property on a land contract? There seems to be no discernible advantage either way. The rights of both the seller and the buyer are essentially the same with either form of ownership. Some owners, however, just feel better when their name is on the title.

Second Mortgage

For a buyer wishing to spend less than the required 20% to 30% down payment to purchase a property the owner might agree to hold a second mortgage for the balance. For example, a buyer wishes to purchase a property for $200,000 and can obtain 70% financing from a mortgage banker. This leaves $60,000 due the seller. But the buyer has only $35,000. The owner might be persuaded to hold a second mortgage for the $25,000 balance in order to complete the deal. Many lenders, unfortunately, will not allow a second mortgage. In such cases, the only way to effect a second mortgage is to do it under the table, so to speak. If the lender discovers the transaction, however, the loan could be called in immediately.

A second mortgage is fully subordinated to the existing first mortgage. This means that in the event of a foreclosure, the holder of the first mortgage will be paid first from the proceeds of a sale and the holder of the second mortgage will be paid from the remaining proceeds. For that reason, second mortgages usually carry higher interest rates, reflecting the increased risk.

Typical second mortgage transaction:

Selling price:	$200,000
Down payment:	$35,000
First mortgage (obtained by the buyer):	$140,000
Interest rate:	10%
Monthly payment:	$1,229
Second mortgage (held by the seller):	$25,000
Interest rate:	10.5%
Monthly payment:	$229
Total monthly debt service:	$1,458

Assuming the Present Mortgage

Sometimes an existing mortgage is assumable, which means that the buyer can take over the mortgage as it exists. If the mortgage holds a low interest rate or if alternative financing is difficult to find, assuming a mortgage can be a viable alternative. If the mortgage is for significantly less than the selling price, the owner might hold a second mortgage for part of the difference. Here is how the deal would look:

Typical transaction involving a mortgage assumption with second mortgage:

Selling price:	$200,000
Down payment (20%):	$40,000
First mortgage (assumed by the buyer):	$80,000
Interest rate:	7%
Monthly payment:	$533
Second mortgage (held by the seller):	$80,000
Interest rate:	10.5%
Monthly payment:	$732
Total monthly debt service:	$1,434

Wrap-Around Mortgage

A wrap-around, or blanket mortgage, can be used when the seller retains title to the property and does not pay off the first mortgage. In such a situation the seller retains the original mortgage, assuming it does not have a due-on-sale clause, and writes a new, larger mortgage for the buyer that "wraps around" the existing mortgage. As an example, if a property is selling for $200,000, the seller might hold a mortgage for 85% of the selling price, or $170,000. The property already has a first mortgage of $80,000, which the seller does not pay off. The new mortgage, then, "wraps around" the original mortgage. The buyer now sends a mortgage payment to the seller each month for the new wrap-around mortgage, while the seller continues to send a smaller mortgage payment to the lender who holds the first mortgage. As with any real estate transaction, everything about a wrap-around mortgage is negotiable.

Here's how it works:

Typical transaction involving a wrap-around mortgage:

Selling price:	$200,000
Down payment:	$30,000
Wrap-around mortgage (held by the seller):	$170,000
Interest rate:	10.5%
Monthly payment (paid by the buyer):	$1,556
First mortgage (retained by the seller):	$80,000
Interest rate:	7%
Monthly payment (paid by the seller):	$533

In Summary

Properties that produce positive cash flow are often less attractive to mortgage lenders, with the result that traditional forms of financing are often difficult to obtain. If, after searching through the yellow pages and the newspapers and talking with other real estate professionals, suitable financing cannot be found, the answer might be owner financing.

Owner financing can take several forms: second mortgage, land contract, purchase-money mortgage, or wrap-around mortgage. The terms of an owner financed loan can be similar to commercial financing, with the advantage that all conditions of the loan are negotiable. Like a commercial loan, an owner-financed loan can be held for a period of up to 30 years or longer. The loan can include provisions for a balloon payment or an adjustable rate, but interest rates can be lower than market rates.

Twenty-Four

■ ■ ■ ■ ■

How Much Cash Will You Need?

In This Chapter

In a typical real estate transaction using traditional sources of financing the purchaser normally must contribute a down payment equal to 20% to 30% of the selling price. Thus, to purchase a property that costs $200,000, the down payment required by the lender would be at least $40,000. Lenders require such a commitment to protect their own interests: a buyer who has invested little or no personal money in a property has little to lose by walking away from an unsuccessful venture. Although it is possible to structure a deal that requires substantially less than 20% down, such transactions normally depend upon one or more specific circumstances: seller financing, other collateral in addition to the property itself, or a long history with the lender. The previous chapter covers several types of seller-financed transactions.

A common mistake when calculating the amount of investment capital that will be required, however, is to overlook the cost of closing the deal. There are three specific types of costs involved with the purchase and sale of real estate: the costs associated with obtaining financing, the fees charged by professionals associated with the transaction, and municipal taxes. None is cheap. Any time a property changes hands, the buyer and the seller will encounter unavoidable fees which, in the aggregate, add a significant amount to the cash investment. These standard fees can cost as much as 3% to 5% of the price of the property. The buyer must be prepared to pay some or all of these fees, depending on how the acquisition is financed.

Costs to Obtain a Mortgage

Lenders typically increase their yield by charging fees in addition to the interest charged on the mortgage itself. If a mortgage broker is involved, some of these fees go to reimburse the broker for services rendered.

Points or loan discount fees: A loan discount, or "points," is a one-time charge used to adjust the yield on the loan to conform with market conditions. A point represents 1% of the loan amount. When shopping for financing, it is essential to determine not only the interest, but also the number of points being charged. On a $200,000 mortgage, one point equals $2,000.

Loan origination fee: Most lenders charge a loan origination fee equal to about 1% of the loan. This fee reimburses the lender for the administrative costs of processing the loan, including securing the loan, preparing the loan documents, etc.

Lock-in fee: When interest rates are at an attractive level, a borrower may want to lock in the current rate, rather than taking the risk that rates will rise before closing occurs. Lenders will usually lock-in a rate for 45 to 60 days, but often charge a fee for doing so. When interest rates are volatile, it is usually advantageous to establish the interest rate at the time of application. Locking in a rate, however, does have its drawbacks. First, the lock-in covers a specific period of time to allow the lender to complete the loan application process. Because the lender controls the process, however, he or she will determine whether the loan is processed within the allotted time. If rates are rising, it requires little effort for an unscrupulous lender to dawdle just long enough to exceed the lock-in period. Second, the lender can also violate the spirit of the lock-in agreement by leaving interest rates alone and raising the number of points required to close the deal. Third, the lender may reserve in the fine print of the lock-in agreement the right to change the locked-in rate in the event that market conditions change. Such a clause obviously voids the intent of the lock-in agreement.

Application fee: Typically, a lender will charge an application fee of $250 to $300, a fee that is normally non-refundable if the loan is denied.

Appraisal fee: Before extending a mortgage on a particular property, a lender must be satisfied that the property is indeed worth what the buyer is paying for it. Thus, a professional appraisal must be done, which the buyer typically pays for. Costs vary, but expect to pay between $250 to $500.

Credit report fee: This covers the cost of running a credit report.

Mortgage insurance: When a buyer invests less than 20% of the purchase price of a property, particularly in an owner-occupied property of one to four units, it is customary for the lender to require mortgage insurance. The first premium for this insurance is normally prepaid at closing. For 5% down, a buyer should expect to pay 1% of the loan amount, or one point, for mortgage insurance. With 10% down, the fee is typically 4% of the mortgage amount. With 15% down, the fee is usually 3%.

Prepaid mortgage payment: The first month's payment on the mortgage will ordinarily be due at closing.

Prepaid insurance: A lender will ordinarily require that the first year's insurance be paid in advance, with proof of insurance, not just a binder, being offered at or before closing. The cost depends on the property being insured.

Prepaid interest: Lenders usually require payment at closing of the interest that will accrue from the date of settlement to the beginning of the period covered by the first mortgage payment.

Municipal Taxes and Charges

Deed recording fee: Ownership of a property passes only when the deal is recorded with the proper government authority, usually the county. The fee for recording a deed is $25 to $35.

Recording taxes: Local governments find a way to tax almost any transaction, and real estate sales are no exception. A stamp tax may be a fixed amount—$250 is common—or based on the amount of the transaction.

Property taxes: When real estate changes hands, the buyer is obligated to pay real estate taxes from the date of the closing. These taxes are pro-rated, meaning the total tax liability is divided by the number of days in a year, and that pro-rated amount is multiplied by the number of days remaining in the year from the date of closing. If the seller already paid the taxes for the entire year, the buyer will rebate to the seller at closing the appropriate pro-rated amount. If taxes are assessed one year and payable the next, the buyer receives a pro-rated credit from the seller at closing. In other words, the seller is giving the buyer the money with which to pay his or her portion of the taxes when they become due.

Fees for Professional Services

Property survey: A current survey checks property lines to make sure there are no encroachments on the land that might hamper a future sale. The cost, which may range from $75 to $150, is ordinarily paid by the seller. That point, however, is negotiable within the framework of the transaction.

Document preparation: If closing is at a title company, expect to pay $50 or so to the title company to cover the cost of paperwork.

Settlement fee: This fee covers administrative costs associated with the closing.

Title search: A buyer should expect to pay approximately $400 for a title search and title insurance. This assures the lender that there are no clouds on the title—no liens against the property and no questions about who the legal owner is. Part of the cost for this service is tied to the price of the property. The title insurance, which is issued by a company specializing in this kind of insurance, assures payment to any claimant in case discrepancies arise regarding title to the property. This fee may be paid by the seller, or, as sometimes occurs, be split between buyer and seller.

Legal fees: A real estate lawyer will normally charge from $250 to $500 or more to handle a closing. If the deal is particularly complex, as when there is a purchase-money mortgage or articles of agreement to be negotiated, the fees will likely be much higher.

Miscellaneous Charges that Affect the Down Payment

Tenant security deposits: If the seller is holding tenants' security deposits, these must be transferred to the buyer. In a larger building, security deposits can add up to a substantial amount and therefore can significantly reduce the amount of money the buyer has to pay at closing.

Pro-rated utilities: If there are any outstanding utility bills due, the seller will grant a credit to the buyer at closing. Conversely, if any of the utilities have been paid in advance, the buyer will credit the seller a pro-rated amount.

In Summary

The down payment is not the only cash that will be required to obtain a property. The cost of obtaining financing and transferring a property can be substantial: as much as 5% of the cost of the property. When purchasing a property for $200,000, therefore, expect to pay as much as $10,000 in additional fees and taxes.

Section IV

■ ■ ■ ■ ■

Some More Things You Need to Know

Twenty-Five

■ ■ ■ ■ ■

Why No-Money-Down Deals Seldom Work

In This Chapter

During the past several years, thousands of would-be real estate investors have adopted the no-money-down concept as a kind of battle cry. No money down is an attractive idea: the ability to make money without investing any of your own money is a seductive notion. The fact is, however, that the vast majority of real estate deals require significant down payments, and often the ones that are structured with no money down are not particularly good investments. Because of that, real estate brokers have long since become weary of the typical no-money-down buyer. Despite their best efforts to dissuade such buyers, however, the idea just won't go away.

No-money-down fever is particularly difficult to extinguish because of the numbers of self-styled, self-made millionaires who aggressively recruit, cajole, and inspire would-be investors with tales of great wealth obtained by following a simple no-money-down formula. Most such strategies involve locating a property that is available at fire-sale prices, negotiating with a highly motivated seller, obtaining one-sided terms from the negotiations, and then acquiring a property that requires no additional investment of capital. Many gurus of the no-money-down formula even promise that the happy investor can obtain financing for more than the price of the property and walk away from the closing with cash in hand. Such deals are within the realm of possibility. It is also within the realm of possibility to win the lottery or to get hit by lightning.

Although some legitimate no-money-down deals exist—and when they come along the advantages are significant—obtaining properties without a down payment should be a minor consideration in your overall investment strategy.

What's Wrong With a No-Money-Down Deal?

There's a line from an old song that goes, "Nice work if you can get it, and you can get it if you try."

It's the same with no-money-down deals: A nice deal if you can get it, and you can get it if you try, and try, and try.

The problem with no-money-down deals and rental properties is that most of them simply do not work. The most important characteristic of a successful rental property is whether it will generate positive cash flow. We have already seen how difficult it is to find one of those. Throw in another criterion—no money down—and the chances of locating a suitable property fall to nearly nothing.

If a no-money-down deal does appear, the additional debt service itself significantly reduces the potential for positive cash flow. On a $200,000 property, for example, a 10% down payment translates into $20,000. If that $20,000 is included in a 30-year mortgage at 8% interest, the additional monthly payment on the mortgage is $147.00. If the $20,000 is held as a second mortgage at 9%, the additional debt service is $161.00. The property must generate nearly an additional $2,000 each year just to cover the extra mortgage payment.

Analysis of a No-Money-Down Deal

To understand some of the fallacies in the no-money-down world, it might be helpful to analyze a simple no-money-down deal as proposed by some of the real estate magicians. A buyer locates a property with an asking price of $200,000. By asking some questions the buyer discovers that the owner is extremely eager to unload this property quickly because he is strapped for cash. The buyer offers $150,000 and the seller accepts. The buyer takes over the existing mortgage for $130,000 and the owner agrees to hold a second mortgage for $20,000.

Typical no money down deal

Asking price:	$200,000
Selling price:	$150,000
Existing mortgage (assumed by buyer):	$130,000
Second mortgage (held by seller):	$20,000
Down payment:	$00

At first glance, this seems like a very reasonable deal. The owner gets out from under a heavy debt; the buyer obtains a valuable piece of property without investing any money. Everyone wins, right?

Fallacy #1: Very few owners can afford to walk away from a property without receiving some cash. Who, for instance, pays the agent's commission? Who pays the closing costs? A seller who is strapped for cash will be unable to pay these expenses. If a buyer brings no money to the deal, the agent's commission will have to be deferred and the owner must agree to pay all closing costs, which, as we have seen, can amount to several thousand dollars.

Fallacy #2: No money down means that the property is fully mortgaged. If the owner is strapped for cash, it means that the property evidently has not been paying its own way with a mortgage of $130,000. If the deal is put together as outlined and the buyer assumes an additional $20,000 debt, ignoring the commission and closing costs, the additional mortgage payment will be approximately $150 per month for a building that has fallen short of paying its bills already.

In order to work, this no-money-down deal must pull together an unlikely set of circumstances: a highly motivated seller, a property that generates positive cash flow, a fully assumable mortgage, an agent willing to defer the sales commission, and a seller willing to pay thousands of dollars in closing costs.

No-Money-Down Deal, Verse Two

A more likely no-money-down deal is for the buyer to pay more for the property and to obtain a new first mortgage, while the seller holds a second mortgage. In this scenario, the seller will receive some cash out of the deal. This is how the deal might look:

A More Workable No-Money-Down Deal

Asking price:	$200,000
Selling price:	$200,000
New first mortgage:	$160,000
Second mortgage (held by seller):	$40,000
Existing mortgage (which is paid off):	$130,000
Down payment:	$00
Cash to the seller:	$30,000

There is, however, a problem with this kind of deal also. Most lending institutions will not allow secondary financing in lieu of a down payment—they want the new owner to be personally responsible for at least 20% of the value of the property—and will call in the first mortgage if they find out (a conforming loan requires 30%). Thus, the second mortgage must be hidden from the primary lender at the closing, even though some kind of down payment must change hands during the proceeding. Federal regulations for conforming loans require that the source of any money used for a down payment be disclosed if the mortgage is to be sold on the secondary market—and the source must be from the buyer's own assets. This requirement effectively precludes any under-the-table deals regarding down payment money in such circumstances. If the lending institution plans to hold the mortgage within their own portfolio as a non-conforming loan, they will nevertheless be circumspect in their determination of where the down payment is coming from. If the buyer is unable to produce evidence that the down payment is taken from his or her account, the loan will likely be refused. If by some sleight of hand the money is accounted for, the action is nevertheless highly unethical and likely illegal, which may jeopardize the buyer, the seller, and any other parties to the transaction, including the attorneys who draw up the deal.

The other problem with this deal is cash flow. If the property is sold under this kind of financing arrangement, it takes on an additional $70,000 in debt. If the original mortgage was at 8.5%, the seller's mortgage payment would have been approximately $1,000 per month. If the new first mortgage is also at 8.5%, the new payment on the first mortgage will be $1,230, an increase of $230 per month. If the second mortgage is at 9%, the payment on the second mortgage will be $322. The total additional debt service is $552 per month, which will significantly cut into any potential cash flow the building might generate.

Existing mortgage:	$130,000	Mortgage payment:	$1,000
New first mortgage:	$160,000	Mortgage payment:	$1,230
Second mortgage:	$40,000	Mortgage payment:	$322
Total additional monthly debt service:			$552

Legitimate No-Money-Down Deals

If a buyer can structure a no-money-down deal on a property that generates positive cash flow, the advantages are obvious: without any investment of cash the buyer has assumed a money-making piece of property. Fortunately, there are ways to structure legitimate no-money-down deals if you happen to find a property that can handle the additional debt. The key in each situation, of course, is to find someone willing to hold the financing for the property. That someone might be a bank or other lending institution, or it might be the seller.

Line of credit: An investor with an excellent track record might negotiate a line of credit with a local bank that can be used for down payment money. This form of financing was covered more fully in Chapter 23. A line of credit requires a strong financial position—which means collateral for the loan that is being extended—and a long-term relationship with the bank. If both such conditions exist, a line of credit can provide the down payment for the purchase of a property.

Full financing: A far less likely scenario is to locate a lender willing to lend the full purchase price of a property. For that to occur, the buyer would have to negotiate a selling price that is 80% or so less than the appraised value of a property. The real estate magicians would have us believe that such deals lie around every corner, waiting to be picked up. Usually, however, such deals—when they exist at all—are reserved for investors who have a history with the lender and a strong track record. A new investor looking for such financing will normally be out of luck.

Equity in other property: An alternative source of down payment money is equity in other property—a home, perhaps, or another investment property. A lender might be persuaded to lend the full price of the new property by holding both properties as security.

Home equity loan: Another alternative is to obtain a second mortgage on your home and use that money as down payment on a rental property.

Bank cards: Some investors have been known to use the line of credit from their bank cards as a down payment for an investment property. Bank-card interest rates are extremely high, making this a kind of last-ditch alternative. If the property can handle the debt, and this is the only way to acquire the property, however, using a bank-card will work.

Owner financing: Owner financed deals are common. Some can be structured as no-money-down deals, particularly if the deal benefits both parties. Such situations are, however, rare. The only reason an owner would structure such a deal is if the property will not sell under a more traditional financing arrangement, which means that the property for some reason is unattractive to most investors. Chances are it will also be unattractive to you.

Profits

If a buyer is able to structure a legitimate no-money-down deal, the key to making it a good investment, as with any real estate acquisition, is whether the numbers work. No money down became particularly popular during the inflationary period of the late 1970s and early 1980s, when it was difficult not to make a good real estate deal. It mattered not whether a building generated positive cash flow. If the owner held on to it for a year, it might appreciate 10% to 20% in value. Therefore, a property that was purchased for $100,000 might be worth $115,000 the next year. If the property were purchased for no money down, and if the income from the property covered the expenses and the mortgage payment, the new owner received $15,000 just for being the owner and spending a little time. Even if the property generated losses each month, the net loss would equal significantly less than the $15,000 capital gain when the building was sold.

In the run-away real estate boom during the last half of the 1980s, a similar strategy would have worked very well. Individuals could literally buy a house one day and wake up the next morning $20,000 richer. If the house could be purchased with no money down, it was even a better deal. As with all speculative bubbles, however, this one burst, leaving many individuals with huge losses.

Conditions Under Which No-Money-Down Works

1.   *The property generates positive cash flow after all expenses and debt service.*
     If you find that unlikely property that can pay its bills, cover two mortgage payments, and still generate a positive cash flow, try to put a no-money-down deal together. Ask the seller to hold a second mort-

gage for the entire down payment (but only if the primary lender will allow secondary financing). Alternatively, try for a wrap-around mortgage (see Chapter 23) for the full purchase price. This works particularly well if the owner does not want to cash out but prefers a monthly annuity from the property. If the seller is willing to hold a first mortgage, look for a source to borrow the down payment.

2. *The property can be made to generate positive cash flow by a change in usage or with proper management.*

    It is possible to find a property, normally one located in a Class III neighborhood, whose only problem is that it has been mismanaged. With proper management, the building will show positive cash flow, but in its present condition is losing money. Usually the owner of such a property is highly motivated to sell, not wishing to incur further losses, and is willing to defer any down payment that may be required. For a buyer willing to assume the mortgage and the risk, this seller might be persuaded to sell with no money down. If the buyer can convince the agent to defer his or her commission, the total cash invested in the property will be the closing costs (plus the capital, if any, required for repairs or upgrading to make the property viable).

3. *The property will appreciate in value and the buyer can afford to make up the losses in the mean time.*

    Normal appreciation of property values can rescue even bad real estate investments over time—but only if there are cash reserves to cover the early losses. As an example, if you pay $100,000 for a property and the property increases 3% in value each year for ten years, you will own a property that is worth $134,392 at the end of the ten years. If you had paid cash for the property, the value of your investment would have simply kept up with inflation, and you would have gained nothing. If you acquired the property with no money down, however, you made a profit of $34,392 on an investment that cost you nothing except some of your time.

    This simplified example assumes that the property pays all of its own expenses as well as the mortgage payment during the ten years of ownership.

    If the property generates a negative cash flow of $200 per month, however, the out-of-pocket investment each year would be $2,400. In ten years, $24,000 would have been invested. Rather than $34,392, the profits upon sale are limited to $10,392. (In actuality, other factors have to be taken into consideration, including the interest paid on the mortgage, increases in income generated by the property, tax consid-erations, and so on.)

A no-money-down deal works well when a property appreciates in value, even if it shows an operating loss during the time it is owned. The key is to have the financial reserves to cover the losses.

4.   *The value of the property can be raised significantly.*

There are two other ways a property can increase in value: through rising demand and through physical improvements. As demand for a property accelerates, so does its value. At the end of a recessionary period, for example, when new construction has typically been slow and demand for housing has seen a decrease because of tight money or high unemployment, the stage is set for real estate values to surge because of so-called pent-up demand. As money becomes available, the population begins buying houses and moving into better apart-ments and this increased demand, coupled with under-supply created by a lack of new construction, drives real estate values upward. If you are lucky enough to buy when prices are depressed and sell toward the end of the appreciation period, your profits will look very good. As most investors have found, though, it is nearly impossible to call the tops and bottoms of price cycles.

Demand is also created by changing conditions in a particular area. A plot of land that is valued only as woods or farmland can suddenly take on a huge appreciation in value when it is located near an inter-change for an interstate highway. A dilapidated little bungalow on a seedy street may double or triple in value when the neighborhood suddenly begins gentrifying. The news that a new sports stadium will be built in a particular location creates a flurry of speculative buying in the area surrounding the site. In such scenarios, if the property were purchased with no money down, the profits to be made are particularly attractive.

Physical improvements: The value of the seedy little bungalow, already driven up by gentrification, may double or triple again if a skilled rehabber reconditions and modernizes it. The woodlot next to an interchange might become home to a Holiday Inn. A venerable old Victorian home in a stable neighborhood can take on new value with the right paint job. A frame two-flat is dressed up with new vinyl siding; a brick apartment building gets a good cleaning and tuckpointing. This kind of forced appreciation through altered use or improvements to the property can provide a substantial pay-off for a no-money-down strategy.

Usually, a strategy of forced appreciation can be accomplished only by an individual or a group that has a good track record and access to significant amounts of financing. If you have the resources to enhance the value of a property, or the foresight to predict with some accuracy that a property will increase in value because of outside influences, and the opportunity for a no-money-down deal exists, take advantage of it. The truth is, however, that very few such deals will present themselves.

Buying Repossessed Property

Some successful investors have followed an alternative strategy for investing with little or no money down—by purchasing repossessed property. At first glance, the strategy seems viable; properties are being repossessed all the time. These properties typically can be bought at excellent prices, often with very small down payments. As with most schemes that seem too good to be true, however, so it is with this one.

First, the strategy requires an excessive amount of time. The list of repossessions, at least in a large city, is quite long and normally includes only an address, not a description of the property. Consequently, a buyer must drive past many addresses to locate a suitable property. Once a potential property is located, the next step is to locate the lender that is foreclosing and negotiate an acceptable deal, all of which requires a significant investment of time.

Second, most such properties have been repossessed for a reason. Usually that reason is that the property generates a negative cash flow—it loses money. Even if an excellent price is negotiated, it is unlikely that the building will generate positive cash flow.

Third, most such properties have been neglected for a long time and will require significant work (read money) to put them into operating condition.

The fact is that there are very few shortcuts to making money with rental properties. No-money-down, repossessed properties, distressed properties—they all are catchy titles designed to lure potential investors with a promise of building vast wealth with very little investment capital. All may play a significant role in a solid investment strategy, but none has viability as a strategy on its own.

Author's Note: Several years ago, I attended a free seminar that purported to teach a fool-proof strategy for locating and investing in repossessed properties. According to the presenters, the idea was a sure thing. All that was necessary was to buy their list of repossessions and go shopping. The list, which was periodically revised from data obtained from public sources, was not expensive. Neither was a subscription for automatic updates. Many participants, eager to put the strategy to work, bought the list as well as the subscription. The "free" seminar seemed to pay off handsomely that night—for the presenters.

After attending the seminar, a close friend—an automobile dealer who had recently sold his share in an Oldsmobile dealership—decided to pursue what he thought was an excellent investment opportunity. He had put in an offer for a new automobile franchise that was to be awarded in his area, and while he was waiting for the deal to materialize he decided to make some real estate deals using the repossession strategy, so he bought the list and started searching. He looked at property after property. Some, he found, were no longer on the market after the lender had restructured the deal with the original mortgagee. Other properties were in very undesirable locations; many needed extensive rehabilitation.

After several months of full-time searching, he finally found a property that looked promising. Then began the search for the lender, which took a few more days. When he finally located the appropriate person, he discovered to his chagrin that the property had already been sold. Now began the entire process all over again.

This was no babe in the woods. This was a sophisticated businessman looking for a legitimate deal, with money ready to invest. He was not the kind to invest his time or money unless there was a good chance that it would pay off for him. He was religious in following up on each property. Yet he spent a full year, working nearly full time, and was able to make no acquisitions. He had the time; he had the money. Yet he was not able to make a deal.

In Summary

No money down is a seductive idea that rarely pays off. Few no-money-down deals are available because most properties are attractive enough to draw qualified investors with substantial investment capital. Typically, only the less attractive properties can be bought with no down payment, and these are the properties that usually will not generate positive cash flow.

Some legitimate no-money-down strategies can be followed, such as using a bank line of credit, negotiating a low price and obtaining full financing, using equity in other properties as collateral for the down payment, obtaining owner financing that provides for no down payment, or using a bank-card line of credit to obtain cash for a down payment. Some investors also pursue repossessed properties in hopes of picking up an under-priced building with little or no money down.

No-money-down deals make sense under one of four conditions: if the property generates positive cash flow after all expenses and debt service, if the property can be made to generate positive cash flow by a change in usage or with proper management, if the property will appreciate in value and the buyer can afford to cover the losses in the mean time, or if the value of the property can be increased significantly in a short time. The fact is, however, that to find a suitable rental property that meets all of our investment criteria is, in itself, a very difficult and time-consuming task. To add an additional criterion—no money down—is to render the strategy nearly impossible.

Twenty-Six

■ ■ ■ ■ ■

What If You've Fallen in Love with a Building But It Generates Negative Cash Flow?

In This Chapter

Sometimes a building just seems right even though the numbers don't work. The neighborhood is strong, the building is beautiful, the location is excellent, the building has been well maintained and well managed, the vacancy rate is low, the future prospects for the neighborhood are good, and the area is on an upswing that should increase property values. The only problem is that the building will not show a profit under the current rent structure. Can a property that generates negative cash flow (translate: loses money each month) still be a reasonable long-term investment? The answer is a qualified yes for three reasons: *inflation,tax deductions, and appreciation.*

Although positive cash flow is the most important characteristic of any property, it is not the only one. There are times when other features are strong enough to make a property a good investment in spite of negative cash flow. When that situation arises a buyer can take advantage of tax laws that are still kind to real estate investors, as well as the inexorable pressure of inflation. Before plunging into such a property, however, a buyer must consider these two qualifications:

1. *Is the property truly a good investment, or are you using this chapter as an excuse to buy a building that you have fallen in love with but which will never make money?*

    Remember the rose-colored glasses of the Urban Pioneer, the Social Worker, the Rehabber? When you take the glasses off, does the building still make a good investment? Review the criteria of a good investment property; how does this property stack up?

2. *Do you have sufficient capital to make up the losses each month?*

    After doing the numbers, you know how much money has to come out of your pocket every month to pay the bills on this property. Review your personal cash flow analysis from Chapter 9. Can you cover the expenses easily without altering your present standard of living?

Investing in a negative cash flow building, while workable, is even more risky than following the recommended rule of buying positive cash flow buildings. It is a strategy that should be limited to those brave souls with substantial liquid capital.

How Inflation and Tax Deductions Can Make a Negative Cash Flow Property More Attractive

If you honestly can afford to make up the losses that a property will generate each month, and if there are good, honest reasons why this building should be considered for a long term investment, then inflation and tax deductions can help out. Keep in mind, however, that neither is a sure thing. We have already seen how property values can decline and Congress likes to fiddle with the tax code.

Author's Note: Relying on either inflation or tax advantages in the purchase of a property is quite speculative. That is why I never do it. But if you're determined to go ahead, I'll show you how the figures can work to your advantage (emphasize the can: this is no sure thing).

Sample Properties: Remember the two sample properties in Chapter 18? The asking price on each property is $350,000. Property #1, however, generates significantly more income than Property #2, even though the expenses are the same for both properties.

Property #1:

Gross monthly income:	$13,750	Gross annual income:	$165,000
Monthly expenses:	$6,613	Annual expenses:	$79,358
Price:	$350,000	Net operating income:	$85,642

Property #2:

Gross monthly income:	$8,196	Gross annual income:	$98,350
Monthly expenses:	$6,613	Annual expenses:	$79,358
Price:	$350,000	Net operating income:	$18,992

How Inflation Reduces Negative Cash Flow Over Time

Property #2 obviously generates negative cash flow. After driving past the building and looking at the neighborhood, however, it appears to be an excellent candidate for a long term investment. Presently the negative cash flow is –$472 per month. Because of inflation, however, rents should increase during the second year of ownership, thereby reducing the negative cash flow. Each year after that, rents should also increase somewhat. Expenses increase at the same time, however; therefore, the inflation strategy depends on keeping expenses under control. The mortgage payment, of course, remains consistent—as long as it is not an adjustable rate mortgage. Here is what might happen over three years.

	Year 1	Year 2	Year 3	Year 4
Income	$8,196	$8,605 (+5%)	$9,035 (+5%)	$9,486 (+5%)
Expenses	$6,613	$6,811 (+3%)	$7,015 (+3%)	$7,225 (+3%)
Mortgage	$2,055	$2,055	$2,055	$2,055
Net income	($472)	($261)	($35)	$+206

During the first year, rental income is $8,196. During the second year, inflation could increase rents by approximately 5%, bringing the income up to $8,605—an increase of $409 for the year. At the same time expenses will increase, but these can likely be brought under control through better management of the property. If the expenses increase by only 3%, the total increase in expenses is only $198. The gap has been reduced by $211. The third year, the gap closes further, and by the end of the third year the negative cash flow has essentially been brought under control. During year four, the cash flow turns positive. All of this, of course, is predicated upon being able to control expenses and keep rents high, which is not a certainty.

Author's Note: As a rule of thumb, if the property is unable to generate a positive cash flow within the first three years, do not invest.

How Tax Deductions Reduce the Impact of Negative Cash Flow

While inflation operates to drive the income side of the equation higher, certain aspects of the tax code operate to reduce the magnitude of the losses each year. In the example property, the first year's operating loss is ($472) per month, or ($5,664) per year. Because of the way the tax code is structured, however, the actual loss is far less than that amount, for two reasons:

First, the building is eligible for a depreciation allowance, which is in effect a paper loss that serves to offset other income.

Second, all interest on the mortgage payment is tax deductible, further reducing your tax liability.

Depreciation

For tax purposes, a property is divided into two parts: the land and the building. Normally, a building is valued at about 80% of the total purchase price of a property, while the land accounts for about 20% of the value. Land, of course, will not deteriorate through aging or normal wear and tear and therefore cannot be depreciated, while a building does age and therefore can depreciate in value. Even though the opposite usually occurs—the building increases in value as long as it is well maintained—for tax purposes the building can be depreciated. Current tax laws allow the depreciation to be calculated over 31 1/2 years on a straight-line basis; that is, the value of the building is divided by 31.5 and that amount is subtracted from the value of the building each year and counted as a tax loss. Using that equation,

$280,000 of the $350,000 purchase price for the property in the example would be eligible for depreciation.

80% x $350,000 (purchase price) = $280,000
(the value of the building alone)

$280,000 (value of the building) ÷ 31.5 (years of depreciation) =
$8,889 (annual depreciation)

On a 31 1/2 year straight-line formula, $8,889 can be deducted each year for depreciation, or $741 per month. In a 28% tax bracket, this translates into $2,489 in tax savings each year.

	Year 1	Year 2	Year 3	Year 4
Income	$8,196	$8,605 (+5%)	$9,035 (+5%)	$9,486 (+5%)
Expenses	$6,613	$6,811 (+3%)	$7,015 (+3%)	$7,225 (+3%)
Mortgage	$2,055	$2,055	$2,055	$2,055
Net income	($472)	($261)	($35)	$+206
(Annual)	($5,664)	($3,132)	($420)	$2,472
Depreciation				
Savings	$2,489	$2,489	$2,489	$2,489
Cash flow	($3,175)	($643)	$2,069	$4,961

Mortgage Interest

Each monthly mortgage payment is divided into two parts: the amount applied to the principal (which reduces the amount of the loan), and the amount that represents interest on the mortgage. The principal is not tax deductible, but the interest is. For the first several years of a 30-year mortgage, the interest portion of each monthly payment represents nearly all of the payment. The amount is not consistent each month because the portion applied to principal increases each month while the amount applied to interest decreases. Nevertheless, for the first five years of the mortgage, it's safe to say that roughly 95% of the mortgage payment goes toward interest. In the sample property, the mortgage payment is $2,055. If 95% of that amount is interest, the interest portion of the payment is roughly $1,952. If you are in the 28% tax bracket, the tax savings on that amount equals $547, which amounts to $6,564 per year.

	Year 1	Year 2	Year 3	Year 4
Income	$8,196	$8,605 (+5%)	$9,035 (+5%)	$9,486 (+5%)
Expenses	$6,613	$6,811 (+3%)	$7,015 (+3%)	$7,225 (+3%)
Mortgage	$2,055	$2,055	$2,055	$2,055
Net income	($472)	($261)	($35)	$+206
(Annual)	($5,664)	($3,132)	($420)	$2,472
Depreciation Savings	$2,489	$2,489	$2,489	$2,489
Mtge Interest Tax Savings	$6,564*	$6,444*	$6,324*	$6,204*
Cash flow	$3,389	$5,801	$8,393	$11,165

This is an estimated figure, used for illustration purposes only. The actual amount will vary somewhat. The amount has been reduced by $10 per month each year to demonstrate that the interest deduction declines in that fashion. Again, the amount represents a rough estimate and is not based on actual calculations of interest payments.

Additional Benefits of Property Ownership

Appreciation: In addition to the above, if the property appreciates at a rate of 5% per year, the owner will enjoy a growth in equity of more than $18,000 per year, not counting the equity growth that occurs as the mortgage is paid down.

In Summary

Negative cash flow can be offset by tax savings and increased rents, all of which, of course, is predicated on continuing inflation that pushes rents higher and a consistent tax code that allows deductions for mortgage interest and depreciation. If rents decrease, however, (which can happen in a recession), the original negative cash flow will only become worse. Buying a property because of a projected improvement in cash flow is risky at best. It is a strategy to be employed only if you can afford to cover the losses each month and if the property is being planned as a long-term investment.

Twenty-Seven

■ ■ ■ ■ ■

When You're Ready to Sell, You Can Save a Lot of Money with a Tax-Deferred Exchange

In This Chapter

With every property there comes a time when the advantages of selling it outweigh the advantages of holding on to it. After several years of operating a rental property, the value of the building will undoubtedly be much greater than the price that was originally paid. When the equity in a building is large enough that it can be better used to re-invest in additional properties, it is time to sell. The deciding factor is the rate of return being generated by the equity. If a property is churning out $1,000 per month in cash flow and the equity in the building is $50,000, the rate of return is approximately 24% ($12,000 per year return on $50,000). If the equity swells to $200,000, however, and the cash flow remains the same, the rate of return on the equity is now only 6% ($12,000 per year return on $200,000). If that same equity were invested in three buildings, each generating $700 per month cash flow, the rate of return would be 12.6% ($25,200 per year return on $200,000). If an investor can double the rate of return on investment by selling one property and buying three more, it is time to sell.

Unfortunately, there is no way to avoid paying income taxes on profits that are generated through selling a property. The increased value of the building is considered a capital gain, which will be taxed when the building is sold. This means the government will take nearly one-third of the money you make on the increased value of the building. Not only that, but the entire amount that has been depreciated will also be taxed. When the building is sold, then, the difference between the *depreciated* value of the building and the selling price will be taxed as regular income. There is no way to avoid paying those taxes. There is, however, a way to *defer* paying them.

Section 1031 of the tax code offers a way to defer paying capital gains taxes by exchanging one property for another, with all proceeds of the sold building being applied to the new building (or buildings). If the code allowed only for the actual exchange of one building for another, however, the limitations imposed by such a deal would render the tax advantages virtually useless for most investors. The possibility of finding a property that meets stringent investment criteria *and* one that is owned by a seller willing to exchange properties is quite remote. Fortunately, the code allows for a *deferred* exchange, which means that all of the proceeds from the sale of the first building can be applied to the purchase of one or more other properties of like kind, none of which must be owned by the buyer of the first property. The procedure is called a "Starker exchange," after a successful court case that established the precedent as well as many of the guidelines. This means that an investor can pyramid his or her investment by applying the proceeds to the purchase of more than one building and defer the taxes on the gain at the same time. To do so, however, requires that the investor follow stringent guidelines *to the letter*.

How to Accomplish a Starker Exchange

The tax code defines a deferred exchange as an exchange in which, pursuant to an agreement, the taxpayer transfers property held for investment (this is the building you are selling, called the "relinquished property") and subsequently receives property to be held for investment (this is the building or buildings you intend to purchase, called the "replacement property"). To meet the requirements of a deferred exchange, the transaction must be an actual exchange, which means a transfer of property for property, rather than a transfer of property for money. Therefore, if you sell a property and collect money for it, then use that money to purchase another property, this is not recognized as a valid exchange, and the proceeds from the property that was sold will be taxed.

There is a way around that requirement, however. Although a seller may not receive the proceeds from the sale, in a Starker exchange a "qualified intermediary" can. This intermediary holds the money in a "qualified trust" until the investor identifies a replacement property, then applies the proceeds from the sale of the first property to the purchase of the new property. As long as the taxpayer does not receive any of the money from the sale of the first property, a deferred exchange can take place.

The deferred exchange process begins *when you complete the contract for the sale of your property*. The sale contract must include a rider, to be signed by both parties to the sale, which specifies that the property to be sold (called the relinquished property) will not be sold to the buyer but rather will be assigned to a qualified intermediary for the purpose of an exchange. At the closing, all proceeds from the sale will be transferred to a trust account, and will be held there until the investor identifies and purchases another property. This property is first transferred to the intermediary who then delivers the property to the investor, thus completing the exchange.

To be considered a valid exchange, all of the transactions must occur within a very tight time-line:

1. The investor must identify the property or properties to be received in the exchange within 45 days after the closing date on the relinquished property.

2. The investor must take title to the new property within 180 days (six months) of the closing date on the relinquished property.

To identify a replacement property, the investor must designate a specific property in writing to the qualified intermediary. As many as three properties of any fair market value may be identified, or more than three properties as long as the total fair market value of all the properties does not exceed 200% of the market value of the relinquished property. If more properties are identified than are allowed by this guideline, the exchange is invalid.

The qualified intermediary may not be related to the investor seeking to complete a Starker exchange. (The intermediary may not be your attorney, accountant, broker or employee.) After establishing the trust, the qualified intermediary then acquires both the relinquished property and the replacement property and effects the exchange. All money must be handled by the intermediary; the investor may not have access to the funds at any time during the transaction.

The rules governing a Starker exchange are very specific and must be followed rigorously. The best course of action is to inform your attorney, prior to the sale, that you intend to do a Starker exchange. If your attorney is not familiar with the details of a 1031 transaction, ask him or her to find someone who is. You or your attorney will need to find someone to act as the qualified intermediary and as the qualified trustee. Normally, a local bank will handle the trust account, for a fee, and a local title company will serve as the intermediary. Not all banks, however, are familiar with the requirements of a tax-deferred exchange. It is in your best interest to locate a bank that is, or allow plenty of time for your attorney to school the local banker in the correct procedures to follow. A mistake by any one of the parties to the transaction might result in a substantial tax liability.

A Starker Exchange Can Test Your Patience

One of the obvious draw-backs with a Starker exchange is the short time-line for purchasing a replacement property. Earlier you were told of the value of patience in searching for and acquiring rental property. A Starker exchange will test your patience to the limits. In the end, you may decide that some short-cuts are called for in order to preserve the tax deferral. (If the money will be lost anyway, why not spend it on a risky property?) That decision is yours to make, but the best advice is to wait as long as possible for the right property. Settling for a building that does not meet your strict criteria might not only negate the tax advantages gained by the exchange, but could lose even more money than was saved by deferring the tax liability.

Author's Note: Not long ago I discovered just how far a Starker exchange can stretch one's commitment to patience. In the course of selling a property that I had held for many years, I decided to complete a tax-deferred exchange in order to preserve a large capital gain. On the day of closing, however, I had not yet identified even one property that I would purchase with the proceeds, and there were only 45 days allowed.

This situation had not developed from a lack of trying. First there had been the rooming house. Owned by an octogenarian, the building had been operated for more than 30 years with the attention normally given to a personal hobby. For several weeks, I had schmoozed and dickered with the clever old guy. The deal was in the bag; I could feel it. He wanted me to have the building. But then at the last minute, he decided not to sell. He was afraid his life would be over if he let the building go.

I tried everything to convince him differently, but to no avail. The deal was dead, and three months of negotiating was wasted.

I continued to shop. After all, my intention was to buy more than one building. But nothing else had turned up prior to the closing. Now, with less than a month and a half to go, I would have to locate at least two properties that would meet my criteria—a task that had taken as long as twelve months for one property in the past.

Within two weeks, fortunately, I managed to locate an owner with several buildings to sell, and was able to identify one of those properties as suitable. I placed that property on my list of identified properties. With well over $100,000 left to spend, however, my job was far from over. I felt much like Richard Pryor in the movie Brewster's Millions—*so much money; so little time to spend it.*

Then I found two other suitable properties and began negotiating. Confident that one of them would materialize, I added them to my list and relaxed. But at the last minute, both deals fell through. Out of four excellent properties, three had been snatched from me at the last minute, and time was running out. The temptation was great to buy virtually anything just to spend the money, but I held on.

Then, suddenly, I received a call from the agent who had handled the one deal that had gone through. He had another building, would I like to see it? With less than three weeks to go, I rushed through the process—doing the numbers (they amazed me, they were so good), walking through the building, learning the neighborhood, making the offer. With owner financing, we were able to close the deal under the deadline, but everyone involved was exhausted by the effort.

For me, the acquisition was particularly sweet: I had been able to maintain my composure, remain patient and wait for the right property, even under the pressure of potentially losing thousands of dollars to taxes. A Starker exchange? The Starker pressure cooker, more like. But we got it done, and it worked out well.

In Summary

When the equity in a property is so large that it depresses the rate of return obtained from the cash flow, it may be time to sell. Selling, however, incurs a large tax liability on the capital gains. The only way to defer paying those taxes is to accomplish a like-kind exchange, known as a Starker exchange. The regulations governing a Starker exchange are specific and provide for rigid time lines within which the exchange can take place. The exchange need not be one building for another. The alternative is to designate a qualified intermediary who holds the proceeds from the sale of your property and uses those proceeds to purchase one or more other properties that you have designated. Although the strict time-lines can stretch one's patience and tempt a buyer to buy substandard properties, holding to your investment criteria is both possible and preferable. When the exchange is complete, the advantages of deferring the tax liability become evident: you are now earning returns on Uncle Sam's money, and that feels good.

Index

About the Author

In a field dominated by male professionals, Susan Underhill (Manisco) has used her arsenal of "street smart" skills to establish herself as a formidable expert in real estate investing, gaining the respect and admiration of her male counterparts along the way. And her success story is even more amazing given the fact that she is entirely self taught.

Underhill grew up in the city with a keen understanding of the neighborhoods and the people who live there. She began her real estate career in 1975 with a small savings account accumulated—with great effort—from her modest earnings as a teacher. Since then she has used her grasp of the real estate markets to parlay that hard-earned stake into a lucrative real estate business.

As a member of various community and professional organizations, Underhill works with local and industry leaders to maintain high standards for herself and other property owners in the neighborhoods. While building her personal real estate empire, Underhill also developed a successful career as a special educator. Having now "retired" from teaching to pursue real estate interests full time, her masters degree and 16 years as a professional educator have proven an asset in her ability to teach her techniques to others.

While it has been said that real estate investing is not for everyone, Underhill has proven, by example, that the right skills—all of which can be learned through persistence and effort—can help virtually anyone achieve success.

About the Publisher

PROBUS PUBLISHING COMPANY

Probus Publishing Company fills the informational needs of today's business professional by publishing authoritative, quality books on timely and relevant topics, including:

- Investing
- Futures/Options Trading
- Banking
- Finance
- Marketing and Sales
- Manufacturing and Project Management
- Personal Finance, Real Estate, Insurance and Estate Planning
- Entrepreneurship
- Management

Probus books are available at quantity discounts when purchased for business, educational or sales promotional use. For more information, please call the Director, Corporate/Institutional Sales at 1-800-PROBUS-1, or write:

Director, Corporate/Institutional Sales
Probus Publishing Company
1925 N. Clybourn Avenue
Chicago, Illinois 60614
FAX (312) 868-6250